The Transparent Event

THE TRANSPARENT EVENT

POST-MODERN CHRIST IMAGES

JOHN P. COCK

tranScribe books

Acknowledgments

No book is ever the accomplishment of a single person. Like everything else, it comes from the direct and indirect efforts of many.

Besides the inspiration of spirit guides and the collegiality of the spirit movement in history, I thank the following special people. First, I acknowledge the care of my wife, Lynda, who loves me and my writings in spite of . . . ; and our sons, John and Jeremiah, who have journeyed with us around the planet and through our life. Finally, I thank my grandchildren, Kaitlyn and Nolan, who give me the great joy of their playful presence.

Dedicated to the
Order: Ecumenical
and
Joseph W. Mathews

Jesus the Man is not nearly so historical as Christ the Event, the transforming event of every person's existence.

—"Epilogue"

Every situation you find yourself in, until the day nobody finds you anymore, calls for a Gautama. You cannot sit around and wait for a Jesus. You must become a Jesus. This is your commission, your assignment, to be Jesus in history. . . .

I had a chance to love the Aboriginal people in Australia. I wrote a bit of poetry—terrible poetry—but it spoke to them about the meaning of their past, including the brutality of the white man. It painted a new possibility of the future of black people across the world. It laid out the meaning of the present in terms of their real demands. That's what I mean by divine love. That's all Jesus did. He opened the future, made new the past, and filled the present full of meaning. And that's our vocation.

—Joseph W. Mathews

One can imagine . . . Arius's . . . answers to Athanasius's arguments. Athanasius argues that God the Father is also God the Son. He says God actually became Jesus despite the fact that, throughout the Gospels, the Son describes himself as being other than the Father and less than Him. He [Athanasius] ransacks the New Testament for evidence to support his position, but the only texts that he can find are two lines from the Book of John: "I and the Father are one," and "He who has seen me has seen the Father." But it is perfectly clear from the context of these statements that Christ is talking about representing God, not about being him.

—Richard E. Rubenstein, *When Jesus Became God*, pp. 117-18

Contents

Section Four: Rethinking My Christology

Section Five: Christ Image Re-creation

Section Six: Edifying Discourses

PROLOGUE

[A]ll of those for whom authentic transformation has deeply unseated their souls must, I believe, wrestle with the profound moral obligation to shout from the heart—perhaps quietly and gently, with tears of reluctance; perhaps with fierce fire and angry wisdom; perhaps with slow and careful analysis; perhaps by unshakable public example—but **authenticity** always and absolutely carries a **demand** and **duty**: you must speak out, to the best of your ability, and shake the spiritual tree, and shine your headlights into the eyes of the complacent. You must let that radical realization rumble through your veins and rattle those around you. . . .

[T]he alarming fact is that any realization of depth carries a terrible burden: Those who are allowed to see are simultaneously saddled with the obligation to **communicate** that vision in no uncertain terms: that is the bargain. You were allowed to see the truth under the agreement that you would communicate it to others (that is the ultimate meaning of the bodhisattva vow). And therefore, if you have seen, you simply must speak out. Speak out with compassion, or speak out with angry wisdom, or speak out with skillful means, but speak out you must.

And this is truly a terrible burden, a horrible burden, because in any case there is no room for timidity. The fact that you might be wrong is simply no excuse: You might be right in your communication, and you might be wrong, but that doesn't matter. What does matter, as Kierkegaard so rudely reminded us, is that only by investing and speaking your vision with **passion**, can the truth, one way or another, finally penetrate the reluctance of the world. If you are right, or if you are wrong, it is only your passion that will force either to be discovered. It is your duty to promote that discovery—either way—and therefore it is your duty to speak your truth with whatever passion and courage you can find in your heart.[1]

—Ken Wilber

I am compelled to jump into the ever-evolving christological dialogue; for christologies over the sweep of 2000 years—original, classical, modern, and post-modern—need to be more grounded in the ultimate reality of life, and in our lives. If our faith is dead, one reason is that the christologies of the tradition have failed us and that we may think, consequently, we have outgrown Jesus the Christ.

I respect the efforts of the newest quest for the historical Jesus, but more and better historical information about Jesus will not get at the spirit malaise of our time. The real question is Who do you say *God* is? That's all that christology is about. If more than 90 percent of the citizens of the USA say they believe in *God*, something is wrong, for that belief system is obviously producing a skewed and unsatisfying quality of life for too many.

I have spent a lifetime preparing to write this book, caught up in a journey of faith that is worth talking about, especially with those of the present generation who see their depth quality of life at risk. I want them to do a faith check. Bob Dylan's *Positively 4th Street* lyrics read

> *You say you lost your faith,*
> *But that's not where it's at—*
> *You have no faith to lose,*
> *And you know it.*

I would change the third line to

> **Your faith is on the blink,**
> *And you know it.*

The faith of our generation may be on the blink—maybe less than self-conscious, or skeptically on hold. But faith is there for sure. Every person has faith in something. Is that *something* substantial? Does it deliver? As Tillich would ask, does it unite us to the mystery, depth, and greatness of life and our lives?

Even as religious fundamentalism swells its ranks globally, there is also a growing number of reflective Christians and enlightened agnostics. This book is for the latter two groups. Or it is for anybody who is struggling to make sense of life in the post-modern era. The *modern* myth of scientific progress that grew out of the Enlightenment (about 1650 on) has hastened the possibility of human and organic destruction on the planet, indicating the need for a new paradigm for the *post-modern*[2] period. The old notion of progress does not work. Many of the old images of Jesus the Christ do not sustain. Therefore, let us consider a new Christ image.

In Sections Two and Three we will compare the christologies of ten theologians of the last half of the 20th century who got it right. (Søren Kierkegaard, 19th century, had much influence on many of the other nine and is therefore included.) I reflect on these ten for two reasons: first, they have been chief guides in my faith journey; second, I judge they could make sense to this post-modern age, and, therefore, I wish to share their thought with a wider audience.

Up front, *my presuppositions* are these: 1) christology is a mystery, never to be finally fathomed or objectified rationally; 2) every Christian has a christology, an image of Jesus as the Christ—a Christ image; 3) no two christologies are alike; 4) there is no right christology; 5) one's christology informs one's life-style; 6) one's christology is always evolving; 7) faith is more response than belief; and 8) Jesus the Christ is an (the) entry into the meaning of *God* for our existence. Although we will never fully understand what we mean by all this, we are driven to the task of creating and re-creating our christologies, our images of Christ. Certainly this is at the heart of what it means to be a Christian—and a human.

As I begin I take Wilber seriously: it is my responsibility to speak the truth that I perceive, right or wrong. As he says, let the "radical realization rumble through our veins."

———————

Before you read further, please do the short **Christ Image Evaluation** *in Chapter 15, page 151. Be honest. You can do it again after you read up to that chapter and see if anything has changed.*

———————

Special Note: Some of the writings quoted in this book come before the revolution of gender-sensitive wording. Some quotes are amended; the longer quoted texts are left intact.

PROLOGUE NOTES

[1] Ken Wilber, "A Spirituality that Transforms," *One Taste*: *Daily Reflections on Integral Spirituality* (Boston: Shambhala, 2000), pp. 33-4.
[2] "Post-modern" (hyphenated), as I use it in this book, denotes that which follows the *modern* period, especially the modern period of theology, and is not used to refer to any particular school of secular *postmodernism* (non-hyphenated). In my use of "post-modern," I am not talking about thought inspired by the likes of Derrida and Foucault. Maybe John Milbank and company are right: *postmodernism* as a system of thought is simply a natural, dark, and unhappy end of the system of thought of *modernism*.

Section One:

"Jesus Christ" in Context

1. My Life Journey With "Jesus Christ"

My images of Jesus Christ were forming before I can remember. When I was born, great Uncle Jethro looked at the shape of my head and declared that I would be a Primitive Baptist preacher. That was a good guess because my great, great, great Grandfather John Cock was ordained a Primitive Baptist preacher in 1836; and my great Grandfather Peter Corn, on my mother's side, was ordained in 1865. Being "called" is in the genes.

I grew up in the First Methodist Church in a small town in the mountains of Virginia. The church was at the center of my life. I attended every service and every family, child, and youth event. From those years I have many images of Jesus, especially Sallman's *Head of Christ* (where Jesus looks like a Middle-Eastern movie star). Following tradition, I wore my father's bathrobe in the Christmas drama and played Joseph, standing beside Mary as we admired our Christ child.

I memorized scripture verses in Sunday school and Bible school. Memorable Jesus scriptures were allusions to Jesus with children; Jesus at age twelve sitting with the elders; the Christmas and Easter narratives; the parables of the Prodigal Son, the Lost Sheep, and the Good Samaritan; and miracles such as the big feedings and Jesus' bringing people back to life.

I learned tens of songs and hymns: *Jesus Loves Me*; *Tell Me the Stories of Jesus*; *Fairest Lord Jesus*; *Just As I Am*; *Stand Up, Stand Up for Jesus*; *'Are Ye Able?' Said the Master*; *The Old Rugged Cross*; *Blessed Assurance, Jesus Is Mine*; *Jesus is Calling*; *I Love to Tell the Story*; *Jesus Saves*; *Christ the Lord is Risen Today*; *He Lives*; *My Jesus, I Love Thee*; *O Jesus, I Have Promised*—an amazing confluence of images of Jesus that deeply informed my early consciousness and are reverberating in me to this day.

When I was in the seventh grade my sister addressed my life by saying I would be a great preacher like Peter Marshall. That was as we walked home from the Rex Theater after we had just seen the movie about his life, *A Man Called Peter*. Later at a Sunday evening service, Rev. Prince Albert Eades called on me to pray, with the introduction that one day he knew I would be a preacher.

More than most youth I knew, I was interested in things spiritual. I relished the deep discussions at the church youth center or at retreats. During several revivals I experienced a genuine urge to go to the altar and "give my life to Christ." At age fifteen, I went to the Carolina mountains to a retreat led by Frank Laubach. His spirituality deeply addressed me, especially as he kept his eyes closed in prayer much of the time when preaching, leading our group, and in personal conversations with me. Jesus must have been like him, I concluded. I also experienced that the spiritual highs and my decisions to follow in Jesus' steps did not last, and that such highs led to spiritual lows, bringing guilt and doubt.

One of my professors at seminary, Norman Perrin, wrote autobiographically about his Christian nurture in the liberal Baptist tradition in England, where he was taught to "believe in Jesus" and the "various forms of proclamation," which produced in him what he calls a "faith-image" of Jesus.

> Part of this faith-image is certainly made up of traits of the liberal historical Jesus. . . . [P]art of the faith-image could be the result of the existential impact of knowledge of Jesus mediated by a modern . . . historic knowledge, for to a believer brought up in this tradition almost anything that talks about Jesus can become kerygma, that is, it can contribute to the faith-image. . . . [L]ike the Christ of the gospels, the Jesus of one's faith-image is a mixture of historical reminiscence, . . . myth, legend and idealism. What gives this faith-image validity is the fact that it grows out of religious experience and is capable of mediating religious experience.[1]

My strong faith-image of Jesus called me to the ordained ministry. I attended a small Methodist college where I soon was put off by the "holy club,' some of whom told me they were praying for me when I stopped participating. I became leery of the overly pious. I further was put off by a very boring New Testament course. At the same time I began to question my Jesus-image, especially the miracles and the resurrection. The "holy club" quoted scripture (which I later found out was the favorite text used by traditionalists and fundamentalists to beat up those of us not believing literally in the resurrection of the dead): "If Christ has not been raised, your faith is futile and you are still in your sins" (I Cor. 15:17, NSV, though they quoted the King James Version, a copy of which I discover I do not have in my library). I came to the point I could not even recite the Apostle's Creed at services; I felt I would have been lying about what I believed, which to me was blaspheming.

Consequently, my struggle with my calling led me to consider leaving college. Instead, with the counsel of a wise professor, I came to the decision to give up the ministry and become an English teacher. After teaching for three years in boys' private schools, I received a Ph.D. scholarship. That did not last long. When John F. Kennedy was assassinated, I was dramatically "called" to the ministry again and immediately enrolled in seminary.

I found myself very skeptical compared to other seminarians. I responded most to the Continental theologians, especially Barth and Bonhoeffer. They not only taught, preached, and wrote, they demonstrated their faith in the face of Nazism and the issues of their time. They and the professors who introduced me to them helped me to establish a set of adult Christian beliefs that made some sense. I was very put off by the fundamentalists at seminary who invited me to their healing services in the chapel. I told them I did not believe in that type of miracle. They said they were doing what the scriptures said to do. I guess I did not believe all the scriptures. Which parts did I believe?

The struggle intensified as I ministered in three Methodist churches in Georgia, North Carolina, and Virginia. I loved the people but knocked heads with the bureaucracy, who, for example, did not ask me what I believed before I was ordained, but whether I smoked. The push for more salary and benefits, more members and new buildings, seemed to be just one campaign after another. Many lay people were ready for a deeper faith journey in all three places, so I spent priority time devising ways for them to grow in their faith, and let the bureaucratic paperwork and campaigns slide.

A new list of Jesus hymns and songs were added to my repertoire by then: *Were You There*; *O Sacred Head Now Wounded*; *What Child Is This*; *Depth of Mercy* (my own); *A Mighty Fortress*; *Come, Thou Long-expected Jesus*; *Jesu, Joy of Man's Desiring; I Sought the Lord*; *Lord of the Dance*; *Lord, I Want To Be a Christian*; and *The Strife Is O'er, the Battle Won.*

Later on in our journey, my wife, Lynda, and I learned of the Ecumenical Institute: Chicago in a *Time* magazine article and attended one of their seminars. We discussed God, Christ, Holy Spirit, and the Church in ways that challenged and motivated us to such an extent that we were soon off to the Institute for an internship year. We stayed on and became a part of that community of faith, living all over the world with our two sons for over sixteen years—usually with the poor whom we helped to empower.

What appealed to us most was the *family order* experiment. The families who performed the work of the Ecumenical Institute called themselves the Order: Ecumenical, or simply the Order. Day in and day out we worshipped, studied, worked, and served together, always experimenting with new forms that we shared with churches, inter-faith groups, communities, and responsive people in general. While in the Order my passion for understanding and communicating the essence of the Christian faith grew, as did my will to reform the church on behalf of the world.

During those years in the Order we corporately studied tens of spirit writers. I came to appreciate deeply Bultmann, Tillich, Bonhoeffer, H. Richard Niebuhr, Kierkegaard, Gogarten, Kazantzakis, R. Otto, St. Ignatius, St. John of the Cross, St. Teresa of Avila,Teilhard de Chardin, Gandhi, J. S. Dunne, C. Castaneda, R. Tagore, S. Ogden, Segundo, and K. Wilber. Joseph W. Mathews, the co-founder of the Order, more than any other, became my mentor through his writing, speaking, priorship, and his faith-style.

After those years, the *Christ event* became the quintessence of my faith-image. I have found no other christological scholarship as compelling as what I found then, whether Rahner, Küng[3], Schillebeeckx, Loewe, Fox, Moltmann, Pannenberg, Robinson, Marxsen, van Buren,

Farmer, Wright, Foster, Macquarrie, Altizer, Hamilton, Hartshorne, Griffin, Cobb, Wildman, Hick, Sanders, Fredriksen, Wink, Crossan, Borg, or Funk.

After leaving the Order, I put my faith journey on hold. I was physically and spiritually scarred, and my greatest cause was no longer. I was in the "desert" for about seven years before my passion oozed again as I began to teach and preach around—and especially to write. I first wrote with pain and doubt about the needed reformation in the church, emphasizing the underlying contradictions and implicit strategies. Next, for six years, I relived my life through writing my memoir,[2] rediscovering my faith journey. I reunited with all my old theologian and poet colleagues (listed above) and realized that the theologizing that I did with them and with my colleagues in the Order has not been enough communicated, especially where my passion lies: the transparent and the contentless dynamic of the Jesus Christ happening. They went further than anyone I know on this subject. I want to share that wisdom and still go further, with the help of spirit guides such as Ken Wilber.

Imaginal education (formulated by the Order out of Kenneth Boulding's *The Image*) says that real learning takes place when an alternate image intrudes to call forth a person's existing image to stand up and enter the debate for truth. Part of what triggered my decision to write this book at this time was my reading of several of the Jesus Seminar books by Funk, Crossan, Borg, and Wink; and attending a recent conference at Duke University, "Jesus in Context," with Crossan, Borg, Sanders, Wright, Fredricksen, and other New Testament scholars. On the one hand I find their research most stimulating. Yet, they need to go further. They are in the long line of scholars over the centuries giving us a more accurate history of Jesus but not giving us any more faith-knowledge,[4] for faith finally does not come from knowing the results of historical research about Jesus. As Günther Bornkamm worte, "Certainly faith cannot and should not be dependent on the change and uncertainty of historical research."[5] At least the scholars would be pleased to know they helped flush me out. Some of them are revolutionaries at heart, trying to reform Christianity through their democratic style of Jesus research and swashbuckling debate. May reform increase through them.

One of the dominant strands of my life is Jesus the Christ, more than just Jesus. Therefore, I feel compelled to put "Jesus Christ in Context," to pull together what I know out of my life and to add it to the age-old witness. My wife calls me *a latter-day John the evangelist*, but she well knows she is not married to a traditional evangelist. I refer to myself as a *post-modern* evangelist.

Special "Jesus the Christ" Note: Like Tillich, I will add the faith article *the* before *Christ* throughout the book because we have become theologically insensitive to the depth understanding of the phrase "Jesus Christ." "Jesus . . . the . . . Christ" reminds us that we are bestowing a christological title on Jesus. "Jesus the Christ" is a faith phrase, meaning "I believe Jesus of Nazareth is the Messiah of *God* for me."

CHAPTER 1 NOTES

[1] Norman Perrin, *Rediscovering the Teaching of Jesus* (New York: Harper & Row, 1976), p. 243-44.
[2] John Cock, *Called to Be: A Vocational Odyssey* (Galax, VA: Gazette Press, 1997).
[3] Hans Küng, *On Being a Christian* (New York: Simon and Schuster, 1976), is a good long read about Jesus the Christ and authentic discipleship. I find him the most helpful Roman Catholic theologian. Rahner next.
[4] N. Thomas Wright, in his essay, "Five Gospels but No Gospel: Jesus and the Seminar," *Crisis in Christology: Essays in Quest of Resolution*, ed. by William R. Farmer (Livonia, MI: Truth, 1995), says it very passionately: "*The Five Gospels* [book by Robert Funk and Roy Hoover, and also the Jesus Seminar] . . . systematically deconstructs its own title. If this book gives us the truth about Jesus, about the early church, and about the writing of the five books here studied [the authors include Thomas as the fifth gospel], there is no gospel, no good news. There is only good advice [alluding to the maxims and aphorisms of Jesus], and we have no reason for thinking that it will have any effect" (p. 147). Wright is a moderate conservative with whom I disagree theologically; yet, his point here is well taken.
[5] Günther Bornkamm, *Jesus of Nazareth* (1960; New York: Harper and Row, 1975), p. 9.

2. Funk's 21 Theses, Thomas, "Q" *et al.*— What To Believe?

Robert Funk, founder of the controversial Jesus Seminar, draws his book *Honest To Jesus* to a close with twenty-one "theses." Reminiscent of Luther, the reformer, Funk also wants to dramatically revolutionize the tradition.

> [I]t is appropriate to . . . ask what we have learned that modifies the future of the tradition inaugurated by Jesus of Nazareth. What real knowledge . . . has this thirst to know the flesh-and-blood Jesus produced? What difference could it possibly make? I propose to elaborate my answer to this question in a series of theses, twenty-one in number.[1]

His theses and titles follow without commentary, except before number 8.

A NEW AGE

1. The aim of the quest is to set Jesus free.
2. The renewed quest prompts us to revamp our understanding of the origins of the Christian faith itself.
3. The renewed quest also has serious ramifications for how we understand the Christian life.
4. The renewed quest points to a secular sage who may have more relevance to the spiritual dimensions of society at large than to institutionalized religion.

BREAKING THE EASTER BARRIER

5. We can no longer rest our faith on the faith of Peter or the faith of Paul.

6. Jesus himself is not the proper object of faith.

7. In articulating the vision of Jesus, we should take care to express our interpretations in the same register as he employed in his parables and aphorisms.

RECOVERING THE ROOTS

> The death of the churches is by no means imminent, yet their demise seems inevitable. . . . The rediscovery and liberation of Jesus could conceivably result in a rebirth. . . . A reformation is imminent when a movement reviews and revises the records of how it got started. . . . I think Christianity is a tradition worth reforming and saving. . . . I have a few suggestions for launching a revision.[2]

8. Give Jesus a demotion.

9. We need to cast Jesus in a new drama, assign him a role in a story with a different plot.

10. We need to reconceive the vocation of Jesus as the Christ.

CHRISTIAN PRACTICE

11. Jesus kept an open table.

12. Jesus made forgiveness reciprocal.

13. Jesus condemned the public practice of piety.

14. Jesus advocated an unbrokered relationship to God.

15. Jesus robs his followers of Christian 'privilege.'

16. Jesus makes it clear that all rewards and punishments are intrinsic.

NICEA REVISITED

17. We will have to abandon the doctrine of the blood atonement.

18. We will need to interpret the reports of the resurrection for what they are: our glimpse of what Jesus glimpsed.

19. Redeem sex and Mary, Jesus' mother, by restoring to Jesus a biological if not actual father.

20. Exorcise the apocalyptic elements from Christianity.

21. Declare the New Testament a highly uneven and biased record of various early attempts to invent Christianity.[3]

Few New Testament scholars come forth with explicit strategies and tactics to reform Christianity and the church. I also commend Funk and the Jesus Seminar for opening up public debate on Jesus of Nazareth and his actual history. The educated masses are at least a part of the Seminar's context for research. The Seminar's research methods are a breakthrough in New Testament scholarship. Why are ministers who are abreast of this new research not passing it on to their laity?

The popular media, more than the established churches, is keeping the masses aware of those who are trying to push the envelope of New Testament research. After crediting Crossan's saying the tomb was empty because Jesus' "body had already been devoured by wild dogs," *Newsweek* (April 8, 1996: 63) goes on to balance out the picture by summarizing what most scholars accept:

> All agree that the New Testament was created by believers whose main concern was to preach the 'good news' of Jesus Christ. All recognize that the Gospel narratives were composed from oral traditions at least 40 years after the death of Jesus, each with its own theological bent. All accept the fact that the Gospel stories . . . reflect controversies within the early church. All acknowledge that the New Testament authors interpreted Jesus in light of various images and beliefs from the Hebrew Scriptures. And all are trained in the intricate historical-critical method of placing specific scriptural passages in their historical context (*Ibid.*, p. 65).

If this is in fact the consensus of radical, liberal, and traditional New Testament scholars—not fundamentalist scholars—then where is the big disagreement? It centers in the arena of sources. The above consensus holds when considering the twenty-seven books of the New Testament as the primary sources.

But that canon is hardly where the radicals and the liberals have been focused lately. The Jesus Seminar has added a fifth "gospel," Thomas. Crossan "relies heavily on the apocryphal Gospels of Thomas and Peter and the secret Gospel of Mark" (*Time*, April 8, 1996: 55). James M. Robinson founded the International Q Project over seventeen years ago, which has done a prodigious amount of research to put together a seemingly "real" Q document (only a hypothetical source for Matthew and Luke, and even Mark, if "Q" in fact dates to the year 50) as yet to be discovered.

The Q Project operates under the auspices of the internationally respectable Society of Biblical Literature and, like the Jesus Seminar, polls its members relative to authentic material. Q Project's cadre of members includes John Kloppenborg, Paul Hoffmann, and major partisans along the way such as Burton Mack and Helmut Koester, and others like Crossan. Upon this hypothetical "Q" foundation is erected such substantial theories as a "non-Christian Jesus," who accomplished no passion, resurrection, atonement, nor had any interest in the end of the world—together the core of Christianity. Compare this with the gospel of Luke—Jesus accomplished the passion, resurrection, atonement, and will come again—and we see the stark contrast. So the sources one believes as authentic make all the difference. Should "Q" exist and ever be discovered, then Christianity could be undermined (Charlotte Allen, *The Atlantic Monthly*, December 1996: 51-68).

Likewise, if filmmaker Paul Verhoeven (*Robocop, Basic Instinct, Showgirls*), who is a ten-year member of the Jesus Seminar, finally makes the Jesus movie out of the presuppositions of the Seminar, what effect might it have? Luke Timothy Johnson, a New Testament professor at Emory University, says,

> "Jesus is the central symbol for Christianity. Reshape Jesus and you reshape Christianity. The seminar's agenda is to change Christianity as a cultural phenomenon by coming up with a different version of Jesus [see Funk's thesis number 9 above]. In this age of mass media, if you can market this Jesus sufficiently, it just might work" (*Emory Magazine*, Autumn 1996: 21).

Russell Shorto (a journalist turned Jesus of Nazareth enthusiast with his current book *Gospel Truth: The New Image of Jesus Emerging from Science and History and Why It Matters*) asks in *G.Q.* magazine (June 1994: 123), "What will the future bring? Will the walls of belief collapse entirely? Will twenty centuries of Western culture be undone in one smart-alecky grunt of scholarship?"

New Testament scholars are no longer hiding their light under a bushel. Each is out to get her or his Jesus into history, often using big-time means. And we thought the Muslims were aggressive in their evangelism. We do need to figure out who Jesus is for us, or somebody else will.

Why is all this so important to everybody? John Dominic Crossan answers this question in *U.S. News & World Report* (April 8, 1996: 52): "There has never been a more empowering figure than Jesus. If you are empowered by Jesus' life, in my judgment that makes you a Christian." Crossan has the zeal to empower people's lives with his Jesus. His Jesus Seminar put in a crowning vote in March 1995: "Did Jesus literally rise from the dead? That such a vote would even take place says a lot about current Bible scholarship; that the result, by an overwhelming majority, was to announce, No, he did not, shows clearly the chasm that has opened between some professors of Scripture and the true-believing flock" (*Time*, April 10, 1995: 66).

As we see, the popular media (including many radio and TV series and interviews) is off and running with this crisis: Who do you say Jesus is? This is the christological question being forced on us by current New Testament research and its promotion or indoctrination. The radicals and liberals are now vying with the fundamentalists and televangelists for control of the Jesus images disseminated to the masses.

What to Believe?

Where do we stand in the context of these reports? Answer ***Yes*** *or* ***No*** *to the following statements and questions.*

1. I "thirst to know the flesh-and-blood Jesus" as Funk does.
2. Was Jesus a "secular sage"?
3. Does my faith depend on the faith of Peter and Paul?
4. Is Jesus a "proper object of faith"?
5. Is the "demise" of the church "inevitable"?
6. Could the "rediscovery and liberation of Jesus" result in Christianity's rebirth?
7. Is Christianity a "tradition worth reforming and saving"?

8. Should we demote Jesus from the Christ?
9. Do most Christians look for "privilege" and "rewards" from their religion?
10. I believe in "blood atonement."
11. I believe Jesus was immaculately conceived of the virgin Mary.
12. If the "apocalyptic elements" were taken out, Christianity would be ruined.
13. The writers of the New Testament were out to "invent Christianity."
14. Jesus' "body had already been devoured by wild dogs" before he was ever taken to a tomb.
15. The first Gospel of the New Testament was written forty years after Jesus' death.
16. Thomas' gospel is as important as those of Mark, Matthew, Luke, and John.
17. The hypothetical "Q" source is reliable for faith-knowledge.
18. Will Christianity be "undermined" by the omission of the passion, resurrection, atonement, and Jesus' coming again?
19. If a different image of Jesus is mass-marketed, could it change Christianity significantly?
20. "Will twenty centuries of Western culture be undone" by the scholarship of the Jesus Seminar and the Q Project?
21. Is Jesus the most "empowering figure" in history?
22. If Jesus empowers my life, am I a Christian?
23. Did Jesus literally rise from the dead?
24. Is it good that the radicals and liberals are vying with the fundamentalists and televangelists for the mass image of Jesus?
25. *Essay Question:* Write in 100 words or less what you believe about Jesus of Nazareth.

CHAPTER 2 NOTES

[1] Robert W. Funk, *Honest To Jesus: Jesus for a New Millennium* (San Francisco: Harper, 1996), p. 300.
[2] *Ibid.*, p. 306.
[3] *Ibid.*, pp. 300-14.

3. Imbalances Within the "Jesus Christ Is Lord" Confession

Jesus Christ Is Lord is one of the earliest confessions of the Christian witness. It is a paradigmatic statement of New Testament christology in that its component parts—*Jesus, Christ,* and *Lord*—hold the inner-structure of Christian faith in *God*: Jesus of Nazareth is the representation of God[1] and is confessed to be the Lord by believers. Or we can say that *Jesus* is the demonstration of radical faith, that *Christ* is the expression of radical faith, and that *Is Lord* is the confession of radical faith. Together, *Jesus Christ Is Lord* is a comprehensive statement of christology guarding against heresy and hypocrisy in every age, including ours.

Below is a holding triangle using the three components of the

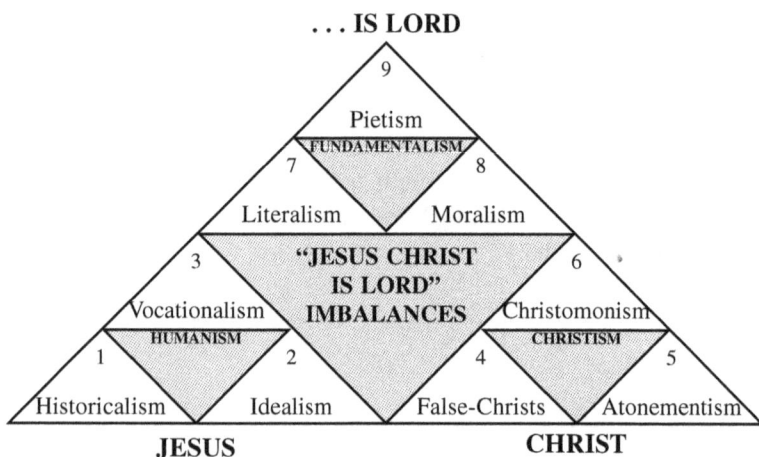

confession to frame nine imbalances (perversions or over-emphases) that I discern in today's popular Christian thinking and practice. From the outset I must advise all who read further that they will be found guilty of living out one or more of these imbalances. This I know first hand, for our human propensity is to try to make *a* meaningful understanding *the* understanding of our lives. Is it any wonder that Christ events are forever slaying our ultimate dogmas that become the center of our faith rather than *God*, to whom they point?

HUMANISM TRIANGLE

On the *JESUS* pole (bottom left of the triangle), the result of the newest "quest"[2] for the historical Jesus, begun in the last two decades, is a *Historicalism* that focuses on the right facts about Jesus of Nazareth. (*Historicism* is close, but focuses more on a verifiable method for rediscovering Jesus; it is subsumed here.) New Testament scholars, some of whom understand their task to be the reform of the Christian faith and religion, illustrate this imbalance by their scientific research of earliest documents. As we read in the last chapter, the founder of the Jesus Seminar, Robert Funk, says in his twenty-first thesis, "Jesus rather than the Bible or the creeds becomes the norm by which other views and practices are to be measured. . . . [W]e will have to start all over again with a clean theological slate, with only the parables, aphorisms, parabolic acts, and deeds of Jesus as the basis on which to formulate a new version of the faith."[3] Maybe *sola historical Jesus* is his stance.

I hardly know what Funk means by "a new version of the faith," but taken at his word his efforts will bring forth a new understanding of the Christian faith based primarily on Jesus of Nazareth, without the christological accretions of the New Testament and the tradition. To this I say that his new historical authority for faith is just another authority, which at best will always be fragmentary and incomplete— intriguing and helpful as his research may be. My questions are How is this new humanistic authority more salvific than other authorities (all *can* be blocks to faith) and How can I appropriate this "new version of the faith"? Not through right historical facts, this I know for sure.

Idealism has held a distinguished role in the history of Christian philosophy and has often sneaked into theology, e.g., old liberalism. I am not taking here the meaning of Plato, Augustine, or Hegel but am suggesting the common meaning: Jesus as the ideal, what one would aspire to, a *goal* or an *ought*. To try to imitate Jesus' deeds and words is to make Jesus a law: Do *this* and you will be saved. This is quite different from, like Jesus, being one's freedom, giving thanks for one's life the way it is, and being obedient to what one judges to be the will of *God*. In these ways we can follow Jesus authentically, being attuned to that gracious presence at the heart of life that we call *God*.

There is a sense in which the *faith of Jesus* dialogue within the historical Jesus movement and contemporary theology (to be discussed in later chapters) can end up imbalanced as well. If one attempts to take on the faith *of* Jesus, again as a goal or an ought, as one's route to salvation, then it is no better than faith *in* Jesus. Both ways will intensify despair. How do I not end up being a humanist, worshipping a saint of my self-styling? Jesus came not to be imitated, but to bring us to faith in *God*, which is the point of the confession *Jesus Christ is Lord*.

The next imbalance on the HUMANISM triangle is **Vocationalism**. The focus here is on Jesus' fulfilling his calling. He most certainly did, I believe, but again, this is not the point. So did Paul, so did Bonhoeffer, so did Mother Teresa. However, none of the three has received the *Christ* claim. There is a world of difference between vocational integrity and christology. Again, Funk illustrates the imbalance, this time in thesis 10: "*We need to reconceive the vocation of Jesus [not] as the Christ.*"[4] By "demoting Jesus" (thesis 8)[5] from the Christ to the vocated one, Funk has definitely humanized Jesus and put him at the head of the this-worldly pantheon of saints. Render to each his due, but do not mention *God* in the same breath.

The HUMANISM triangle of imbalances leaves Jesus with much less than exhalted status. This JESUS pole is to accentuate the authentic humanity of Jesus, but not in order that we become humanists. As the dictionary states, a *humanist* is one who has an interest in high human values and a philosophy that stresses "an individual's dignity and worth and capacity for self-realization through reason." No doubt the Jesus of the newest historical "questers" has these values, stresses individual dignity and worth, and will lead us to a kind of self-realization through our reason, if we give him our allegiance. And we can worship him down at the Meeting House of Jesus of Nazareth, but not at the Church of Jesus the Christ Our Lord.

CHRISTISM TRIANGLE

On the **CHRIST** pole (bottom right of the triangle), the imbalances come close to home for the believer. The **False-Christs** imbalance focuses on the multiple saving modes within Christianity, such as dogmatism: believe the right things and you will be saved. *Dogmatism* is more an imbalance among Protestants, while the false-christ of *traditionalism* belongs more to the Roman Catholics, and *sacramentalism* to the Orthodox. Right beliefs, right lineage, and right practices do not save, and if one thinks they do, one is farther from salvation than when he or she began the journey of self-conscious faith. Let us be very clear. If one believes that *God's* grace alone is the agent of salvation, and repeats that creed religiously Sunday after Sunday, and thinks that this *belief* will save him, he is believing in a false-christ: believing that belief itself can save. If one does what the church says and gives all her money to rebuild the Vatican, and thereby believes this will "get her into heaven," she is believing in a false-christ: believing the church can save. If one believes that the bread becomes the body and the wine becomes the blood, and if by properly receiving the Eucharist one receives eternal life, that person is believing in a false-christ: believing the sacrament can save.

Atonementism focuses on Jesus as the Savior, as though his vocation was to shed his blood and die to atone for our sins, for our *crimes against God*. This does not make sense to us today.[6] I agree with the historical Jesus scholars here: he understood himself "not dying as an atoning sacrifice, but probably for a cause,"[7] the cause of *God's* reign. N.T. Wright said there exists "2000 years of atonement theology that Jesus did not know."[8] Dominic Crossan was more outspoken: "the Atonement is transcendent child abuse."[9] The point is, Jesus is not the Christ because he is said to have sacrificed himself for our sins.

The word **Christomonism**[10] focuses on the imbalance of Jesus as *God*, which is probably the most universal heresy of Christians from the beginning till today. Jesus was not, is not, *God*. Jesus is not equal to *God*. Jesus reveals *God*, is transparent to *God*, but is not the object of faith. He himself had faith in *God* alone, which is "radical monotheism."[11] To have faith in Jesus is idolatry. To have faith in *God* alone is the message and mission of Jesus whom we call the Christ.

The CHRISTISM triangle leaves Jesus too exalted, even more exalted than *God*. The so-called divinity (Christ) pole of the big triangle—supposed to be held in tension with the humanity pole, especially in the *Chalcedon formula* that follows—has been overwhelming the humanity pole since the beginning of the Christian church:

> Following the holy Fathers we teach with one voice that the Son [of God] and our Lord Jesus Christ is to be confessed as one and the same [Person], that he is perfect in Godhead and perfect in manhood, very God and very man, of a reasonable soul and [human] body consisting, consubstantial with the Father as touching his Godhead, and consubstantial with us as touching his manhood; made in all things like unto us, sin only excepted; begotten of his Father before the worlds according to his Godhead; but in these last days for us men and for our salvation born [into the world] of the Virgin Mary, the Mother of God according to his manhood. . . .[12]

As a consequence, our Christ image has become ungrounded and supernatural, in spite of the dialogue of the first councils as they tried to maintain the tension between "true man" and "true God." The *Nicene Creed* (325 C.E.) below—over a century before the above *Chalcedon formula* (451 C.E.)—stresses Jesus' divinity even more:

> We believe in one God,
> > Father Almighty,
> > maker of all things visible and invisible;
> and in one Lord, Jesus Christ,
> > the Son of God,
> > begotten of His Father,
> > only begotten, that is of the *ousia* [essence] of the Father,
> > God of God, Light of Light,
> > true God of true God;
> > begotten, not made,
> > of one substance with the Father,
> > by whom all things were made,
> both things in heaven and things in earth. . . .

On the humanity (Jesus) pole, we recite up to and through the word "suffered," when the divinity (Christ) pole takes over again:

> who for us men and for our salvation,
> came down from heaven
> and was made [became] flesh
> and was made [became] man,
> *suffered* and rose again on the third day,
> ascended into the heavens
> and comes to judge living and dead.[13]

One immediately sees that the tension between the two poles of humanity and divinity was hardly held in these creedal formulations that were out to slay heresies on either side, e.g., Arianism (heresy losing the divinity pole tension) or Sabellianism (heresy losing the humanity pole tension). Nevertheless, Jesus' divinity has outweighed his humanity from the beginning, mainly because of the power of the life-transforming faith catalyzed by Jesus and the aggressive promotion work by the church, i.e., Athanasius and the Nicene Christians of the 4th century.[14]

We have never been able to keep the Christ dimension of the earliest creed, *Jesus Christ is Lord*, in balance. Unfortunately, the "enlightened" have over-reacted in the last three hundred years through scientism and humanism and have thrown out the baby (Christ) with the bathwater (supernaturalism). Why? One big reason: the other-worldliness of christism—Jesus being God—makes little sense in our post-modern worldview.

FUNDAMENTALISM TRIANGLE

In the top triangle of the creedal statement *Jesus Christ Is Lord*, the imbalances come even closer home to the contemporary believer. This is the confessional triangle and the ***IS LORD*** pole. When one starts critiquing its three sub-triangles, Pietism, Literalism and Moralism, an uproar begins, for the vocal majority rules this triangle of FUNDAMENTALISM. If the likes of the Jesus Seminar own the Humanism triangle, and if the traditional denominations own the Christism triangle, the right wing of Christianity owns this top one, *Fundamentalism*[15]—even though we all live in it to some degree as our religious rootage. The imbalances of Literalism, Moralism, and Pietism are the intensification of the other two main sub-triangles, Humanism and Christism.

For example, *Literalism* is a short hop, skip, and jump from historicism. I perceive that the newest "questers" for the historical Jesus are becoming literalistic in their research consensus and will not give credence to any words not in red or pink (the color of voting pills), verifiably the words, they vote, Jesus *probably* spoke. This type of new literalism is just a little better than the old literalism of the fundamentalists who claim that every word of the Bible is the inerrant—"inspired" is not strong enough for them—Word of *God*. The Bible for a fundamentalist is to be understood literally, even if that means one believes creation happened about 6000 B.C.E. (before the common era) and the scientific community consenses that the Big Bang happened about fifteen billion years ago—the Bible is right and science is wrong, they must believe.

What most of these literalists have in common, as I judge, is nitpicking over such issues as whether it is biblical for a woman to be ordained and homosexuality, and on the other hand, seeming blindness relative to the substantive verses of scripture that tell one to give away all he or she has to the poor or to take up one's cross and follow Jesus. They generally nitpick the scriptures that do not demand a sacrifice of their lives. What disturbs me most about the inerrancy believers is that they divide churches and Christendom, and they run off the would-be thinking Christians who want nothing to do with literalistic interpretations that make no sense to a 21st century worldview. The literatists preach that salvation depends upon one's literal belief of the Bible, and most times the King James Version at that.

Moralism seeks for its authority the keeping of the law, doing what is right, earning one's salvation by good works, equating righteousness with morality, pleasing *God* by doing what the church and Bible say. Some say Christianity is a moralistic guilt trip and the pseudo-righteous will be with us forever. The Bible becomes a rulebook rather than a book of grace. At a deeper level, one's responsibility is cut off from one's confession of faith: one lives out of cultural and institutional oughts rather than an authentic response to *God*.

A goodly percentage of the hymns in the *Cokesbury Hymnal*,[16] that I sang out of until I was out of seminary, are built on salvation through moralism, i.e., "Shun evil companions, Bad language disdain; God's name hold in reverence, Nor take it in vain; Be thoughtful and earnest, Kind-hearted and true; Look ever to Jesus, He'll carry you through" (hymn *Yield Not to Temptation*). The church becomes a community of moral principle—more like a Boy Scout troop with its laws—rather than a community based on the awesome and uncontrollable Word and Grace of *God*.

Then there are the hymns that point to the world after this world, an elaborate mythology in song. *Pietism*[17] is the ninth imbalance and is a big umbrella. Under it are those thousands of heavenly hymns, sawdust aisles and altar calls, personal saviorism, born again-ism, emotionalism, individualism, new age spiritualism, faith healing, etc. If I had to put the focus on any one thing, it would be the authority of the individual religious experience, often times an escape from the life of radical faith.

An old high school friend buttonholed me recently to witness to his new life. He said, as he wrote out on a piece of paper, "In 1962 I got my B.S. degree from the university; in '75 I got my real B.S.—Been Saved; in '98 I got my B.A. degree—Born Again; last week I got my B.H.G.—Born of the Holy Ghost. These last degrees are the ones that matter." He was pointing to that saving religious experience that is associated with conversion. I cannot say such experiences are not authentic religious experiences. But is such a stereotypical experience the primary presupposition for faith in *God*?

To say one has to have such an experience, to say one has to operate out of a certain set of principles, or to say one has to believe in the Bible literally is to be a fundamentalist. FUNDAMENTALISM operates out of a known, verifiable authority: a book, a law, or an experience. These are idolatries of the Christian faith, which tolerates no earthly authorities, gods, or idols. Believing in some worldly authority or idol takes the place of faith in *God*.

Reflection

To over-emphasize any one of the elements of *Jesus Christ Is Lord*—the humanity of Jesus, the divinity of Jesus as the Christ, or the confession of Jesus as Lord—is to change the meaning of the creedal

statement of faith in *God*. To over-emphasize *Jesus* is to call for a
confession of faith in *the man*, which is idolatry. To over-emphasize
Christ is to call for a confession of faith in *the Christ*, which is idolatry.
To over-emphasize *Is Lord* is to call for a confession of faith in some
earthly authority, which is idolatry. All three idolatries exist today and
contradict authentic Christian faith in *God*.

To confess that *Jesus Christ is Lord* is to confess faith in *God*
as Lord. It is fair to say that the nine imbalances detract from our
confessing faith in *God* alone, and if so, they block our faith in *God* and
are therefore even sinful. Some will say our falling into these imbalances
is natural; well, so is sin. Our stating these nine imbalances hopefully
brings to consciousness perversions of faith. If so, this analysis will
help us to see that what seems to us as righteousness is in fact our
religious sin, separating us from *God* and creation.

Stating the nine imbalances that stand in the way of authentic
and radical faith *in God* is an important context for the rest of this book.
Major questions of faith indicated by these imbalances are

1. What does it mean to confess *Jesus Christ is Lord*?
2. What does it mean to call Jesus the Christ?
3. What does faith in *God* look like practically?
4. How does one come to such faith?
5. What difference does such faith make?

In the following chapters we will seek to answer these
christological questions in order to awaken faith. Reflecting on the
christologies of the ten theologians I have chosen will hopefully help us
to sort out and rebuild our own christologies. None of the ten has
outgrown Jesus. All ten would probably confess that their christologies
are inadequate, but let us not forget they have given their lives to articulate
their faith in Jesus the Christ meaningfully for themselves and following
generations. Two are still alive, Schubert Ogden and Jon Sobrino. All
are "alive and well" through their written confessions of faith in Jesus
the Christ. They are now a part of the tradition of Christian faith,
maybe as important to that tradition, as far as I am concerned, as Paul,
Mark, Matthew, Luke, John, Augustine, Aquinas, Luther, and Wesley.

Maybe I need to give some *warning* here. The next ten chapters
will be slow reading, as theology always is. I have sought to present in
summary form the christologies of the ten theologians. There will be
many quotes and footnotes—really endnotes at the end of chapters to be
less distracting. Don't miss their quotes for they are key to their
christologies. I will make some reflective remarks in each of these
chapters and will pull their christologies together in Chapter 15, before
I present my own, and will list major points again in Chapter 23. (If you
bypass the theology, at least read the *Edifying Discourses* in Section Six
before beginning the exercises of Section Five.)

I choose the word *reflection* rather than *critique*, mainly because
these ten have given me the most help in creating and re-creating my
own christology. *Critique* has such a combative and negative slant in
our Enlightenment mode of education and research. That is not to say I
agree with the theologians all the time; they don't agree with each other
all the time either, as we will see. Every christology for itself, finally,
for each reflects the faith of each unique individual. No two are alike,
yet all are similar in the main.

If you decide to skip these ten (or eleven, including mine—
Chapters 16-18), by all means read the summaries: Chapters 15 and 23.
Make notes in the margins that will help you in Section Five to rewrite
your own christology. At least put a "+" sign beside comments with
which you agree and a "?" mark where you don't. As Leslie Weatherhead
said many decades ago, what you can't honestly believe, put it away in
your "agnostic box," to be brought out and looked at later. In other
words, believe what you can believe now and bracket the rest.

Let your reading be an intentional journey of faith dialogue
with these companions of Jesus the Christ. And let us remember with
St. John that *whoever sees Jesus sees* God*, and whoever honors Jesus
honors the One who sent him.*

CHAPTER 3 NOTES

[1] Schubert M. Ogden, *Christ Without Myth* (New York: Harper & Row, 1961;
Dallas: SMU Press, 1991), p. 160.
[2] Some of the Jesus Seminar do not prefer the title "new quest for the historical

Jesus," following on the second quest begun in the 1950's and led by Ernst Käsemann and James M. Robinson, and the original quest begun in the late 18th century, stimulated by H. S. Reimarus' posthumous writings.

[3] Robert W. Funk, *Honest to Jesus* (San Franciso: Harper, 1996), p. 301.

[4] *Ibid.*, p. 309.

[5] *Ibid.*, p. 306.

[6] Alister E. McGrath, *Christian Theology: An Introduction* (1994; Cambridge, MA: Blackwell Publishers, 1997), p. 388. "The term [atonement] was used especially extensively in the nineteenth and early twentieth centuries. However, there is increasing evidence that this term is seen as . . . unhelpful by many modern Christian writers, across the entire spectrum of theological viewpoints."

[7] Amy-Jill Levine, *Jesus in Context: Who Was He?* conference, sponsored by Duke University, Omni Chapel Hill Hotel, February 19-21, 1998.

[8] *Ibid.*, N. T. Wright.

[9] *Ibid.*, John Dominic Crossan.

[10] Lonnie D. Kliever, "The Christology of H. Richard Niebuhr," *The Journal of Religion*, Vol. 50, Number 1 (Chicago: University of Chicago, 1970), p. 47. In this article, Kliever cites as well the word "Jesusolatry." "Niebuhr recognizes that popular theology and practical piety often simply identify God and Jesus. But he maintains such christomonism and Jesusolatry are contrary to the biblical witness, trinitarian thought, and radical faith," p. 47.

[11] H. Richard Niebuhr, *Radical Monotheism and Western Culture* (1960; New York: Harper & Row, 1970).

[12] "Definition of the Faith of Chalcedon (451 C.E. [common era] or A.D.)," *A History of Christianity: Readings in the History of the Early and Medieval Church,* ed. Ray C. Petry (Englewood Cliffs, NJ: Prentice-Hall, 1962), p. 68 (brackets by editor).

[13] "The Creed of the Council of Nicaea (325 C.E.)," *Ibid.*, p. 63 (brackets by editor).

[14] Richard E. Rubenstein, *When Jesus Became God: The Struggle to Define Christianity during the Last Days of Rome* (New York: Harcourt, 1999).

[15] "Fundamentalism" is used loosely here. One definition reads: "extreme dispensationalism; excessive emotionalism; social withdrawal; fear of cultural challenges to the gospel; neglect of ethical issues; theological pugnaciousness; pietistic individualism." Harvie M. Conn, *Contemporary World Theology: A Layman's Guidebook* (Phillipsburg, NJ: Presbyterian and Reformed, 1979), p. 121.

[16] *The Cokesbury Worship Hymnal*, Methodist Publishing House (Nashville).

[17] "Pietism" here does not specifically denote a movement begun by Philip Spener in the seventeenth century.

Section Two:

Comparative Christologies

4. Schubert Ogden: Christology of Re-presentation

In Chapter 3, we talked about how the early confession of Christendom is now perverted—*imbalanced* is less blunt. What then does it essentially mean that *Jesus Christ Is Lord*? Schubert M. Ogden, Emeritus Professor of Theology at S.M.U, says it well: "to affirm that Jesus Christ is Lord is to affirm . . . solely the promise of God's unending love to all who will but receive it. Likewise to affirm that Jesus Christ is Lord is to affirm . . . God's love for us and thereby be freed to fulfill his command to love all the others whom he also already loves."[1]

To affirm that *Jesus Christ is Lord* has everything to do with God and his love and finally nothing else. This is theocentric or God-centered christology. What is "Jesus the Christ" all about? Revealing God. Showing us God's love. Calling us to receive God's love. Sending us to love whom God loves. God loves—receive it. Do it. It's that simple for Ogden, though he never says it that simply.

"[T]he redemptive grace of God is always given to us and to all men in every situation of our lives, and therefore the authentic existence in faith and love it continually makes possible is something for which each of us is primordially responsible."[2] Said more plainly and inclusively, God's redemptive grace is always given to us, and our responsibility is to accept it. To me this is our first and greatest responsibility as human beings. The second is like it: to witness to God's grace and act out of it with love.

These two quotes from Ogden make the point of christology clear: to focus on God and our relationship with God. When we say *Jesus Christ Is Lord*, we are saying that God is our only god. Thus Jesus lived and died to relate us to God. Why else? Certainly not to become another god or to claim equality with God. This is so basically true. Ogden continues, "this theme [the reality of God] is, in the last analysis, the *sole* theme of all valid Christian theology, even as it is the *one* essential point to all authentic Christian faith and witness."[3]

Therefore, Ogden's understanding of christology is monotonously consistent. In *The Point of Christology* he says "that Jesus is the decisive *re-presentation* of God, in the sense of the one through whom the meaning of God for us, and hence the meaning of ultimate reality for us, becomes fully explicit."[4] Who is Jesus? He is the one who answers in his totality the right question, "Who is God?" Jesus is the one who shows us enough that the meaning of God for us is understandable. "Jesus . . . explicitly authorizes *faith in God* as our authentic self-understanding."[5] Again, said more plainly, Jesus tells and shows us that faith in God is our key to understanding our own existence.

We cannot interpret Ogden's theology, including his christology, without assuming that every word off his pen is moving toward an existentialist interpretation. He began with translating and interpreting Rudolf Bultmann. He is not as exciting as Bultmann in thought and expression—as an American, Ogden's writing structure often seems more German than Bultmann's complex sentences. Though Ogden's complex style discourages the lay person, there is gold in his mines. He is even more the existentialist than Bultmann, who is an avowed Christian existentialist. Ogden is borderline Christian existentialist and secular existentialist. He can be interpreted either way.

His existentialist interpretation of christology and his difference with Bultmann is highlighted when Ogden criticizes Bultmann (fairly or not we will consider further in Chapter 5) for *not* demythologizing the "event Jesus Christ." Said another way, Bultmann finally believes that the "Jesus Christ event" is a necessary condition to authentic faith in God. Jesus as the Christ is the mythological exception, Ogden says, that Bultmann does not apply to existentialist interpretation. He therefore says Bultmann erred on two counts: 1) he was not finally consistent in his demythologizing project of the New Testament—he left a "remainder"[6]; and 2) he put a condition on faith. Ogden is emphatic on the second point as he cites the heart of the Reformation: *grace alone— faith alone.*

To be sure, the deepest conviction of Christian faith is that God's saving action has been decisively disclosed in the event Jesus of Nazareth; and, in this sense, Jesus is indeed God's 'work' of salvation. But when this conviction is so expressed that the event of Jesus becomes a condition apart from which God is not free to be a gracious God, the heretical doctrine of works-righteousness achieves its final and most dangerous triumph.[7]

If his critique of Bultmann is true, the "Humanism," "Christism" and "Fundamentalism" imbalances in Chapter 3 are at play here, blocking authentic faith in God. Jesus the Christ becomes the object of faith rather than the transparency of faith. Faith in God has no conditions, else it becomes also faith in that condition, which becomes a competing object of faith—an idol. So we are back to our point, that Jesus the Christ focuses us on faith in God—alone.

Aware of his theocentric focus and his existential orientation, we can pull these two together in his use of the word *re-presentation* (see quotes above). For Ogden, God constituted authentic existence in the beginning with his self-presentation to all people by building into the hardware of life its very meaning. Jesus the Christ decisively *re-presents* or makes manifest what God originally presented or constituted.

His christology can even be referred to as a re-presentational christology. What does this mean? Grace did not begin with Jesus, but with God. Jesus *re-presents* it. Jesus is not the absolute truth about life, but *re-presents* it. Before Jesus the Christ the possibility of salvation was already existent.

[U]nless the *theocentric* basis and sanction of 'christocentrism' is explicitly acknowledged, emphasis on Jesus Christ can be a snare and a delusion and a mere travesty of authentic apostolic faith. . . . [T]he New Testament does *not* affirm that in Christ our salvation 'becomes possible.' It affirms, rather, that in him what has always been possible now 'becomes manifest,' in the sense of being decisively presented in human witness.[8]

Jesus the Christ re-presents and reveals God's salvation. He does not establish salvation. Ogden would ask Why does Jesus have to establish it to be the Christ? He can be God's re-presentation without having to be pre-existent with the Father or the second person of the trinity. "[T]he point . . . is not that the Christ is manifest only in Jesus and nowhere else, but that the word addressed to man everywhere, in all events of their lives, is none other than the word spoken in Jesus and in the preaching and sacraments of the church."[9]

Ogden points out that Paul's christology makes one basic claim: "the human word that speaks to men in the event of Jesus . . . is the same word always addressed to them in God's original revelation."[10] "I understand it to belong to the very essence of the Christian witness to attest that the fundamental option for salvation that is decisively *re-presented* solely through Jesus is also *implicitly* presented to every human being as soon and as long as he or she exists humanly at all."[11] And Ogden means from the very beginning to the very end. By *existence* Ogden means the history of existence as well as our personal existence.

As far as our present existence is concerned, John Macquarrie says the essence of Ogden's *The Point of Christology* is that "The gospel tradition tells us not who Jesus *was* in a historical sense, but who he *is* in his existential significance for us in the present."[12] Ogden, like Bultmann and all existentialists worth their salt, says that it is finally all up to us to decide for or against authentic existence as it is revealed to us.

Ogden says that God has made existence possible for every bit of creation through grace and "boundless love."[13] And more, that we can experience now God's unconditional love if we but receive it. How do we know this? *Explicitly*—often after the fact—God's graciousness has become abundantly clear to us through Jesus, whom we therefore call the Christ. Consequently we have experienced and affirmed faith in God.

If Abraham did not know about Jesus, was faith possible for him? Ogden would say, "Of course." How so? Because, from the beginning, life has at least *implicitly* manifest itself as gracious, full of possibility; and there have been those in every generation who have manifested this understanding, as Abraham did. Every human at least senses life is worth living, that life is a gift, that faith in the profound reality of life is possible, and that he or she can opt for authentic living, which includes honoring and serving the rest of creation.

Reflection

Let us talk about Ogden's significance for us from this brief introduction. We have quoted enough of his writings to reflect seriously upon his christology. What of Ogden's christology makes us reflect deeply?

1. Jesus the Christ is not the object of our faith.
2. Grace did not begin with Jesus.
3. Jesus *re-presents* what God has always presented.
4. The Word spoken through Jesus is final revelation for all—though not the exclusive revelation.[14]
5. The point of *Jesus Christ Is Lord* is to bring us to faith in God.
6. Therefore, christology deals with our relationship with God.
7. The gospels have more to do with Jesus' significance for our present history than with Jesus' past history.
8. Jesus' word deals not only with our existence but with the whole history of existence, for it re-presents God's Word from the beginning.
9. God's Word is built into our existence and encounters all humans.[15]
10. The word of Jesus—and therefore God's Word—encounters us in every human event, whether or not we are conscious of it.
11. If the event of Jesus the Christ becomes a condition for our faith in God, it is an idol.
12. Jesus' mission is to relate us to our only God.
13. Jesus shows us God's love, calls us to receive God's love, and sends us to love those whom God loves—everyone and every bit of creation.
14. Everyone experiences God's love either explicitly through Jesus the Christ or implicitly through the way existence is created.
15. Why stick with Jesus, knowing there are other disclosures of God?
16. Was Abraham's faith in God as authentic as the faith of one who professes Jesus as the Christ?
17. Can one know God's "boundless love" as strongly without Jesus the Christ?

We rightly will struggle as we reflect on these christological insights and questions coming out of our dialogue with Schubert Ogden. That is as it should be. Whether we agree with Ogden or not, it is refreshing to meet a Christian theologian who gets to the heart of the matter and stays there. What else is there to talk about as a Christian except one's authentic relationship with *God*, and that finally revealed through Jesus the Christ? Ogden has spent his adult life coming at this from multiple directions, and when his book of systematic theology is printed, I feel sure it will be more of the same. He is chaste in that all his Christian existentialist reflections are *God*-centered.

Let us end as we began, standing before Ogden's theocentric understanding of christology:

> Thus to affirm that Jesus Christ is Lord is to affirm that the final promise in which we place our confidence is none of the many promises of the so-called gods of heaven and earth, but solely the promise of God's unending love to all who will but receive it. . . . *To affirm this promise . . . is the real meaning of affirming the lordship of Jesus Christ. . . .* [16]

> [T]he affirmation whose meaning I have tried to interpret is fundamentally an affirmation that each of us must make not only with his mind and lips, but with his 'heart,' with the whole weight of his existence as a self through a free, personal decision. [17]

CHAPTER 4 NOTES

[1] Schubert M. Ogden, *The Reality of God and Other Essays* (New York: Harper & Row, 1963), pp. 203-4 (emphasis added).

[2] Schubert M. Ogden, *Christ Without Myth: A Study Based on the Theology of Rudolf Bultmann* (New York: Harper & Row, 1961; Dallas: SMU Press, 1991), p.141.

[3] *The Reality of God*, p. x.

[4] Schubert M. Ogden, *The Point of Christology* (San Francisco: Harper & Row, 1982), p. 82 (emphasis added).

[5] *Ibid.*, p. 83 (emphasis added).

[6] *Christ Without Myth*, p. 112.

[7] *Ibid.*, p. 145.

[8] *Ibid.*, p. 143.

[9] *Ibid.*, p. 156.

[10] *The Reality of God*, p. 203.

[11] *The Point of Christology*, pp. 83-4 (emphasis added).

[12] John Macquarrie, *Jesus Christ in Modern Thought* (London: SCM Press/ Trinity Press, 1990), p. 332.

[13] *The Point of Christology*, p. 119. Ogden uses the phrase "boundless love" repeatedly to point out "that *Jesus meant love*—that the basic motif expressed both by his proclamation of God's reign and his summons to repentance and faith and by his implicit claim for their decisive significance was the motif of God's prevenient love as the gift and demand of authentic existence in faith and returning love." A summary mouthful and a glorious run-on sentence!

[14] *Christ Without Myth*, pp. 123-4. Here Ogden does not dispute that the "event Jesus Christ" is the decisive event of faith, but does dispute that it is the *only* event of faith. This is his primary dispute with Bultmann.

[15] John Macquarrie, *Christology Revisited* (Harrisburg: Trinity Press, 1998): he says Jesus is the Jew in relation to Judaism, the Lord in relation to the church, and the authentic human person in relation to the human race, p. 106.

[16] *The Reality of God*, pp. 203-4.

[17] *Ibid.*, p. 205.

5. Rudolf Bultmann: Christology of the Word

Ogden's God-centered christology is complementary to Rudolf Bultmann's Christ-centered christology, or christology of the Word of God in Jesus the Christ. Having said this, I do not infer that Bultmann is talking about our having faith in Jesus rather than God.[1] To get hold of Bultmann's thoroughgoing Christian existentialist interpretation, I will use his lecture *The Crisis of Faith*,[2] which in its first three sections talks about God's activity, faith in God, and Christian faith in God.

In his **section** on **God**, Bultmann sums up the paradoxical activity of God this way:

> *God is what limits mankind*, who makes a comedy of his care, who allows his longing to miscarry, who casts him into solitude [even 'final solitude'], who sets a limit to his knowing and doing, who calls him to duty, and who gives the guilty over to torment. And yet at the same time it is God who forces one into life and drives him into care; who puts longing and the desire for love in his heart; who gives him thoughts and strength for his work, and who places him in the eternal struggle between willfulness and duty. God is the enigmatic power beyond time, yet master of the temporal; beyond existence, yet at work in it.[3]

Who does this limiting, this cutting off? Bultmann repeatedly makes a point to call it a dark or mysterious power. And what does he name this power? *God*.[4] Likewise, who drives us into life and care? Again, the mysterious power whom he names *God*. He is saying that this paragraph illustrates more than a dozen ways *God*—who is beyond time and existence—acts in the existence of all human beings.

In the **second section** on *faith in God*, he begins by asking

Why give the enigma, the mystery which drives us this way

and that and hedges us in, any other name than simply 'the enigma', or 'fate'? Does the name 'God' not gloss over the fact that we are in the dark, and are at the mercy of fate? Or, if there must be a name, why not equally well that of the devil? Does not this power play a cruel game with us, destroying and annihilating? Is not unfulfillment the mark of every life? Is not death, nothingness the end?[5]

Bultmann does not back off from saying that the power that drives us this way and that is *God*, but is quite aware that we do not like it the way it is and want it some other way. However that may be, this is the way life is for us all, to be limited, driven, and fenced in by *God*.

And is it not to the point, in face of the enigma and the darkness, to insist on the meaning of life with a cry of 'Nevertheless!'?
. . . [T]his 'Nevertheless' is . . . the meaning of faith in God. It is the courage to designate that dark enigma, that sovereign power as God, as my God. It is the courage to assert that in the knowledge of this power every being acquires its meaning, that . . . I also realize I belong to it, and that the limit which fences my being about is inwardly removed. This will, of course, happen when I give up my pretense to make my own way; when I submit to this power as that which brought me into existence, when I can say 'Yes' to it. Faith in God is the courage which utters this 'Nevertheless.'[6]

Bultmann goes on to talk about why a *worldview* is not faith in God, for

Knowledge of the power which creates and limits existence is not theoretical knowledge but is the knowledge which breaks in on us in critical moments of our existence itself. . . .
Real faith in God always grows out of the realization of the *questionableness* of existence, . . . which comes to consciousness in the *moment* of living . . . by holding to a proper detachment from things and by carrying out that humbling, that 'Yes': 'Not my will, but yours be done.'[7]

Then he talks about why *mysticism* is not faith in God.

> His [God's] *otherness* is the otherness of one having power over the temporal and the eternal, the otherness of the *power* which creates and limits our life, not the otherness of a substance or of a void with which the soul unites and into which it is swallowed up as it soars above the world in devotion, abstraction and ecstasy. . . . [O]ne who wishes to escape from himself is only flung back on himself. . . . It knows that what one *has done* and *does*, his decisions, constitute him in his very being, that temporality is his essence, and that wishing to escape from the temporal simply means wishing to escape from his own reality, and therefore from God, who is met by him nowhere else but in this temporal reality. . . . [One hears] in the call of the moment the call of God, and is always to carry out his obedience to God in *decision*, in *action*. In such obedience he is to gain his freedom from the world, from bondage to the world in anxiety and thoughtlessness, in self-deception and vanity. . . .[8]

At this point the existentialist is sailing along saying, "Here, here!" And then Bultmann goes on to the **next section**, **Christian faith in God**, not just faith in God. But before he does, he points out the difference between an existentialist faith in God and stoicism, which is really "faith in humanity."

> [For stoicism, is not] this 'Nevertheless!' simply the Nevertheless of defiance, of the courage bred by despair? In fact: faith as it has been described [up to this point] need not be anything but faith in humanity, that is, fundamentally not a faith in an otherness, but a human attitude, a disposition of the soul, which in overcoming despair and resignation, stupidity and thoughtlessness, takes stock of the reality in which it exists, saying 'Yes' to it in awe and gratitude, proudly and humbly at one and the same time, refusing to be discomfited, but, on the contrary, going on its way composedly and courageously.
> . . . Such faith of course speaks of God; indeed, it even speaks *to* God. But for it, God is the undefined, is fate, and in any event, is not the God of Christian faith.[9]

Stoicism, as Bultmann sees it, has within it what I will call an *existential yearning* for something more. Bultmann quotes Luther: "'For outside Christianity, even if people have faith in and worship only a true God, yet they do *not* know what his intentions are towards them, and they cannot look to him for any *love* or *good*. . . .'"[10]

Bultmann adds emphatically that "It is for this very reason that the *Word* [of Jesus the Christ] was [and is] needed."[11] If we in our human existence of being driven this way and that cannot see any "love or good," we are left with the stoic's gutting-it-out or the secular existentialist's boot-strapping-it. Neither is the worthy promise for authentic humanness—rather, just sheer unrelenting demand.

So what is this *Word* all about that *makes all the difference*? Bultmann says

> *Christian faith* has its distinctiveness in speaking of an event. . . . The event is *Jesus Christ*, in whom, as the New Testament says, God has spoken, and whom the New Testament itself calls 'the Word'. That is, in what happened in and through Christ, God has decisively manifested[12] himself to humanity, and in this event a message is grounded and legitimated which confronts one as *God's Word*, not teaching him a new concept of God, but giving him the right to have faith in the God [of love and good] in whom he would like to have faith. . . .
>
> In order to understand this . . . we need to reflect further on *how* this Word tells one that he may have faith in God. It tells him by its promise of *forgiveness of his sin*; and in saying so, it is also telling him that submission[13] to the power which calls us into life and makes us finite, and that saying 'Yes', is only real and radical, and what it should be, when it is at once a confession of sin and a plea for grace. Here we are not to think of sin as immorality, but as the human claim to seek to exist in one's own right, to be one's own master, and to take one's life into one's own hands.[14]

Bultmann finishes this third section by pointing to the flip side of God's Word, the "command to love," for in our sin we have said *No* to the neighbor.

[C]aught up in a life of lovelessness and hate . . . [man] is guilty and impure because so much callousness and ingratitude, falsehood and meanness, thoughtless spoiling of the joys of others, and selfish neglect of the other person, so much coolness towards others and insistence on his own rights, all lie behind him. No, rather they do not lie behind him but cling to him unforgiven, and make him impure. . . .[15]

That my guilt, that—in God's eyes—my sin, is forgiven, is what the Word of the Christian proclamation says, and only to the one who accepts this forgiveness, submitting to its judgement and taking upon oneself the demand of love, does it give the right to speak of God and to God.[16]

Reflection on Bultmann's Lecture, *The Crisis of Faith*

Through these excerpts from the eleven full pages of the three sections of his lecture, we have a condensed context for Bultmann's christology of the Word.

Section one lays out the way existence is for every person, according to Bultmann. To deny that life is this way is to go against the consensus of our experience. To say that it is God who drives us this way and that may not be a consensus, especially not among fundamentalist Christians and those who say they do not believe in God in the first place. Bultmann's confession that it is God who puts us in this situation, that God constituted existence this way, is the beginning of wisdom. *For this is **the way life is**; if God is absent from it, then God is out of it and life is without love.*

- Are we *limited*? Of course.
- Are we limited by *everyday care for the morrow*? Of course.
- Are we *fools* because we lay up *stores for tomorrow*? Of course and of course not.
- Will we ever get the *care for tomorrow* done? Of course not.
- Do we *long for the true and the beautiful*, for an *eternity of pleasure*? Of course.
- Do we *long for love*? Of course.
- Do our *longings ever miscarry*? Of course.

- Do we experience *loneliness*? Of course.
- Are we aware of a *final solitude, death*? Of course.
- Do we have an *impulse toward knowledge*? Of course.
- Do we ever *know enough*? Of course not.
- Do we have an *impulse to action, to work*? Of course.
- Do we ever *complete our work*? Of course not.
- Does our *work* ultimately fulfill our lives? Of course not, we finally find out.
- Are we *called to duty* by *conscience*? Of course.
- Do we experience *guilt* because of *thoughtlessness, wasted time, lost opportunity, impure thoughts, and mean actions*? Of course.
- Are we *forced into life* or *driven to care*? Do we just care?[17] Of course.

What would you call a movie about the situation suggested by the above questions? What would the man on the street call such a situation? Is it good or bad? Where are you in this situation of being driven this way and that? What do you call it?

Then he begins **section two** with some hard questions, which add up to Who do you say put you in this situation? Enigma? Fate? Devil? Destroyer? Annihilator? What would you call someone who put you in this situation? Be honest. What name do you call the power that has put you here? Bultmann says *God*. What do your honest answers say about you and your faith? What does Bultmann's answer say about him and his faith? It makes all the difference in the world what we name the power that puts us here in this existence. What would it mean to say "Nevertheless!" to this situation? Can you say "Yes" to that power who put you in this situation? Are you able to say God put you in this human situation and to give thanks? If so, you have faith in God, Bultmann says. Or are you only able to say "Nevertheless!" defiantly out of courage bred by despair? Are you able to honestly say God constituted this existence? Or are you only able to say honestly that whatever caused existence to be this way is not worth bowing before, so I'll do the best I can with faith in humanity? Am I a stoic or a secular existentialist without faith in God? Are these the alternatives?

Then Bultmann goes to **section three** to talk about an event that manifests that God has intentions of love and good toward us humans in this God-given life situation; and that this happening, that the Christian tradition has called Jesus the Christ, or the very Word of God, calls us to a "Yes" response to God who forgives us as we confess our not wanting to have life the way it is and rebelling against it, even showing hate toward our neighbors. Bultmann says that this Christian faith is accepting God's love and taking upon oneself the demand to love.

In this lecture Bultmann explains what faith in God is not and what it is. He explicates existence, God, existentialist faith in God, worldview, stoicism, and Christian faith in God. By dealing with his remarks seriously we can better discover where we stand in relationship with God, for his spectrum of faith is clearly differentiated. Finally, Bultmann wants us to know that the *crisis of faith* is always with us in this existence, ever calling us to a new decision of faith.[18] These crises in our existence always come to a head through the non-Gnostic Christ, Bultmann says:

> In place of cosmic dualism [of Gnosticism] steps a dualism in decision: life and death are not determined from all time on natural grounds, but depend on the decision of faith and of unbelief. The Redeemer therefore does not bring a knowledge that illuminates men as to their true nature; rather he reveals to man his sin, and sets him before the decision to live on the basis of the created world or from the Creator.[19]

Reflection on Bultmann's Christology

We need to further reflect on Bultmann's understanding of the *event of faith*, at the heart of his christology, knowing that his lecture above was mostly context for this event.

Let me try to articulate in a hundred words Bultmann's dynamics of the faith process both existentially and theologically: (1=) *Existentially* the *historical* (general history) becomes *historic* (eventful) and encounters me in my *historicity* (my history) in order to challenge me with a decision for *authenticity* out of a new *self-understanding* (understanding of existence). *Theologically* God's Word—the eschatological event of Jesus the Christ based on the cross/resurrection kerygma (proclamation)—

brings me to the moment of decision to receive new life and reject my old willful life; if I say "Yes," grace has brought me to faith, to a new image of myself wherein I freely let God determine my life through my obedience as I lovingly serve my neighbor (=100).

Ogden in Chapter 4 says that Bultmann made an exception to his demythologizing task by stating that the "event Jesus Christ" was a requirement for authentic life. Ogden based his argument on Bultmann's saying that human authenticity was in principle possible without the Christ event, but was in fact not really possible without it. This is similar to what Bultmann said in his lecture above, the difference between faith in God and Christian faith in God: one can have faith in God, but is left with an existential longing for a sure knowledge that his or her God is loving and good, which the Christian faith in God proclaims. Also, Bultmann did demythologize the Christ event by existentially interpreting "eschatology" *from* the myth of the end-time crisis *to* the fact of a present crisis born of an event that brings us to decision for faith—simply, a "Yes" or "No" decision now; end time is always now.

Ogden cannot say much, for as I interpret him, he too prefers the Christian faith in God of "boundless love," though he does not say the "Jesus Christ event" is a requirement for faith. He says a great deal about love and observes that humans generally experience God's love in their existence, which he says God put there primordially without Jesus' having to manifest it to them. Bultmann does not observe naked existence as full of love as Ogden does.

As I read them, they end up about the same place, both preferring to proclaim a loving God who is decisively manifest in the Christ event, which is really a demythologized Christ, though Bultmann does put forward the condition of the proclamation of the Word based on the cross. Ogden cannot go this far and says God constituted his "boundless love" in existence with or without the Word—but says he himself believes the Christian proclamation.

They both speak truth. Yet, I too observe that there is that existential longing in those who come to faith in *God*, a longing to know that the mysterious power that drives us this way and that is a *God* of love and grace. Also, Bultmann, not Ogden, places much emphasis on confession of sin and forgiveness out of the Word. I call both *Christian existentialists* and add that Ogden puts a condition on this title.

Many Christians would say that neither is a Christian, primarily because they demythologize most major tenets of traditional Christian faith, e.g., virgin birth, miracles, resurrection, second coming, heaven, hell, ascension, and atonement. Again, what we mean by this is that both theologians existentially interpret these myths, or transpose their supernatural content into our life context. As said earlier, the "eschatological event," which is at the heart of Bultmann's christology, is transposed *from* the mythology of the final judgment and Jesus' second coming *to God's* judgment of us at this moment, calling us to a decision to end our old ways of self-will and begin a new life in obedience to *God's* rule—in other words, taking a future-oriented doctrine out of the past of the New Testament and saying it has to do with our lives right now, which is the end time.

Through such a method of interpretation I was brought again to faith. At a time in my life when I threw the New Testament out because of its unbelievable myths, Bultmann and others of his ilk brought me back to faith and to the church.[20] I found that I could demythologize the Testaments and the creeds and hymns in a way that made sense to me, that again put me in dialogue with ultimate truth about life.[21] That is what Bultmann and Ogden are out to do through their interpretations, to bring us to authentic faith in *God.* If the mythology of the three-story universe (heaven/this world/hell) of the 1st century is the stumbling block, re-interpret it into our 21st century one-story universe of existence and let our "Yea" or "Nay" to *God's* Word become the issue—here and now.

What does demythologizing have to do with Bultmann's christology of the Word? Through it we are allowing the Word to be the Word rather than arguing over this or that belief. As Bultmann reminds us, the Word is an event in our lives, not a belief system that becomes a law to be fulfilled. His demythologization of salvation gets at the heart of his thought. "The entire salvation-drama—incarnation, death, resurrection, Pentecost, the parousia—is concentrated into a *single event*: the Revelation of God's 'reality'. . . in the earthly activity of the man Jesus combined with . . . man's accepting it in faith."[22] This is radical in that there is no revelation, or Jesus is not the Christ for me, unless I accept this in faith—christology depends on my decision. Salvation is the coming together of *God's* reality, through Jesus, by our faith. Jesus as the revelation of *God's* reality, through our faith, begins to delineate Bultmann's christology. *Jesus is the Christ through this event of revelation and our faith*—he is the fact of *God's* revelation and the fact of our faith. Macquarrie says that in Bultmann "Christ's deity is the *event* that takes place when the *word of Christ* is heard as *word of God*. In Bultmann, *God* too is understood as *event*. . . . The miracle of Christ is that a human word is heard as a divine word,"[23]—or when the Word-event really speaks to me, I hear the Word of *God* and respond in faith. Bultmann's is a christology of the Word revealed in our real lives and the Word received in our decision of faith.

Now, hopefully, we can better understand Gogarten's great summary sentence of the core of Bultmann's christological faith: "the decision for what takes place in this eschatological event, that is, the making possible of new life, in the 'obedience of faith' in which the possibility is apprehended, brings with it a decision for the historicity of one's own existential life."[24]

CHAPTER 5 NOTES

[1] John Macquarrie, "Christology in Dialogue with Existentialism," *Christology in Dialogue*, ed. by Robert F. Berkey and Sarah A. Edwards (Cleveland: Pilgrim Press, 1993), pp. 269-274. In this essay Macquarrie makes very clear that Bultmann sees hardly any references in the synoptic Gospels or Paul's epistles that would indicate we have faith in Jesus as our God. Macquarrie reminds us that Bultmann wrote a sharp criticism of the 1951 World Council of Churches christological statement that the WCC "is composed of churches which acknowledge Jesus Christ as God."
[2] Rudolf Bultmann, "The Crisis of Faith," *Rudolf Bultmann: Interpreting Faith for the Modern Era*, ed., Roger Johnson (London: Collins Liturgical, 1987), pp. 240-56.
[3] *Ibid.*, p 243.
[4] Bultmann uses the word *God* with deliberation, often describing an activity of reality first, and then saying, "That's what I am pointing to when I use the word *God*." Likewise, I will be deliberate in my use of the words *God* or *Christ* or *Spirit* as pointing to some reality experienced in existence.
[5] *Op. cit.*, p. 244.

[6] *Ibid.*

[7] *Ibid.*, p. 245.

[8] *Ibid.*, p. 247.

[9] *Ibid.*, p. 248.

[10] *Ibid.*, p. 249 (emphasis added).

[11] *Ibid.*, (emphasis added).

[12] "Decisively manifested" is like phrases Ogden borrows from Bultmann, Ch. 4.

[13] Later on Bultmann says that "submission is impossible without *confession of sin* and *forgiveness.*"

[14] *Ibid.*, p. 249.

[15] *Ibid.*, p. 250.

[16] *Ibid.*, pp. 250-51.

[17] The emphasized words are out of Bultmann's first section.

[18] Dietrich Bonhoeffer, *A Testament to Freedom: The Essential Writings of Dietrich Bonhoeffer* (1990; San Francisco: HarperSanFrancisco, 1995). Like Bultmann's *crisis of faith*, Bonhoeffer makes the point of daily faith: "You do not have your belief once and for all. Your belief . . . demands to be won anew with every new day. God gives us always just precisely so much faith as we need for the present day. . . . Either we receive it anew everyday, or it decays. One day is long enough to keep faith. Every morning brings a new struggle to push through all the unbelief, through all the littleness of faith, . . . to reach faith and wrest it from God. . . . Belief *is* a decision" (p. 295). The crisis of faith is a daily decision for faith in God.

[19] Rudolf Bultmann, *The Gospel of John: A Commentary* (Philadelphia: Westminster, 1971), p. 9.

[20] I find it interesting that many of the noted scholars of our generation—the generation after Bultmann—whom I take seriously, also found much of their faith stimulation through studying under him or dialoguing with his thinking: Friedrich Gogarten, Norman Perrin, Joseph Mathews, Schubert Ogden, John Macquarrie, Gerhard Ebeling, Ernst Käsemann, Günther Bornkamm, James Robinson, Willi Marxsen, Robert Funk, etc.

[21] John P. Cock, *Called to Be*, pp. 193-94.

[22] Rudolf Bultmann, *Theology of the New Testament*, Vol. II (New York: Charles Scribner's, 1955), p.58 (emphasis added).

[23] John Macquarrie, *Jesus Christ in Modern Thought*, p. 295 (emphases added).

[24] Friedrich Gogarten, *Christ the Crisis* (Richmond: John Knox, 1970), p.15.

6. H. Richard Niebuhr: Christology of Radical Faith

When we think of H. Richard Niebuhr we think of sociology, ethics, and ecclesiology before we think of theology and christology. Yet, his theology is as helpful to me as anyone's, probably because his christology revolves around his understanding of faith, or better, radical faith. Again, like Ogden and Bultmann, his christology cannot be understood apart from a theology of God. Like them also he is a Christian existentialist.

As in the chapter on Bultmann, we will enter Niebuhr through one piece of his writing, ***Faith in Gods and in God***,[1] easily one of my ten favorite theological essays. I will splice together key quotes and will then go on to reflect upon his essay from the standpoint of his christology of radical faith. In the ***introduction*** he raises the existential question, "How is faith in God possible?" This is a key question, a very personal, existential question for us, for we are asking it out of our real life situation rather than from some abstract perch.[2]

Niebuhr launches into his ***first section***, ***What Is Faith***, by saying *we cannot live without a cause, without some object of devotion, some center of worth, something on which we rely for our meaning.* In this sense each of us has faith. *To have faith and to have a god is one and the same thing. When we believe that life is worth living, by the same act we refer to some being which makes our life worth living. And this being, whatever or whomever, is properly termed our god.*[3]

In ***section two***, ***Who is God***, we arrive, then, at the problem of deity by setting out from the universal human experience of faith. As Luther reminds us, *Trust and faith of the heart alone make both God and idol. . . . For the two, faith and God, hold close together. 'Whatever then the heart clings to . . . and relies upon, that is properly thy God.'*

Natural religion is polytheistic, having many gods. *The private faith by which we live is likely to be a multifarious thing with many objects of devotion and worship.* The most common is the self. The self becomes the center of value. *But this self is never an adequate god.* There are many other gods: *Mothers make gods of their sons and daughters.* There are the gods of *home, sex, country, ideologies, democracies, civilizations, churches, art, truth, moral values, ideas,* and *social values. One of the beings on which institutionalized faith relies for deliverance from meaninglessness is religion itself.*

What is the tragedy here? That *none of these values or centers of value exists universally, or can be the object of a universal faith. None of them can guarantee meaning to our life in the world save for a time. They are all **finite**.* None of our gods is able *to save us from the ultimate frustration of meaningless existence.*

Our inner conflicts stem from our having *many sources of value.* All cannot be served: we fight for *America, liberty, solidarity, equality, order,* and *fraternity. But none of these gods is universal and therefore devotion to one always implies exclusion of another. So the gods are divisive socially as well as within the person.*

We dream of integration, of a great pantheon in which all the gods will be served. But synthesis is never achieved, *for each god in turn requires a certain absolute devotion.* More than this, *we practice a kind of successive polygamy, being married now to this and now to that object of devotion.*

The tragedy of our religious life is not only that the many gods divide us *within ourselves and from each other. There is a greater tragedy—**the twilight of the gods**. None is able to supply continuous meaning and value. The causes for which we live **all die**. The great social movements pass*; our *ideals* are *relative; the empires and cities all decay. At the end nothing is left to defend us against the void of meaninglessness. We try to evade this knowledge, but it is ever in the background of our minds. The apocalyptic vision of the end of all things assails us. All our causes, all our ideas, all the beings on which we relied to save us from worthlessness **are doomed to pass**.*[4]

In *section three*, **GOD**, he asks *What is **it** that is responsible* *for this passing, that dooms our human faith to frustration?* Some of *its* names are *nature of things, fate, reality, law of things,* the *way things are,* and the *void out of which everything comes and to which everything returns. Against **it** there is no defense. **This reality** . . . **abides when all else passes. It** is the source of all things and the end of all. **It** surrounds our life as the great abyss. What **it** is we do not know save that **it** is and that **it** is the supreme reality with which we must reckon.*

> [O]ur faith has been attached to that great void, to that enemy of all our causes, to that opponent of all our gods. The strange thing has happened that we have been enabled to say of this reality, this last power in which we live and move and have our being, 'Though *it* slay us yet will we trust *it*.' We have been allowed to attach our confidence to *it*, and put our reliance in *it* which is the one reality beyond all the many, which is the last power, the infinite source of all particular beings as well as their end. And insofar as our faith, our reliance for meaning and worth, has been attached to this source and enemy of all our gods, we have been enabled to call this reality *God*.
>
> Let us raise three questions about this fact that faith has become attached to the void and the enemy which surrounds our life. The first one is, What does it mean to attach faith to this power? The second, How does such faith come about? And the third, What are the consequences of such faith?

*First, to have faith in this reality means that, having been driven away from our reliance on all the lesser causes, we have learned to conceive of and rely on this last power, this nature of things, as itself the greatest of all causes, the undefeatable cause. . . . 'For this cause was I born and therefore I came into the world that I might make glorious the name and exhibit the power of this last cause.' To have faith in something as able to give value to our lives is to love it. **Without such love there is no faith.** And to have faith is also to live in hope. To have hope of this One is to have hope that is eternal. **This being cannot pass away.** And to hope for the manifestations of its judgments and its love is to hope to eternity.*

Professor Whitehead has said that *'religion . . . is transition from God the void to God the enemy to God the great companion.'* *When we say that we conceive faith in the great void and the great enemy we mean that we have learned to count on it as **friend**. We have learned to rely on it as a **cause to which we may devote our lives**, as that which will make all our lives and the lives of all things valuable even though it bring them to death.*

*   *Second, how is such a faith possible? How does it happen that this void, this enemy, is recognized as friend, that faith attaches itself to the last power, to the great hidden mystery, and calls it God,* that we can lose ourselves *in adoration of this being, saying with the Psalmist, 'Whom have I in heaven but thee? and there is none upon earth that I desire beside thee?' or with Job, 'Though he slay me, yet will I trust him'?*

Having faith in this God *has happened in our human history and it does happen in personal histories. There can be no doubt of the fact that it has happened and that it does happen.*

How does it happen to us as individuals? We struggle intellectually and morally (with our *transgressions*), for we discover the *inadequacy* of all our *gods* and are *driven to despair in life's meaning.* We must go through the *experience of frustration, of noting the death of all things*; *the experience of the internal division* from worshipping many gods; *the experience of the great social catastrophes which show the weakness of the great causes and beings* in which we *trusted as **saviors of life***; the experience of *something we must call spiritual, . . . something which is . . . like the **flash** of recognition of truth. All these elements are involved* in the *transfer of faith to the ultimate being.*

But for most of us *another element is involved—the concrete meeting* with others *who have received this faith, and the concrete meeting with Jesus Christ. We confront in the **event of Jesus Christ** the presence of that last power which brings to apparent nothingness the life of the most loyal man* [Jesus]. *Here we confront the slayer* [through the cross], *and here we become aware that this slayer is the life-giver* [through the resurrection]. *He does not put to shame those who trust in him. In the presence of Jesus Christ we most often conceive, or are* *given that faith. We may try to understand how we might have received the faith without Jesus Christ; but the fact remains that when this faith was given Jesus Christ was there.*

> This faith in the One has had its occasional manifestations elsewhere. But it has happened in history that it has been conceived and received where a people who regarded themselves as chosen suffered the most cruel fate, and where a Son of man who was obedient to death actually suffered death. Here the great reconciliation with the divine enemy has occurred. And since it has occurred, there is no way of getting rid of it. It is in our human history.

*   **Third**, *the consequences of faith in the one, final, and only God are not automatic* nor *a possession.* It *lives* in us and is that by which we *live.* It is a basis for all thinking, but it is not itself a thought. It is the reliance of a person on a person.*
    The moral consequences of this faith is that it makes relative all those values which polytheism makes absolute. A **new sacredness** *attaches to the relative goods. Whatever is, is now known to be good, to have value, though its value be hidden to us. The moral consequences of faith in God is the universal love of all being in him. This is the requirement: that all beings, not only our friends but also our enemies, not only* humans *but also* animals and the inanimate be met with reverence, for all are friends in the friendship of the **one to whom we are reconciled in faith**.[5]

*   **Conclusion**: **Faith in God** *involves us in a permanent revolution of the mind and of the heart, a continuous life which opens out infinitely into ever new possibilities. It does not, therefore, afford grounds for boasting but only for simple thankfulness. It is a gift of God.*[6]

Reflection

Niebuhr's essay is a journey to faith in God: we move from faith in the many gods to the happening of faith in the only God. A summary follows.

Faith in many gods
- many centers of value
- divisiveness of the gods causes conflict
- dream of integration of the gods
- warring of the gods is ongoing tragedy

But there is only one God
- enemy of all the gods
- twilight of the gods
- void of meaninglessness
- only the final reality does not pass away

The happening of faith in God
- intellectual and moral struggle
- despair in life's meaning
- despair of noting the death of all gods
- spiritual event, like a flash
- transfer of faith to the ultimate God
- concrete meeting with others of faith
- in the event of Jesus Christ we are given faith in God

The permanent revolution of faith in God
- friend of the One who was the enemy
- relativizes all goods and gods
- reverence for all beings
- revolution of heart and mind: life of new possibilities
- thanks for faith in God, which is a gift

---

20 QUESTIONS

Hopefully this spirit exercise will help us gain clarity on our faith. Written answers help us in our reflection.

1. Americans are devoted to which five gods?
2. Which of these five gods is probably number one?
3. How do these gods divide groups?

4. Name five gods in your life.
5. Which of these gods war against each other?
6. What difference does their warring make in your life?
7. Name gods you were devoted to which have died.
8. Name a time you suffered greatly when one of your gods passed.
9. Which of your present gods gives you the most meaning?
10. Which one of your gods drives you almost without mercy?
11. Which one of your gods would be the hardest to live without?
12. Name one of your gods you could not give up.
13. Which one of your gods most interferes with your devotion and service to GOD?
14. Which one of your gods is likely to pass away next?
15. How do you protect your gods from GOD?
16. Recall a time when one of your gods died and you experienced new freedom.
17. Recall an event in your life that relativized the power of your gods and later gave them back to you as companions of wholesome affection.
18. Describe your experience of the happening of Jesus Christ.
19. What is your existential feel having answered these questions?
20. What does this spirit exercise tell you about your faith in GOD?

On the way toward radical faith in God, Niebuhr takes us from corrupted faith to reconstructed or radical faith[7] through the happening in Jesus the Christ. In doing so, he lays out his dynamical understanding of faith.

Niebuhr says, "The experiences of the twentieth century have brought into view the abyss of 'faithlessness' into which men can fall." He therefore raises the prophetic question of Jesus, "When the Son of man comes will he find faith on earth?" (Luke 18:8).[8] In his writings he answers with a qualified "yes." He says each of us has faith in something, "faith in the little gods." Only, this natural faith is misdirected, fallen, sinful, idolatrous, false, corrupted, perverted, or immature.[9] "Sometimes they [we the polytheists] live for Jesus' God, sometimes for country and sometimes for Yale. For the most part they make gods out of themselves or out of the work of their own hands, living for their own glory."[10] This kind of human faith is not wrong or bad, it just becomes the source of despair. As Niebuhr paraphrases Tolstoi in his *Confession*, "If . . . man does not see the temporality and futility of the finite he will believe in the finite as worth living for; if he can no longer have faith in the value of the finite he will believe in the infinite or else die."[11] When our corrupted faith becomes a dead-end, we have run into God. Or better, God brings our faith in all the little gods to a dead-end.

But why do we continue whoring after finite gods until they are run off the street? Niebuhr says it is because we distrust God: in our great anxiety of life we doubt God's goodness and power.[12] But not until we have to—when our little gods are proven impotent—do we consider God, and this not on our own. We are left helpless as it were, asking How is faith in God possible? At the death of our gods sometimes the miracle of faith happens, just when we think that faith in something of final worth and trust is impossible.

Sometimes the Christian community's paradigm of radical faith is revealed to us in that moment. Even though we first see Jesus' crisis of abandonment in death on the cross as a confirmation of our own distrust in God's goodness, Jesus exemplifies radical faith in spite of God's apparent faithlessness, until we hear the rest of the paradigm—in the resurrection[13] God sustains Jesus' faith against the ravages of nothingness.[14] This paradigm of cross and resurrection explains our situation to us existentially. We too sense ourselves over against the faithlessness of the gods and God, over against nothingness, when sometimes a moment of revelation happens that convinces us of the possibility of faith. Niebuhr says that the "incarnation" of Jesus' faith is the key to the reality of faith that happens in human history.[15]

In the life and death of Jesus we confront the radical faith of Jesus and the radical faith of God. Jesus in his life and death had radical faith in God's goodness and radical faith in God's cause, even though he was denied, betrayed, and abandoned. His faith did not depend upon the knowledge of a resurrection. His was truly radical faith, believing that God had to be both good and powerful, neither of which he knew for sure. Now we know that God can be trusted. More than this, we have the history of the radical faith of his followers. So we have the radical faith of Jesus, the show of God's power over nothingness, and the radical faith of his followers—from then to this day—to launch us in our faith leap. Is radical faith in God possible? Yes! Do we have a better chance for radical faith than did Jesus and his followers? No! But just as good a chance. Finally, "faith in God cannot be based on anything except itself."[16] Knowing radical faith is possible, we still have to decide and leap.

To sum up, our faith in the gods is transformed into faith in the one God, and therefore we are unified—rather than torn and quartered by multi-devotions. We have integrity, for there is now the *integer* in our life, that which gives meaning to the whole. Putting an end to the strife with the warring gods and transvaluing their existence, God reconciles us in faith through goodness and power.

We thus have the major clue to Niebuhr's christology. He indicates that Jesus the Christ is the linchpin holding God and us together, which is the point of christology: our joining Jesus in his faith in God, and God's joining us in his faithfulness toward Jesus. I have no better way of thinking of our faith in God than remembering Jesus; likewise, I have no better way of remembering God's faithfulness to us than remembering Jesus. Therefore, God does not have special significance for *me* without Jesus. Because of all this Jesus is the Christ, for me. This is a confessional[17] christology of radical faith.

CHAPTER 6 NOTES

[1] H. Richard Niebuhr, an essay retitled from "The Nature and Existence of God," *Motive*, December 1943, included as a supplementary essay in *Radical Monotheism and Western Culture: With Supplementary Essays* (1960; New York, Harper and Row, 1970). I prefer the original title, which is more apt in that it tells us that we will discuss what God is like in our existence. Yet, I like the new title, for it adds the word "faith," which is at the heart of the essay. A still better title would be "The Existential Journey to Radical Faith in God."
[2] *Ibid.*, p. 116.
[3] *Ibid.*, pp. 116-19 (emphasis added). [Niebuhr's words from his essay are in italics, except where indented. To help flow, ellipses marks are not added.]
[4] *Ibid.*, pp. 119-22 (emphasis added).

[5] *Ibid.*, pp. 122-26 (emphasis added).

[6] *Ibid.*, p. 126 (emphasis added).

[7] Niebuhr uses "corrupted" and "reconstructed faith" in *Faith on Earth* and "radical faith" in several of his works, especially *Radical Monotheism and Western Culture*. These words indicate that faith is a natural or human fact before its transformation.

[8] H. Richard Niebuhr, *Faith on Earth: An Inquiry into the Structure of Human Faith*, ed. Richard R. Niebuhr, (New Haven: Yale University Press, 1989), p. 1.

[9] *Ibid.*, p. 46. "In the light of faith in God it appears that there was never a time when faith in Him was wholly absent from our existence though it was present in perverted and immature form."

[10] H. Richard Niebuhr, *The Meaning of Revelation* (New York: Macmillan, 1941), p. 57.

[11] *Ibid.*, p. 56.

[12] *Faith on Earth*, p. 100.

[13] Niebuhr's understanding of resurrection as the "miracle of faith," *Ibid.*, pp. 96-99.

[14] Kliever, *The Journal of Religion*, p. 50.

[15] H. Richard Niebuhr, *Christ and Culture* (New York: Harper & Row, 1951), p. 255.

[16] *Faith on Earth*, p. 26.

[17] Niebuhr calls his a confessional rather than an ontological christology.

7. Sobrino and Segundo: Anthropological Christologies

Two Latin American theologians, Jon Sobrino and Juan Luis Segundo, emphasize the humanity of Jesus as their anthropological starting point for christology. As liberation theologians, often understood by outsiders to mean taking scriptural license to do one's political agenda, neither fits this caricature. Niebuhr would have categorized their christologies under "Christ the transformer of culture" in his typology.[1] They are both Jesuits who have done their christological work as though it makes all the difference to brothers and sisters of Christ.

JON SOBRINO began his major writing with *Christology at the Crossroads* (1978),[2] which is less radical politically than his later works, and understandably so, for he was an advisor for Archbishop Romero, who was assassinated in 1980; Sobrino was absent the night his six Jesuit brothers were gunned down about nine years later. Obviously more political passion was unleashed and is reflected in his writings after those personally close atrocities. Yet, this is all the more reason I choose the earlier work: it can be more fairly reviewed under the purposes of this book as not so much a political motivation for liberation theology's "fanaticism" with the poor.[3] In addition, the major theological bases of his christology have not changed.

In essence his christology revolves around the "faith of Jesus" and our following in his way, or "discipleship." As one trained in Continental theology, he tells us first what his christology is *not*: 1) not *dogmatic*, meaning not based on abstract doctrine, i.e., atonement; 2) not *idealistic*, meaning not based on exalted myths, i.e. Son of God; 3) not *existential*, meaning not based on personalistic decision-making in relation to a proclamation event (Bultmann's christology is suspect to Sobrino for the reason "interior *metanoia*" may not be turned into something "real" in the world.[4]) Sobrino says that existential interpretations do not take the historical Jesus seriously and have often left Latin America with "dehistoricized Christs" used by those in power to manipulate and oppress the poor.[5]

For this and other reasons, Sobrino is quite unbending when he starts his christology with the historical Jesus. He says the Chalcedonian formula assumes the believer knows who and what God and we humans are. Not so, for the human Jesus challenges both assumptions.[6] History of Jesus here is not what we usually think. It has to do with Jesus' history of faith more than with the other facts of his life. Sobrino disagrees with Aquinas that Jesus did not need faith because he was conceived with a full knowledge of God, and agrees with Leonardo Boff (a co-founder of liberation theology of "praxis" over "orthodoxy" along with Gustovo Gutierrez in the early 1970's) that the key to Jesus' existence was his "extraordinary faith" in God.[7] Sobrino assumes that a primary reason we can relate to Jesus now is because of his human faith journey then.

We can certainly relate to Jesus as like us in every way (Heb. 4:15). Sobrino takes some time to trace Jesus' human journey of faith. He points out how the Gospels talk about the growth in Jesus' life and consciousness, his temptations, failures, "the rupture in his faith," his "self-identity crisis," his conversion, his surrender to God, his learned obedience, his agonies, his growth in faith up through his ultimate faith on the cross when he was abandoned.[8]

The Letter to the Hebrews is a prime source for this understanding. In Hebrews we hear loud and clear that we along with Jesus are all sons and daughters of God, and that he is the *first born*[9] of the household of faith in God (Heb. 1:6; 2:17; 3:6; 12:2). The point is, Jesus is our first born sibling and is our pioneer of faith in God. He is the first born not only of the resurrected but also of believers.[10]

"First born" suggests Jesus' relationship with the Father—as son—and his relationship with us—as brother; and if we are his brothers and sisters, it follows that we are God's sons and daughters. This is our christological bond, historical and relational rather than ontological, which is abstract and deals with the second person of the trinity. The divinity of Jesus is bound up in his showing and facilitating the way to the Father,[11] is bound up in his being the Son: "being 'firstborn' is part and parcel of Jesus' divinity." What is the difference between our brother Jesus and us? "Jesus is the one who has lived faith in all its pristine fullness, who has opened up the pathway of faith and traversed it to the very end. We might also say that he is the one who has lived hope absolutely, precisely insofar as he experienced the Father's total abandonment on the cross."[12]

So how do we enter into brotherly communion with him as the Father's Son? By following the path of his faith. He writes, "one can, and in my view must, say that Jesus was an extraordinary believer and had faith. Faith was Jesus' mode of being."[13] Together with him on the way to God in faith do we begin to understand Jesus' divinity and his difference from us. "The most radical and most orthodox affirmation of *faith in Jesus* is affirming that the *faith of Jesus* is the correct way to draw nearer to God and realize his kingdom, and then acting accordingly."[14] Through brotherhood with Jesus on the way do we come to God as our Father.

Going one step further, Sobrino says, "The Spirit of Jesus is the one who paradoxically prompts a re-creation of Jesus' human history. . . . We are saying that Jesus, as the firstborn Son, is capable of making people his brothers and sisters in every historical situation. . . . [T]he most profound reality of the historical Jesus is his ability to open up a wholly new history through his followers."[15] And what is their mission? As always, to bring about the kingdom of God as did Jesus.

Again, the point of this christology is following Jesus in his faith. This is how we profess Jesus Christ as Lord, following him. Is it not absurd to profess that Jesus is the "eternal Son of God if his reality were not capable of unleashing a history of sonship"?[16] Jesus' divinity is living "for" the Father by living "for" human beings by revealing to them the way to the Father, not the Father himself. This should be the true meaning of the christology of the creeds, "that every human being in every historical situation is offered the possibility of being a son of God if he or she follows the way of Jesus."[17]

Discipleship is therefore "the general paradigm of Christian existence."[18] "Discipleship is no longer the following of some Messiah. . . . Now it is the following of Jesus on his journey to the cross."[19]   There are five aspects to this discipleship: 1) it is a praxis, action similar to that of Jesus in collaborating with the kingdom of God; 2) this action is structurally akin to that of Jesus, directed toward concrete manifestations of politics, bodily life, and the cosmos; 3) its applications will vary because sin, misery, and alienation will keep cropping up in history in different ways and will consequently demand new ways of overcoming them in practice; 4) we will experience the same sort of structural conflict that Jesus did, both in the political and religious sectors—and God's silence and relative historical impotence in the face of evil will be the same; and 5) "the one outstanding difference between the follower and Jesus is that Jesus suffered and died in solitude whereas his followers suffer and die in communion with him."[20]

Sobrino says his christology only makes sense as we experience it from the inside of discipleship, not from speculation. The subjective starting point of christology is our faith, whereas the objective starting point is the historical Jesus: his person, proclamation, activity, attitudes, and death by crucifixion. Instead of asking questions of Jesus in some abstract, creedal way, Jesus calls *us* into question. He offers us the possibility of attaining our true identity by facing up to a crisis and undergoing a conversion. Only in this way can the kingdom come about. Therefore, in relation to the christological creedal statements, "the correlate of Jesus' person is not God but the 'reign of God,'" which is the urgent call of liberation theology in Latin America.[21]

We cannot conclude our summary of Sobrino's christology without mention of the cross and resurrection. The cross was the end of the early followers' faith in Jesus, yet shortly afterwards they are preaching about Jesus and are willing to give up their lives, which is evidence of the resurrection power. As a result of this power comes the universalizing the significance of Jesus for all peoples in the world. And because of this power his followers interpreted Jesus to be at one with God, pushing the relationship descriptively, almost without bounds, to include pre-existence, conception, baptism, transfiguration, lordship, etc.[22]

But we cannot forget that Jesus who becomes the Christ for them and us is the *way* to the Father and can have meaning only for someone who follows the same road of service "for" God and service "for" human beings.[23] *Discipleship in the faith of Jesus is where we find out exactly who the Son is and who the Father is, and therefore who we are, brothers and sisters of Jesus the Christ.* Is this imitation of Christ? No, impossible, for he was in a different history from ours.[24] No, this is not imitation but discipleship, which only makes "christological epistemology possible at all." "We can come to know Jesus as the Christ only insofar as we start a new life, break with the past and fight for the justice of God's kingdom."[25]

The christology of **JUAN LUIS SEGUNDO** is harder to get hold of. He writes less systematically and more intuitively. He seems to be in dialogue with myriad currents of human thought simultaneously, which gives the impression of lack of focus at times. Yet, Latin America lost one of its most creative theologians with his death in 1996.

I will not come at his christology directly but will focus more on his methodology as it applies to christology. Segundo writes about a "bridge of anthropological faith"[26] that connects Jesus' own "effective faith" with ours twenty centuries later. Both he and Sobrino are anthropological in their christology as we have said, stressing our reliving of the faith of Jesus through our discipleship, hence coming at Jesus as the Christ from our common human experience rather than from some point of doctrine. Segundo's is kin to the christologies of Bultmann, Ogden, and Karl Rahner in regard to what Jesus has to say to human existence: his significance for the human being's faith comes prior to any claim for divinity.[27]

"Through Jesus, says Bultmann, the Absolute continues to appeal to our lives, to place them in crisis, and to oblige us to make radical decisions as to how to be a human being or a better human being." Segundo picks up on Bultmann's "*preunderstanding* to their hearing of the word, be it a human or a divine word."[28] God knocks at the door of our lives through some event, person, or writing as the word of God, and we either accept or reject according to that attitude of our heart, our preunderstanding.[29] Rahner comes at this another way by saying "the hope of an absolute savior is unavoidable for the human being because it is a part of transcendental anthropology, a *prerequisite condition* for being human."[30] At any rate, all of us receive Jesus as the

Christ out of some pre-understanding or presupposition of humanness. At this point Segundo throws in his new word "anti-christology" to describe his work and to shed light in the same direction as Bultmann and Rahner. Segundo says we need to free the Christ from all the "false pretensions" of human beings, especially Christians, who try to possess him by boxing him into classical categories, and thereby "strip him and his cross of their bite and scandal."[31] But Jesus would not and will not let us define him aside from our faith.

Furthermore, Segundo makes one of his strongest points regarding christology: Jesus always reaches us already interpreted by some person or group.[32] All New Testament writings are interpretations based on faith, and the interpretations of Jesus do not agree. Here is where Segundo begins to discuss the "hermeneutical key" to the works of scripture, or the key to interpretation. For example, "We know that Paul's analysis of the human being was done in the light of the Christ event, even though his key was certainly anthropological."[33] In that earliest period and throughout the Christian tradition, different interpretations of Jesus as the Christ have emerged; naturally Segundo asks why *we* cannot create meaningful christologies as well.

Segundo talks about the "preunderstanding for interpreting scripture" or the "hermeneutic circle" (which he says is an improvement on Bultmann's) as the change in our interpretation of scripture through the change in our understanding of reality, both individual and social. Created out of our experience of reality, he lists his four steps of the circle:

1. suspicion of the operating ideology
2. which leads to suspicion of the whole ideological superstructure in general and its theology in particular
3. which leads to a new manner of experiencing theological reality
4. which leads to a new way of interpreting (new hermeneutic) the source of our faith, the scriptures (i.e., Christ-event and faith of Jesus)[34]

Segundo uses James Cone's *A Black Theology of Liberation* as a good illustration of the hermeneutic circle:

1. Cone is questioning the operating ideology of America's partial commitment to the black community's struggle for freedom
2. arrives at high suspicion of the whole American superstructure, including its dominant white theology
3. must destroy the corruptive influence of the present white oriented theology
4. new theology built on both the revelation of Jesus Christ *and* the liberation of black people[35]

For *my* own journey leading up to this book

1. I questioned the belief systems manifested in the American churches
2. and realized the sticking point is christology
3. in that too many churches are teaching a mythology that says Jesus is God—which of course is idolatrous—and therefore try to persuade us to worship Jesus; if Jesus is God, we are off the hook of discipleship, for in no way is Jesus like us
4. I perceive that our existence is changed through a gracious and transparent event (Christ event) that calls forth vocational expenditure in the context of care for creation

As I understand Segundo's interpretive method, it goes from 1) questioning one's tradition, to 2) realizing its corrupted theology, to 3) discerning its deeper reality, to 4) proposing a theology that is realistic or authentic. Or maybe we can simply reduce his hermeneutic circle to

1. suspect vision
2. radical analysis
3. depth insight
4. new hermeneutic (or new method for interpreting the source) for a new style of existence.

Segundo has searched out a human method for not only scriptural interpretation but for individual and social transformation. He is not content for our theology and in particular our christology to be an exercise, but wants it to be a radical stimulus for our future and the "universal context for evolution," which is a key phrase from a later book.[36]

Reflection

What have we mined from the christologies of Sobrino and Segundo? Neither is classical in the sense of building on the second person of the trinity or the saving works of Christ. Sobrino takes a third foundation, discipleship in the faith of Jesus, as the key to christology. Although Segundo appreciates this human foundation, he is less clear on any one foundation; he emphasizes the freedom of the faithful to choose their way guided by Jesus, the scriptures, the proclamation through the ages, and reflective human methods. If he were pushed hard, he would maybe choose the Christ event as described by Paul and Bultmann as his key to understanding christology, though he would be uncomfortable in doing so. Both Segundo and Sobrino would rather talk about the human's relationship with God that is pioneered and catalyzed by Jesus. Through Jesus we understand God and ourselves. Neither theologian would give up the understanding that Jesus is finally any different from us humans, and if so, he cannot be the Christ for us. Therefore, we call theirs anthropological christologies.

Many would follow by saying that neither has a christology but only a Christian philosophy of life. Why talk of a christology if one does not take the divinity of Jesus seriously through the person and works of Jesus? This would be a traditionalist asking the question, possibly one who believes that Jesus is not really like us humans—a clue that such a christology is really a *christism*, as we discussed in Chapter 3. Sobrino and Segundo are among contemporary Christians struggling to articulate a non-miraculous understanding of christology, unless one says with Niebuhr that faith itself is a miracle. These two Latin Americans are trying to keep one foot in the tradition and one in our contemporary worldview. Why? Because they want to effectively evangelize the emerging human being who honestly declares a non-miraculous universe, wherein pre-existence, virgin birth, resurrection, ascension, and second coming can be meaningful myths to be interpreted rather than miracles to be believed.

I am not totally satisfied with their christologies, but I take their struggle and their starting points seriously. Key points for dialogue are

1. hermenuetics relative to individual and social transformation
2. Jesus comes to us always interpreted
3. creating a new christology that attracts contemporaries
4. Jesus defied fixed, classical categories which preclude reinterpretation
5. each human has a pre-understanding through which to hear the word
6. our knowing Jesus as the Christ happens only in the act of following in his faith, unto the cross
7. our knowing Jesus as the Christ does not come as an illumination, an experience, or a rational insight in the first place
8. only in the journey of our discipleship does revelation of Jesus as the Christ happen
9. Jesus reveals the rule of God, not God
10. our true identity is found in the faith *of* Jesus, not in faith *in* Jesus
11. not imitating Jesus or walking in his steps (which is a faith justification)—different from our having the faith *of* Jesus
12. faith *of* Jesus, unto the cross, is easier for us than it was for Jesus, for we have Jesus as our companion

Who was Jesus? Just a Jewish layman,[37] says Sobrino. And who was Abraham? Neither Jew nor Christian,[38] says Segundo, interpreting Paul. Jesus and Abraham are human beings like us, except in the quality of their faith, which of course is a possibility for us and every human. The big question: Is Jesus really the Christ for us, or can we, like Abraham, come to faith in *God* without him?

CHAPTER 7 NOTES

[1] *Christ and Culture*, pp. 190-229.
[2] Jon Sobrino, *Christology at the Crossroads: A Latin American Approach* (Maryknoll, NY: Orbis Books, 1978).
[3] I have shared such a fanaticism as well, living with the poor in ghettos and third-world villages around the world, and this too out of the self-

understanding of my christology.

4 Eileen M. Fagan, *An Interpretation of Evangelization: Jon Sobrino's Christology and Ecclesiology in Dialogue* (San Francisco: Catholic Scholars Press, 1998), p. 94.

5 *Ibid.*, p. 229.

6 *Christology at the Crossroads*, pp. 81-3.

7 *Ibid.*, pp. 79-80.

8 *Ibid.*, pp. 92-9; 366.

9 Segundo comes at the anthropological image of "first born" out of Romans when he says that "the destiny to be brother or sister [to Jesus] was on the scene primordially through the Spirit, which made possible the saving and liberating attitude known as Faith, thus for Abraham and the [last human being]." Juan Luis Segundo, *The Humanist Christology of Paul*, Vol. III (Maryknoll, NY: Orbis Books, 1986), p. 153.

10 *Christology at the Crossroads*, p. 91.

11 *Ibid.*, p. 106.

12 *Ibid.*, p. 107.

13 Jon Sobrino, *Jesus the Liberator: A Historical-Theological View* (Maryknoll, NY: Orbis Books, 1993), p. 154.

14 *Christology at the Crossroads*, p. 108.

15 *Ibid.*, p. 138.

16 *Ibid.*, p. 342.

17 *Ibid.*, pp. 387-88.

18 *Ibid.*, p.389.

19 *Ibid.*, pp. 361-62.

20 *Ibid.*, p. 256.

21 *Ibid.*, pp. 346-57.

22 *Ibid.*, pp. 350-78.

23 *Ibid.*, pp. 390-95.

24 *Ibid.*, p. 132.

25 *Ibid.*, pp. xxiv-xxv.

26 Bryan P. Stone, *Effective Faith: A Critical Study of the Christology of Juan Luis Segundo* (Lantham, MD: University Press of America, 1994), p. 91.

27 *Ibid.*, p. 114.

28 Juan Luis Segundo, *The Historical Jesus of the Synoptics*, Vol III (Maryknoll, NY: Orbis Books, 1985), p. 32 (emphasis added).

29 *Ibid.*, pp. 34-5.

30 *Ibid.*, p. 38 (emphasis added).

31 *Ibid.*, p. 39 (emphasis added).

[32] *Ibid.*, p. 17.

[33] *Ibid.*, p. 155.

[34] Alfred T. Hennelly, *Theologies in Conflict: the Challenge of Juan Luis Segundo* (Maryknoll, NY: Orbis Books, 1979), p. 109.

[35] *Ibid.*

[36] Juan Luis Segundo, *An Evolutionary Approach to Jesus of Nazareth*, Vol. V (Maryknoll, NY: Orbis Books, 1988).

[37] *Christology at the Crossroads*, p. 384.

[38] *The Humanist Christology of Paul*, p. 152.

8. Friedrich Gogarten: Christology of Jesus' Faithful Obedience

Friedrich Gogarten has played a significant role in the development of 20th century theology, first, in his lifelong dialogue with Barth, Brunner, and Bultmann, and, second, in his theological presentation of *secularization*. One of his last books is set amidst the emergence of the second quest for the historical Jesus, championed by students of Bultmann, who were not content to let their professor's summary of proclamation—it's enough that Jesus came and was crucified—stick. After the second quest began in the mid-1950's from Käsemann's lecture and James Robinson's book, about a decade went by before Gogarten's book *Christ the Crisis*[1] entered the confusing debate to bring clarity. He entered on the side of the New Testament, Luther, Bultmann,[2] and a couple of Bultmann's students, especially Gerhard Ebeling. It is a difficult book because of his repetitious style, and like most theologians, he does not ground his concepts in our experience of life. He has a bit of an excuse in that he was an eighty-year-old when this book was published in Germany in 1967.

Sobrino's *Christology at the Crossroads* is definitely kin to Gogarten's book and to Ebeling's *Word and Faith*,[3] for all three, plus Niebuhr's *Faith on Earth*, place a strong emphasis on the faith *of* Jesus. Likewise, one of Gogarten's overall themes is *sonship*,[4] which is also a major point in Sobrino, though Gogarten puts more emphasis on our sonship than Jesus'. One of my favorite professors at Emory, Theodore Runyon, along with his professor, Carl Michalson, helped make Gogarten's work known in English and have written much about his theme of sonship.[5]

Using Ebeling, who wrote an analysis of the faith of Jesus about this time, Gogarten interprets Jesus' faith. Ebeling says that the reality of the human being Jesus is to be sought in the fact that in him faith "came to expression." It is this faith of Jesus which is "the one absolutely decisive and all-determining characteristic in the life and message of the historical Jesus."[6] Gogarten takes Ebeling's insight of the faith *of* Jesus as a key to the task of christology. We can say with Ogden's "re-presentation" the same for Ebeling: our faith is the "re-expression" of the faith that came to expression in Jesus. In the following important but difficult quote to understand and which is later explained, Gogarten—spinning on Ebeling's insight of the faith *of* Jesus in God—writes:

> We have described the task of christology as that of saying who Jesus is, and describing in new terms the faith which came to expression in him as that which sustained his whole existence. . . . In christology, the faith which came to expression in Jesus must be brought to expression in such a way as to make clear that it sustains our whole existence and is the decisive element in it. At the same time our own existence, in its wholeness as that which is sustained by faith, must also be brought to expression. *Only then is the task of christology fulfilled.* The faith which came to expression in Jesus must so take hold of us in our existence that this existence is brought to wholeness as an existence which is attentive to Jesus, and is therefore saved or, by denying Jesus, abandons itself to evil. Otherwise we are not speaking of Jesus and his faith in christological terms, but in historical terms—in the way in which one speaks of anything which has nothing directly to do with our existence, and to which one can adopt any attitude one pleases, of acceptance or rejection.
>
> The task of christology, which consists of bringing the faith of Jesus to expression in this way, has always existed since it came to expression in Jesus himself. For once what had happened to him had been realized, it was felt necessary to understand this faith in such a way that it was possible to pass the knowledge of it on to others. What we nowadays call the primitive Christian kerygma, or the New Testament witness to Jesus Christ, was the first attempt on the part of primitive Christianity to fulfill this task. It was an attempt on the part of the Christians of the early church to bring this faith to expression as that which sustained their own existence. . . .

But, as we have already seen, this faith is not the acceptance of certain dogmatic ideas, but affects the existence of man as an existence sustained and determined by this faith. When this faith is brought to expression as such, in it the existence of Jesus is also brought to expression. But this is only possible, in so far as his existence was an existence sustained by this faith. His existence here does not mean the detailed historical facts of his life, but his existence in the distinctive wholeness into which his faith, by bringing it about and sustaining it, concentrates it and draws it into a unity.[7]

Through the following outline I will try to make more plain what Gogarten and Ebeling are saying in these quotes.

EVOLUTION OF THE EXPRESSION OF THE FAITH OF JESUS AND ITS RE-EXPRESSION

- Jesus' expression of *faith centers upon God alone*
- the faith of Jesus leaves *Jesus' humanity intact*
- Jesus becomes the transparency of faith, for through his faith one sees clearly the *dynamics of authentic faith in God:*
    1. initiative of God's *call* through a faith event
    2. Jesus' response of *Yes*
    3. radical *obedience*, unto the cross
    4. demand [God's call] of faith [Yes] transformed [through his obedience] into the *gift of God* that
        a. *determined* his whole existence
        b. *sustained* him
        c. *focused* his mission
        d. drew others to the power which *unified* his life of faith in God
- others took up the faith of Jesus and became *followers* who lived the same dynamics of authentic faith in God
- because of the faith of Jesus' power upon others to "save" and because of its power to determine, sustain, focus and unify their lives, the *New Testament kerygma* was written; the history of his faith quickly (Gogarten

says too quickly) became the basis of their claim "Jesus
is the Christ"

- because his followers re-expressed the faith of Jesus
  in their lives, still others came to re-express the faith of
  Jesus and formed a *movement*
- and because of the witness of the faith of Jesus in the
  kerygma from then *till now*, still *others* have re-expressed
  the faith of Jesus
- and the faith of Jesus has become, consequently, a
  historic event, calling all to the same faith in God who
  hear the witness and see his followers' faith—in fact,
  the faith of *Jesus* has become a *call-of-God-event* in
  history, therefore leading many to profess Jesus as the
  Christ

This is the evolution of the christology from the "faith of Jesus" to the
"Christ of faithfulness."

Gogarten and Ebeling later in the book point out that Jesus said
little about his own faith. Neither is the idea introduced in the synoptics.
They are clear that *Jesus did not call for faith in his own person, but
always faith in God*. Ebeling in essence said it is impossible to understand
Jesus without focusing on his faith in God—to deny it is to say his
preaching was inspired in some extraordinary way, that he was equipped
with a knowledge of the past and future which did not require faith. He
and his preaching could be based only on his own faith. He spoke from
his faith, and in his preaching his faith speaks in such a way that it
brings with it the event.[8] One can even say that Jesus is faith personified,
having several meanings: he is the expression of faith; he is the foundation
for faith; he calls others to follow in his faith, catalyzing the literature
and the tradition of Christianity through his faith. Yet, he did not call
for faith in himself, only faith in God.

Niebuhr, Ebeling, Gogarten, and Sobrino—in that order—talk
about the faith *of* Jesus (in distinction from faith *in* Jesus) as a key to
our coming to faith in God and, secondly, a key to our understanding the
relationship of Jesus as the *Christ*, or Jesus as the *one who brings us to
faith in God*. If Jesus became the embodiment or the expression of

faith in God in history, then he is the Christ.

Gogarten talks about this faith *of* Jesus as "responsibility to God/responsibility for the world" throughout his book *Christ the Crisis*. But these are just neat, moral phrases—"double responsibility" or "twofold responsibility" (Gogarten's code names)—without the faith of Jesus. In Chapter 7, "The Historical Basis of New Testament Christology," Gogarten makes sure we do not take Jesus' faith lightly and therefore grounds it in the image of the "event of Jesus' obedience" and how that event transforms our existence.

In Chapter 6, Gogarten cites Paul's references to Jesus' obedience to God.

> This relationship is not a metaphysical relationship between two natures, a human and a divine nature, but one which is exercised in the obedience of the man towards God. This obedience actually takes place between Jesus and God. For by Jesus's becoming 'obedient unto death, even death on a cross', his humanity was fulfilled (Phil 2.7f). Thus Paul can sum up the redeeming work of Jesus Christ in the following sentence: 'by one man's obedience many will be made righteous' (Rom. 5.19). The Epistle to the Hebrews likewise describes this obedience as the sacrifice which Jesus, as the high priest installed by God, offered to him: 'In the days of his flesh, Jesus offered up prayers and supplications, with loud cries and tears, to him who was able to save him from death . . . although he was a Son, he learned obedience through what he suffered' (Heb. 5.4-8).[9]

In Chapter 7, Gogarten points out that

> the primitive Christian church was equally certain that what God did in and through Jesus did not take place without Jesus's own will. Just as Paul says of Jesus that he was given up by God, he can likewise say . . . that Jesus 'gave himself for our sins to deliver us from the present evil age' (Gal. 1.4; 2.20). Or, as we read in the Epistle to the Ephesians, 'he gave himself up for us, a fragrant offering and sacrifice to God' (5.2), or in the Epistle to the Hebrews: he 'offered himself' (9.14). And

in many other passages, the same thing is said in a similar way. . . .

This obedience brings about a transformation which takes in the totality of the world: the 'old world' becomes the 'new'.[10]

And then Gogarten makes a radical christological statement:

But if these happenings [crucifixion and resurrection] form part of the event which, in our view, is the content of the kerygma, then they, too, must be understood in terms of this event. That is, what took place in them in accordance with their proper historical meaning is in fact the event of Jesus's obedience towards God, and nothing else.[11]

Here Gogarten has essentially rested his case, and the remaining 230 pages of *Christ the Crisis* explicate his christology of the event of Jesus' obedience to God. What follows from the event of Jesus' obedience, according to Gogarten? Not only the transformation of the old world to the new in our existence, but more, to "make possible for the believer's faith an obedience which is in accordance with that exercised" by Jesus.[12] So what is the task of christology? Jesus' expression of faith and obedience become God's event to bring forth our re-expression of his faith and obedience. *When we, for example, re-express Jesus' faith and obedience, the claim of christology is fulfilled.*

It is very important for Gogarten to ground the faith of Jesus in Jesus' obedience, for we Protestant Christians, especially, still think faith and obedience are separate, or one can have the faith *of* Jesus in God without the obedience *of* Jesus to God. This is the heart of Bonhoeffer's book, *The Cost of Discipleship*: "Only he who believes is obedient, and only he who is obedient believes. . . . Faith is only real when there is obedience, . . . and faith only becomes faith in the act of obedience."[13]

This is not enough said to guard against our tendency toward justification by works, or our imitation of Jesus.[14] Gogarten clearly understands that we can make a mockery of faith. He therefore says "the event of Jesus' obedience" occasions our faithful obedience to God. Here Gogarten agrees with Bultmann's understanding of "event," which is always and only God's event or act which calls for decision and obedience. Faith "is only possible on the basis of participation in something that happens."[15] Again, "This existence is called into question, and the person is thereby faced with his destiny, and the decision he must make . . . whether to submit to the fate and double responsibility God has destined for him, or to refuse to do so."[16] And again, "the faith of which Jesus speaks is likewise possible only in this encounter."[17] So what is the *crisis* that is the Christ? Since Jesus' faithful obedience, "man has been faced with the decision either to be responsible to the world . . . or to be responsible to God"[18] for the world. This is the transformative question of existence that comes with Jesus.

How is it that Jesus is *the Christ* for us, according to Gogarten? If we decide that the life-changing event of Jesus' faithful obedience is the meaning of our lives, then we too will orient our lives to faith in God rather than in this world (of which we are the center). We will take responsibility for the "doom"[19] of the world, which has ultimate faith in itself rather than in God (Gogarten's definition of "sin"[20] or "false god"[21]). We will stop living the "lie" ("religious veneration of this world")[22] of the "good life" and will become, as Jesus, faithfully obedient to God by giving our lives for the redemption of those who live the "lie"—even if we have to descend into hell with Jesus[23] where God's ultimate power of resurrection "calls into existence the things that do not exist."[24]

Reflection

What Gogarten has helped us to see is our being trapped in this world, the old world, our giving over our freedom and destiny to the power of the "lie": this world will give us our heart's desire, will save us. Mark 8:36 asks, "What does anyone gain by winning the whole world at the cost of his or her life?" Jesus lived and died to abolish the illusion that the things of this world will deliver final meaning to our lives, are worth our living and dying for. This is what "responsible *to* the world" meant to Jesus, according to Gogarten. Another way to say this is that we are not free, we are bound by this world; or we have given over our freedom and destiny to the reign of this world.

So how do we get freed from the death-dealing illusion of this world? By the possibility for entering the new life of the new world.

This is where the "faith *of* Jesus" and "the event of Jesus' obedience" come to "save us." Jesus' existence was riveted to God. He was "responsible to God" alone, not to the world. His faithful obedience therefore was to do the will of God, which was to be "responsible *for* the world." He took on the doom of the world—our being lost in our attachment to the world as our god. And by all he said and did through his life and death, he freed us from that doom. He expressed faith in God and called us to the same possibility through our re-expression of faith in God; and showed us what it looks like for us to take responsibility for people living the lie, under the reign of illusion rather than truth.

Jesus' radically new image of what it means to be "responsible *to* God *for* the world" became historical, called others to decide for his way of faith and obedience through his word and deed, and let loose a revolution of faith in reality rather than unreality. What was and is that reality? That one is responsible to *no thing* as a free person and responsible for *every thing* as a free person. This is what it means to be the faithful son or daughter of God. The event that breaks us free is Jesus as the Christ: our perceiving the faithful obedience of Jesus; our being called out of the old world into the new world of that same faithful obedience; our repenting or deciding to break with the lie, to operate out of reality rather than illusion; and our being the faithfully obedient one, like Jesus, responsible only to God and only for abolishing the doom of the world. Losing one's life in this way is its very meaning.

Gogarten says the ultimate words of christology when he talks about the uniqueness of Jesus that grows out of his faithful obedience to God:

> And since this faith and destiny determined his whole life from beginning to end, it was in this life and in what took place in it that God revealed himself in his action in man as he has never done elsewhere. In the life of Jesus, this fate and destiny form the very event on which the world and its salvation depend, to a degree that can scarcely have occurred in anyone else. And in the same way the action of God as revealed in the life of Jesus affected not only his life but thereby affected the salvation of the world and of those who live in it.[25]

To sum up, Gogarten declares that the faithful obedience that Jesus expressed—and that is written about and re-expressed in his followers till this day—is the event which encounters us and demands our decision. This event determines our whole existence. Jesus' task in history was to call *us* to decide to live the new life of faithful obedience to God—as he decided to. By bringing us to such a decision—a critical juncture or crisis point—Jesus the Christ is our crisis of faith.

By making all this clear, Gogarten has solved the theological debate that would pit those chasing the *historical Jesus* against those who say the *Christ of the kerygma* is enough. What is his answer? The Christ-event of Jesus' faithful obedience to God, or Jesus' responsibility *to* God *for* the world. The facts of Jesus' life and death alone will not bring us to faith; the proclaimed Word of Jesus as the Christ alone will not bring us to faith; more than either of these, Jesus' faithful obedience to *God* encounters *us* with *our* decision to be responsible *to God for* the world. Only as the facts and the Word bring us to this critical decision are they authentically the facts and Word of Jesus as the Christ.

CHAPTER 8 NOTES

[1] Friedrich Gogarten, *Christ the Crisis* (Richmond: John Knox, 1970).
[2] Gogarten says in so many words it was Bultmann who launched the post-modern theological debate around 1953 with the English publication of *Kerygma and Myth*, where he says on page 208 it is not the historical Jesus, but Jesus Christ the crucified, who is the Lord. *Ibid.*, p. 11.
[3] Gerhard Ebeling, *Word and Faith* (Philadelphia: Fortress Press, 1963).
[4] *Christ the Crisis*, p. 163.
[5] Theodore Runyon, "Friedrich Gogarten," *A Handbook of Christian Theologians*, ed. by Dean G. Peerman and Martin E. Marty (Cleveland: World, 1965); Carl Michalson, *The Rationality of Faith* (New York, Scribners, 1963).
[6] *Christ the Crisis*, p. 44.
[7] *Ibid.*, pp. 45-6 (emphasis added).
[8] *Ibid.*, pp. 240-43.
[9] *Ibid.*, p. 61.
[10] *Ibid.*, p. 69.
[11] *Ibid.*, p. 73.
[12] *Ibid.*, p. 71.

[13] Dietrich Bonhoeffer, *The Cost of Discipleship* (London: SCM, 1959; New York: Macmillan, 1963), p. 69.

[14] Rudolf Bultmann, *Faith and Understanding I*, ed. Robert W. Funk [founder of the Jesus Seminar] (New York: Harper & Row, 1969), p. 277. I prefer to use "the event of Jesus' *faithful* obedience."

[15] *Christ the Crisis*, p. 93.

[16] *Ibid.*, p. 237.

[17] *Ibid.*, p. 238.

[18] *Ibid.*, p. 262.

[19] *Ibid.*, p. 67.

[20] *Ibid.*, p. 68.

[21] *Ibid.*, p. 139.

[22] *Ibid.*, p. 67.

[23] *Ibid.*, p. 280.

[24] *Ibid.*, p. 76.

[25] *Ibid.*, p. 253.

9. Norman Perrin: Christology of the Risen Lord

Having just completed his book *The Resurrection*[1] days before, Norman Perrin's life ended much too soon at age fifty-six. Marcus Borg calls him "the most prominent Jesus scholar in North America at the time of his death."[2] From my days at Emory University, I remember him as a man definitely on a mission to bring the authentic New Testament proclamation to our time. As he spent much of his adult life wrestling with the theology of Bultmann and his school, Perrin considered him to be "the greatest New Testament scholar of the twentieth century, and perhaps the greatest of any century."[3] He understood Bultmann better than any other scholar I have read. In his later years, Perrin especially came to find compatibility with Bultmann's view.[4]

I have chosen Perrin's *Rediscovering the Teaching of Jesus*, and especially the long last chapter, "The Significance of Knowledge of the Historical Jesus and His Teaching,"[5] as the primary source for his christological insights. In this chapter he gives an excellent analysis of the debate over the historical Jesus, from Reimarus to Perrin (c. 1778-1970). Bultmann's New Testament theology is a focus of the chapter, and everyone else is precursor of, student of, to the right of, or to the left of him, except Perrin, who is in the center with Bultmann because "we have come to distinguish faith and faith-knowledge from history and historical knowledge, largely under the influence of Bultmann."[6] Bultmann differentiates kinds of knowledge as an outgrowth of the two words for "history" in the German language, *historie* and *geschichte*.[7]

Just before the 20th century, Martin Kähler proffered the debate's question till now: what is the relationship between the Christ of faith and the historical Jesus?[8] After spending many pages laying out arguments from many sides, Perrin intends to clarify the scholars' positions by presenting the three kinds of knowledge that are involved in the debate: historical, historic, and faith.[9] Let us go through these in order.

First, the descriptive *historical knowledge* of Jesus of Nazareth, by which he means "post-Enlightenment" historical knowledge, or "hard" knowledge that exists independently, or "nothing but the facts." His examples are Jesus, Socrates, and Capt. Oates of Scott's Antarctica expedition. Historically verifiable are the facts that all three died as the consequence of their actions: Jesus from the proclamation of the Kingdom and his fellowship with sinners; Socrates from his utter commitment to his innermost convictions; and Oates from his hope to save his companions as he walked out into a blizzard. These are consensed upon historical facts. But historical facts can change with further discovery. "So it is theoretically possible, however practically doubtful, that we may one day have to concede that Jesus was carried to the cross, railing against God and his fate."[10]

Second, any of the above facts can become significant for us, connecting the knowledge of the past to our present. For example, existential knowledge easily speaks from one human to another through the medium of common existence. *Historic knowledge* is historical knowledge that has in some way influenced one in the present: all three examples above could have "touched" or "moved" us in some significant way. Historic knowledge becomes personal, which moves into interpretation of the facts for our lives. "[T]he cross of Jesus is as 'historical' as that of any other Jew executed by the Romans, but it is also 'historic' in the significance it came to have for future generations in a way the others did not. . . . But then we must go on to recognize that there is another side to the historic Jesus; that is, there is the historicity of human existence in the world as affected by the historic Jesus and by the response of an individual to the impact of that aspect of Jesus."[11]

Third, *faith-knowledge* is significant only to religious faith, belief, or commitment. For example, this is knowledge that is meaningful to a particular group and is not necessarily historical knowledge, but can be.[12]

> 'Faith-knowledge' depends upon special worth being attributed to the person concerned, so that knowledge of that person assumes a significance beyond the historic. Historic

significance can be attributed to almost any number of people from the past, certainly to all three of our examples, but 'faith-knowledge' could be attributed only to the one figure who comes to be of special significance in terms of revelation, religious experience, religious belief. Also, the use of these categories necessarily introduces a reference to a transhistorical reality—strictly speaking, a non-historical reality—in that it introduces the idea of God and his activity. So, for the Christian, it is possible to say: 'Christ died for my sins in accordance with the scriptures.' This, however, is a statement of faith, not of history in the normal sense. It is faith-knowledge, not historical knowledge. . . . None of this is history in the post-Enlightenment sense of that word. . . . The value here ascribed to that death is not ascribed to it because of what Jesus did, but because of what God is regarded as having done. The death of Jesus is not efficacious for 'my sins' because he died nobly, or because he showed confidence in God, but because the cross is believed to have fulfilled the purpose of God. That Jesus died nobly or showed confidence in God are historical statements, subject to the vicissitudes of historical research.[13]

Perrin then says Bultmann is understandable in this context, for we can know Jesus in all three types of knowledge.

He grants that we have historical knowledge of Jesus, although limited in extent and not including any knowledge of how he understood his own death. So also we have historic knowledge of him; we can encounter him as historical phenomenon at the level of historic significance. Finally, we encounter him as the eschatological phenomenon in the proclamation. True, this Jesus of the kerygma, this Jesus of faith-knowledge, encounters us in our historic situation, but he is not the historic Jesus, he is the Christ, the eschatological Jesus. Our encounter with him is not like an encounter with the historic Socrates, or with any other historic figure, but it is an eschatological encounter: it changes everything for us and brings our old history to a close, opening up for us a new history and a new future as no other encounter with a figure from the past could do. Even this figure from the past can only do so because, as the eschatological figure, he becomes present for us in the proclamation, and present for us as eschatological act of God.[14]

In light of this, Perrin then categorizes those to the right and left of Bultmann again, but this time using the three kinds of knowledge. Those to the right want historical knowledge of Jesus of Nazareth and faith-knowledge to be closer together than Bultmann will allow. For example, they want much more than the cross to be faith-knowledge, i.e., ministry and preaching of Jesus—and if one does not believe the "red letters" of the Bible are faith-knowledge, watch out. Bultmann stops with saying Jesus has come and he was crucified: this is the heart of the proclamation of the early church, of kerygma, of "faith-knowledge." The eschatological encounter or event is based upon this presupposition, "that there was a Jesus and that he was crucified."[15] Perrin himself spends most of his book, *Rediscovering the Teaching of Jesus*, talking about in what way the synoptic gospels can be "faith-knowledge." But his point here is to understand the dynamics of faith-knowledge.

Those to the left are really saying faith-knowledge is not faith-knowledge but historic knowledge, "so that Jesus becomes not the eschatological, but only a (or, the) supreme historic, figure." And later on Perrin says they "cannot think in terms of a knowledge of Jesus that is different *in kind* from knowledge we may have of other historical persons. So either Jesus becomes an example of an existential relationship with the transcendent, supreme but capable of being imitated (Jaspers), or he becomes the 'decisive' manifestation of that which may also be known elsewhere (Ogden)."[16]

As said earlier, Perrin aligns himself with Bultmann in the center, thus advocating the emphasis upon faith-knowledge as an event or act of God in our history, bringing us to the decision of faith. "Bultmann achieves this by abandoning the historical Jesus to the vicissitudes of history and by claiming that Christian faith is not in fact necessarily related to that historical Jesus but, rather, is dependent upon something which lies beyond historical investigation, namely, the eschatological act of God *in Jesus* and in the Christian kerygma."[17]

Perrin describes more in depth faith-knowledge that arises in response to the challenge of the many forms of proclamation of the church. These forms (Bible reading, sermons, church school lessons, hymns, creeds, church history, etc.) must have the "ability to mediate the encounter of faith with the Christ." Here Perrin begins to talk autobiographically, distinguishing between "kerygmatic Christ" and "historical Jesus." "[A]ll the various forms of proclamation to which we have been subject have served to produce for us what we would call a 'faith-image' of this Jesus."[18] Perrin does not tell us the difference between "faith-knowledge" and "faith-image" but uses them somewhat interchangeably. Let us use again a quote of Perrin from Chapter 1 of this book, where he talks about his own nurture in the liberal Baptist tradition of Great Britain:

> Part of this faith-image is certainly made up of traits of the liberal historical Jesus. . . . [P]art of the faith-image could be the result of the existential impact of knowledge of Jesus mediated by a modern . . . historic knowledge, for to a believer brought up in this tradition almost anything that talks about Jesus can become kerygma, that is, it can contribute to the faith-image. . . . [L]ike the Christ of the gospels, the Jesus of one's faith-image is a mixture of historical reminiscence, . . . myth, legend and idealism. What gives this faith-image validity is the fact that it grows out of *religious experience* and is capable of mediating *religious experience*.
>
> Historical knowledge of Jesus, then, is significant to faith in that it can contribute to the formation of the faith-image. . . . The main source will always be the proclamation of the Church, a proclamation arising out of a Christian *experience* of the risen Lord.[19]

To Perrin, "religious experience" is significant. In 1970, Victor Furnish, in a pull-together of articles and reviews, traced a ten-year pilgrimage of Perrin's christology, and towards the end of the essay writes,

> As his work has proceeded he has shown less interest in identifying within the church's preaching a concern for the specifically 'historical Jesus,' and increasingly more interest in the church's response to the resurrected Christ. . . . Perrin

suggests 'that we should emphasize . . . the fact that Christology is a product of Christian *experience* and the possibility that the synoptic tradition is a product of Christian reflection.' [At the head of his list of *experience* and reflection is the] importance of Jesus' resurrection. From the context of his work it is clear that he is not thinking of the resurrection as an event of the past to which the earliest Christians looked back. Indeed, he specifically says that christology was 'not so much' produced from reflection on 'the past event of Jesus' as from 'the present "experience" of Christians.' It is then, within the post-Easter community that christology has its roots. . . .

[H]e is concerned lest it be forgotten that the earliest Christians identified their risen Lord 'absolutely and completely' with the earthly Jesus; for this reason he believes that the message of the historical Jesus requires attention.[20]

In line with the articles and reviews cited above, Perrin in *Rediscovering the Teaching of Jesus* uses the "early Christian equation": earthly Jesus of Nazareth = risen Lord of Christian experience, or more simply, "earthly Jesus = risen Lord." He also uses the equation "situation in earthly ministry of Jesus = situation in early Church's experience."

Incidentally, we have recently had some striking historical evidence for the validity of this equation in that the intensive discussion of the eschatology of Jesus and of earliest Christianity in recent New Testament scholarship has shown that there are remarkable parallels between these eschatologies: *both challenge men to a new relationship with God in face of a decisive act of God in human experience (Jesus: Kingdom of God; early Church: Christ as eschatological event),* and in both the believer stands in a situation theologically the same. . . . If the believer in response to the kerygma stands in a relationship with God parallel to that in which a Galilean disciple stood in response to Jesus' proclamation of the Kingdom of God, which the synoptic gospels necessarily claim, then teaching addressed to that latter situation is applicable to the former. In this way historical knowledge of the teaching of Jesus becomes *directly applicable to the believer in any age.*[21]

Perrin ends his book with a proviso connected to the last sentence: "that we can solve the practical problems involved in crossing the barrier of two millennia and radically different *Weltanschauungen* [worldviews] necessary to do this."[22]

One way Perrin solves these "practical problems" is to write passionately a book about Bultmann's thought, in order to make this and other points with him, it seems to me:

> God did not bring the world to an end in that way [through the second coming of Jesus on a cloud as Son of man to judge the world]; he brought it to an end by making authentic existence possible. . . . Now God has made authentic existence possible by acting in Jesus Christ so 'Jesus Christ is the eschatological event, the action of God by which God has set an end to the old world.'
>
> The phrase 'the eschatological event' is very important to Bultmann [and Perrin]. It means 'that event (or series of events) by means of which God brings to an end the old world of sin and establishes a new world of grace. . . .' For Bultmann, however, such an event [the end of the world] never did take place, and never will take place, because actually the crucifixion of Jesus, the cross of Jesus, as proclaimed by the church fulfills this function. The action of God in the cross of Jesus and in the proclamation of that cross by the church is the eschatological event. . . .[23]

As Perrin's life came to an end while he was writing about the resurrection in the synoptic gospels, let us end this summary of his christology of the risen Lord with his redactive theological reflections on Paul, Mark, Matthew, and Luke. This is Norman Perrin's most final public witness.

> *Paul* is the one witness we have whom we can interrogate about his claim to have seen Jesus as risen, and our assumption has to be that if we could interrogate the other witnesses [the three evangelists] their claims would be similar to his. In some way they were granted a vision of Jesus which convinced them that God had vindicated Jesus out of his death, and that therefore the death of Jesus was by no means the end of the

impact of Jesus upon their lives and upon the world in which they lived. Very much to the contrary, since Jesus as risen commissioned them to new tasks and to new responsibilities, they found confidence in themselves and in the future of the world in which they lived precisely because they were responding to Jesus as risen, and because they were now living in a world in which Jesus was risen. If I personally were asked in connection with the resurrection of Jesus, What actually happened? it is in these terms that I would speak.[24]

I am reluctant to say more than that because I believe that I have reached the limits of what the testimony of Paul entitles me to say, and because I am moving far beyond the intent of the gospel narratives. My concern throughout has been the intent of the gospel narratives of the resurrection, and here I am glad to close my discussion by affirming once more the intent of those narratives as I understand them. *Mark* is attempting to convince his readers that they can experience the ultimacy of God in the concreteness, the historicality of their everyday existence; that wherever they are, God is also there, and he is there in the form of the figure of Jesus known from the gospel stories. *Matthew* is attempting to convince his readers that the eternal ship of the church is the vehicle of salvation for all people everywhere, and that aboard that ship the risen Lord effectively sustains those who believe in him. *Luke* is attempting to convince his readers that Jesus effectively lived out the life of the first Christian in the world, and that the resurrection means that his spirit now empowers those who follow him truly to imitate his life. These are the meanings of the resurrection so far as the evangelists are concerned, and as such they are more important than the question of 'what actually happened' in terms of appearance stories and empty tomb traditions.[25]

Reflection

There are four strong clues to Perrin's christology above: 1) the risen Lord, 2) faith-knowledge/faith-image, 3) religious experience, and 4) the event of Christ. Through all of these he puts himself in the camp of faith in the kerygmatic Christ, not the historical Jesus, though he takes quite seriously the faith role of the latter as well. Cursory reading of Perrin could be a turn-off for thoroughly post-modern human beings, for he uses much of the old language, i.e., risen Lord, religious experience, resurrection, Kingdom of God. But so did Bultmann, who catalyzed the post-modern christological debate. Both of them chose their words carefully and are never to be understood speaking other than as men of the 20th century worldview. Needless to say, they spent their lives demythologizing and doing redaction criticism, but what else can one do with New Testament texts of a three-story universe and enable meaningful dialogue to happen in the present? In his resurrection interpretations above, Perrin did not leave his post-Enlightenment worldview while at the same time honoring the 1st century worldview.

By "christology of the risen Christ" we understand him to be standing in a position similar to where Bultmann stood with the crucified Jesus: *God* was and is acting in our history through the encounter of the Jesus the Christ event to enable us to live our lives with "confidence in [ourselves] and in the future of the world" in the "historicality of everyday." How do we know this? Through the witness of the church and through our own experience in our response of faith.

CHAPTER 9 NOTES

[1] Norman Perrin, *The Resurrection: According to Matthew, Mark, and Luke* (Philadelphia: Fortress Press, 1977).
[2] Marcus Borg, *Jesus in Contemporary Scholarship* (Valley Forge: Trinity Press, 1994), p. 189.
[3] Norman Perrin, *The Promise of Bultmann* (Philadelphia: Fortress Press, 1979), p.4 (quote by his wife in the Foreword, written after her husband's death).
[4] Victor Paul Furnish, "Notes on a Pilgrimage: Norman Perrin and New Testament Christology," *Christology and a Modern Pilgrimage: A Discussion with Norman Perrin*, ed. Hans Dieter Betz (Missoula: Scholars' Press, 1974), p. 62.
[5] Norman Perrin, *Rediscovering the Teaching of Jesus* (New York: Harper & Row, 1976), pp.207-48.
[6] *Ibid.*, p. 238.
[7] Perrin offers a meaningful understanding of these types of history in two of his books, *The Promise of Bultmann*, pp. 33-41, and *The New Testament: An Introduction* (New York: Harcourt Brace Jovanovich, 1974), pp. 27-9.

[8] *Ibid.*, p. 216.

[9] *Ibid.*, p. 234.

[10] *Ibid.*, p. 236.

[11] *The New Testament*, p. 28.

[12] *Rediscovering the Teaching of Jesus*, pp. 234-37.

[13] *Ibid.*, p. 237.

[14] *Ibid.*, pp. 238-39.

[15] *Ibid.*, pp. 221.

[16] *Ibid.*, pp.239-40.

[17] *Promise of Bultmann*, p. 48 (emphasis added).

[18] *Ibid.*

[19] *Ibid.*, pp. 243-4 (emphasis added).

[20] *Christology and a Modern Pilgrimage*, pp. 69-70 (emphasis added).

[21] *Rediscovering the Teaching of Jesus*, pp. 246-47.

[22] *Ibid.*, p. 248.

[23] *Promise of Bultmann*, p. 42.

[24] John Macquarrie in *Christology Revisited* speaks of the resurrection in a meaningful way: after he states we cannot "explain what happened on Easter Day" (p. 112), he writes, "This process of a growing awareness of the glory of God in Christ had reached its climax at the cross, the revelation of the 'pure unbounded love' of God in the Crucified One. The eternal life of God himself, untouched by death and imperishable, had met them [the disciples] in the man from Nazareth" (p. 113).

[25] *Ibid.*, pp. 83-4 (emphasis added).

10. Søren Kierkegaard: A Radical Existentialist Christology

When we think of Søren Kierkegaard, we think of his existential "leap of faith." Contrary to what some of his critics would have us think, he certainly believed that the reality of God existed apart from his own faith. Yet, he has made it clearer than most in the last two hundred years that God is not real to anyone without faith. Kierkegaard's famous formula for faith, in non-religious language, is this: "By relating itself to its own self and by willing to be itself, the self is grounded transparently in the Power which constituted it."[1]

Though he uses secular language here, he understands its meaning as religious. "In faith the self wills to be itself."[2] Kierkegaard (to be referred to as *SK*) in several places in his writings refers to the *leap*: the leap of God to us in grace through Christ; the leap of despair; the leap *to* faith. He does not use "leap *of* faith," for one leaps in the midst of his or her despair or sin *to* faith, in response to the prior leap of God. Through one's passionate leap, instigated by grace, one moves to a new existence, leaving behind the old self in that moment.

SK quoted an unidentified German poet's phrase, "a blessed leap into eternity,"[3] which suggests leaping into and being supported by the Power that *constitutes* or *posits* one. What does this mean? What is it like? The leap is not unlike a small boy who cannot swim jumping for the first time into the arms of his father waiting in the deep water; or not unlike one's making a first jump into the outstretched hands of a swinging trapeze catcher—with no net underneath; or not unlike one's jumping from a third-story window into a stretched canvas, held by neighbors, to escape the raging fire. In these examples one is jumping toward something she trusts will save her, or will not let her come to harm. Nevertheless, the leap is always experienced as a terrifying risk. It demands a radical decision.[4] Finally, one must leap. In the leap one can talk about the "leap *of* faith," when one is actually in the air, so to speak. There is no faith to SK without the act, the leap. At that point one has jumped from the old into the new. In the leap one has grounded the self transparently in the Power that constituted it. In a real sense, one becomes at-one with the Power, trusting it with one's life. This is "grounding" faith in actuality rather than in some theory or doctrine, which usually requires no risk. Faith is only the individual's faith as he or she leaps.

This, in essence, is what SK means by becoming "contemporaneous with Christ." SK says Christ helps us to become our true selves: "[Man] is in his own self a self. Hence Christ would first and foremost help every man to become himself . . . so as then to draw him unto Himself. . . . He would draw him only as a free being, and so through a choice."[5] Faith in Christ is an *act of the self* in response to the Christ, not a belief in him as one who saves us without our free act of choice to be the selves we are. In sum, SK is saying that the coming of the Christ to us is out to change our lives by calling us to choose to be our true selves. Therefore, in Christ the self is actualized.

Another way to look at SK's formula is to consider it as the dynamics of consciousness. The Order: Ecumenical called the formula "consciousness of consciousness of consciousness." As I am conscious (1) of my disobedience to the truth of existence, I stand as the disobedient one. By some means I become conscious (2) of my guilt in relationship to my disobedience. If I decide consciously (3) to be the disobedient-guilty one and passionately live my guilty life in obedience to the truth I understand, I thereby authenticate my real self, or I ground myself transparently in the Power that constituted, or constitutes, me.

Said religiously, I cannot choose to be a self other than the one I actually am—just as I am—and that self is always a self in disrelationship or sin. If through revelation I perceive my life in sin and hear the call to repent and to live true selfhood in Christ, I am given through grace the possibility of new life. Then I must actualize that possibility by deciding to leap into it or not. If I do, at that moment of faith I experience new life. This is consciousness of consciousness of consciousness, or "By relating itself to its own self (consciousness 1) and by willing to be itself (consciousness 2), the self is grounded transparently in the Power (consciousness 3) which constituted it."

Again, all of this process is initiated from beyond the self, not by the self, for the self is lost in a deathly sickness.

In rebelling against Hegel's synthesis in abstraction, SK articulates the message of "existentialism" and is called its father by most, although he borrowed from Friedrich Schelling's existentialism. Paul Tillich, as a theology student, was among the generation first impacted by SK, starting around 1905.[6] He describes SK's existentialism this way: "Kierkegaard would not deny the possibility of scientific truth, but this is the truth of detachment. It is not the truth of involvement; it is not existential truth. Existential truth is objective uncertainty and personal, passionate experience or subjective certainty, but a certainty which can never be objectified. It is the certainty of the leap."[7]

In diagnosing the sickness of our time, Tillich says we have become objects or things—"its," Martin Buber says. "The protest of subjectivity does not mean the protest of willfulness. It means the protest of freedom, of the creative individual, of personality, of man who is in the tragic situation of having to decide in a state of estrangement, in the human predicament. In these ideas we have almost the whole summary of Kierkegaard's theology."[8] Tillich goes on to say that there is "one content to which he [SK] refers all the time, and this is the appearance of the Christ. Thus the leap which is necessary to overcome the situation of doubt and despair is the leap into the reality of the Christ."[9]

But there is a problem here in that SK says only "one thing matters: In the year A.D. 30, God sent the Christ for my salvation. I do not need any more theology; I do not need to know the result of historical criticism. It is enough to know that one thing. Into this I have to leap."[10] Tillich says the problem is that we cannot leap back two thousand years, and that we do have a direction; therefore, the leap is "not a sheer leap any more." "[W]e have more than subjectivity and paradox. . . . [I]f you already know in which direction to jump, in the direction of Christ, for example, then you must have a reason for this. This reason may be some experience with him, some historical knowledge, some image of him from church tradition, etc., but in any case, you have some content."[11] "Kierkegaard wanted to solve the problem of historical criticism by this concept of contemporaneity. You can do this if you take contemporaneity in the Pauline sense of the divine Spirit present to us, and showing the face of Jesus as the Christ. But you cannot escape historical criticism by becoming contemporaneous with Jesus himself. This is the fundamental criticism which we must make from a theological point of view."[12]

Tillich declares where he stands in this regard. By saying we cannot know Jesus of Nazareth personally, even if historical research discovers a large body of historical facts about him, he dismisses the historian's route to our knowing Jesus as the Christ. We can be influenced by Jesus through the witness of those who were closer to him in time, for example, the gospel writers, by perceiving the historic impact Jesus had on them and those they write about. But to be authentically encountered by Jesus in our existence we can only experience the Spirit of Christ, through revelation, as did Paul on the road to Damascus. We must remember that Paul had no historical contact with Jesus, but like him we too can become Apostles of Jesus the Christ. The important thing is this: the Spirit of Christ comes to us, for there is a large gap of separation between us and God. By grace, Jesus the Christ comes to us in our estranged state, at which moment we are left with the decision to leap in his direction. Like Paul, we can experience the reality of Christ to such an extent that our lives are transformed. As SK would say, we can become contemporaneous with Christ.

Tillich is right, we do have direction. Yet, I would say we still have a sheer leap, not into blinding darkness, but into blinding light, which is finally no less terrifying or no less a risk to our ego. Leaping into the direction of the Christ, knowing what we know about Jesus and his followers' existence, we are leaping with total abandonment. This terrifies those whose egos obsessively seek the "good life." Nevertheless, grace brings this choice to leap to faith and find one's true self. SK says there is no other way to really know oneself. He would laugh at all the psychological and new age perversions of knowing oneself in our era, and would be vindicated in doing so by the very strong debate going on today over the validity of Freudianism.

Let us finish this short look into SK's christology by considering what is truth. SK writes, "within me (that is, when I am truly within myself, not untruly outside myself) truth is, if it is at all, a being, a *life*. Therefore it is said, 'This is life eternal, to know the only true God and him whom He hath sent', the Truth. That is to say, only then do I truly know the truth when it becomes a life in me."[13] He later adds that truth is *not* understanding, *not* knowledge through comprehending, speculating, or reflecting.[14] SK makes his point by referring to Jesus' sermonette to Pilate. "'If my life', He [Jesus] might say [to Pilate], 'does not open thine eyes to what truth is, then it is of all things the most impossible for Me to tell thee what it is. Herein lies the difference between Me and all other men: doubtless what some other man says in answer to the question, "What is truth?" is not always quite true, but I am the only man that cannot reply to this question at all, for I am the truth.'"[15]

SK says that "Christianity understood, the truth consists not in knowing the truth but in being the truth."[16] One cannot *know* the truth. Christianity is all about *being* the truth. Truth is being "when it is 'the way.'" "Christ was the truth, He was the way, or He was the way in the sense that the truth is the way. The fact that He has travelled the way to the end does not alter anything in the situation of the successor [us], who, if he is of the truth and desires to be of the truth, can be so only by following 'the way'."[17] Therefore, those *on* "the way" are the only true Christians, the "followers," not the "admirers."[18]

To sum up, as followers on the way we are contemporaneous with Christ, we have leapt to faith, we are our true selves, we are being the truth, we are Christians.

Reflection

SK was so radical in his time that he was not read widely until early in the 20th century. And when he was read, he was censored formally (by Pope Pius XII in 1950) and informally as a threat to the Christian tradition.[19] Why? He understood that christology has to do with our decision of faith more than it does with the objective history of Jesus and the doctrines of the tradition. As Carl Michalson, a student of Gogarten, writes about SK, "the quickest way to falsify the truth of God is Christendom's way, treating God as the object of belief. . . . [For SK] Christian faith is not a teaching about God but a mode of existence."[20] To him faith is "objective uncertainty." Therefore, "it was necessary for Christ to go away before the Disciples could follow Him."[21] "Faith being a decision for subjectivity does not affirm that God is, but that God exists. . . . God only exists in faith."[22] "Faith is existential knowledge of God because it is God's way of being present in existence, the eternal's way of being contemporaneous."[23] "[T]he emphasis in Kierkegaard's Christology, as in theology today, is more along [this line]: 'The God-Man is the Unity of God and an individual man in an actual historical situation.'"[24]

> It is true that the rich young ruler was asked to give up his worldly goods. The irony in the incident is that he felt he could not afford to give up the world, yet, if he had taken the movement of faith, 'he would have gotten every penny back," [*Fear and Trembling*] as Abraham got Isaac back when he acted in faith. 'He who when he has the world is as one who does not have it, then he has the world, otherwise the world has him [*Edifying Discourses,* I]."[25]

Michalson is getting at the radicality of SK's christology when he says for SK, "God only exists in faith." *God* does not exist for me except through faith. Everything else is academic, objective speculation. If *God* does not exist for me through my decision of faith, then he does not exist for me. We can talk about *God's* "isness" and *supreme being* and *existence* all we want to, but without our faith it's all useless chatter, like answering a survey question *Yes* that asks Do you believe in a supreme being? And who is it that convinces us that faith is radical abandonment? Jesus the Christ and his followers, not his admirers sitting in church pews saying creeds in unison. To become contemporaneous with Jesus the Christ is to decide like Abraham. He became the Knight of Faith for SK. Abraham was saved by his faith in Jesus the Christ, long before Jesus was born. Abraham embodied radical faith and consequently experienced the reality of *God's* existence for him. Paul calls him the father of faith (Rom. 4).

CHAPTER 10 NOTES

[1] Søren Kierkegaard, *The Sickness Unto Death*, translated by Walter Lowrie (Princeton: Princeton University Press, 1941), p. 216.
[2] Perry D. LeFevre, *The Prayers of Kierkegaard* (Chicago: University of Chicago Press, 1956), p. 171.

[3] Donald D. Palmer, *Kierkegaard for Beginners* (New York: Writers and Readers Publishing, 1996), p. 134.

[4] Wesley J. Wildman, *Fidelity With Plausibility: Modest Christologies in the Twentieth Century* (Albany: State University of New York Press, 1998), p. 360. Wildman points out that after Kierkegaard human decision became fundamental in theology and the social sciences.

[5] Søren Kierkegaard, *Training in Christianity*, trans. Walter Lowrie (1941; Princeton: Princeton University Press, 1944), p. 160.

[6] Paul Tillich, *Perspectives on 19th and 20th Century Protestant Theology* (New York: Harper & Row, 1967), p. 162.

[7] *Ibid.*, p. 174.

[8] *Ibid.*

[9] *Ibid.*, p. 175.

[10] *Ibid.*

[11] *Ibid.*

[12] *Ibid.*, p. 176.

[13] *Training in Christianity*, p. 202 (parentheses and italics not added).

[14] *Ibid.*

[15] *Ibid.*, p. 200.

[16] *Ibid.*, p. 201.

[17] *Ibid.*, p. 204.

[18] *Ibid.*, p. 247.

[19] Carl Michalson, "Subjectivity and the Reality of Faith—Søren Kierkegaard's Theology," *Worldly Theology: The Hermeneutical Focus of an Historical Faith* (New York: Charles Scribner's, 1967), pp. 114-15.

[20] *Ibid.*, p. 117.

[21] *Ibid.*, p. 121.

[22] *Ibid.*, p. 122.

[23] *Ibid.*, p. 123.

[24] *Ibid.*, p. 124 (from *Training in Christianity*, p. 123).

[25] *Ibid.*, p. 126.

11. Paul Tillich: Christology of New Being

Paul Tillich, at the age of forty-seven, was dismissed from the faculty of the University of Frankfurt in 1933 when Hitler became German chancellor. Tillich, with his family, came to teach at Union Theological Seminary in New York, "without even a minimum knowledge of the [English] language,"[1] at the invitation of the Niebuhr brothers. Since then he has become the preeminent theologian of the United States of the 20th century, writing his three volumes of *Systematic Theology* in English. He was profoundly thankful to Union for shelter, its offer of a job, the fellowship with faculty and students, and its worshipping community, where Tillich preached many of his sermons, printed in three volumes.[2]

His most famous sermon, *"You Are Accepted,"* points to the essence of Tillich's christology. Let us reflect upon its last paragraphs.

'Where sin abounded, grace did much more abound', says Paul in the same letter [*Romans*] in which he describes the unimaginable power of separation and self-destruction within society and the individual soul. He does not say these words because sentimental interests demand a happy end for everything tragic. He says them because they describe the most overwhelming and determining experience of his life. In the picture of Jesus as the Christ, which appeared to him at the moment of his greatest separation from other men, from himself and God, he found himself accepted in spite of his being rejected. And when he found that he was accepted, he was able to accept himself and to be reconciled to others. The moment in which grace struck him and overwhelmed him, he was reunited with that to which he belonged, and from which he was estranged in utter strangeness.

Paul described this "most overwhelming and determining experience" as grace, which happened in his greatest separation.

Accepted in spite of, he was reunited to all. Not mentioned here, we know that Paul became the most motivated Apostle for Jesus the Christ, living with abandon his new mission until his martyrdom. Tillich recounts Paul's grace narrative and then asks,

> Do we know what it means to be struck by grace? It does not mean that we suddenly believe that God exists, or that Jesus is the Saviour, or that the Bible contains the truth. To believe that something is, is almost contrary to the meaning of grace. Furthermore, grace does not mean simply that we are making progress in our moral self-control, in our fight against special faults, and in our relationships to men and to society. Moral progress may be a fruit of grace; but it is not grace itself, and it can even prevent us from receiving grace. For there is too often a graceless acceptance of Christian doctrines and a graceless battle against the structures of evil in our personalities. Such a graceless relation to God may lead us by necessity either to arrogance or to despair. It would be better to refuse God and the Christ and the Bible than to accept them without grace. For if we accept without grace, we do so in the state of separation, and can only succeed in deepening the separation.

In this second quote Tillich is talking about "graceless" or would-be humanly earned grace that leads to arrogance or despair, or a situation worse than before. Grace does not depend upon anything from us, not even belief in God, Jesus, or the Bible; not even a moral accomplishment as great as giving away all that we have, even our very lives. This is a radical statement. Separated humans cannot save themselves, and the more we try the more we intensify our state of separation—and despair.

> We cannot transform our lives, unless we allow them to be transformed by that stroke of grace. It happens; or it does not happen. And certainly it does not happen if we try to force it upon ourselves, just as it shall not happen so long as we think, in our self-complacency, that we have no need of it. Grace strikes us when we are in great pain and restlessness. It strikes us when we walk through the dark valley of a meaningless and empty life. It strikes us when we feel that our separation is

deeper than usual, because we have violated another life, a life which we loved, or from which we were estranged. It strikes us when our disgust for our own being, our indifference, our weakness, our hostility, and our lack of direction and composure have become intolerable to us. It strikes us when, year after year, the longed-for perfection of life does not appear, when the old compulsions reign within us as they have for decades, when despair destroys all joy and courage.

We absolutely cannot transform our lives. We can only allow them to be transformed by grace, but we have no control over grace. Then Tillich goes through the litany of separations in our existence that we all experience more or less intensely. He seems to know what he is talking about. If we cite particular examples from our own lives, our separation becomes palpable. Remember, there is nothing religious here, *per se*.

> Sometimes at that moment a wave of light breaks into our darkness, and it is as though a voice were saying:
> 'You are accepted. You are accepted, accepted by that which is greater than you, and the name of which you do not know. Do not ask for the name now; perhaps you will find it later. Do not do anything now; perhaps later you will do much. Do not seek for anything; do not perform anything; do not intend anything. Simply accept the fact that you are accepted!'

This is the announcement of the secular word of grace that comes from somewhere. Who says we are accepted? Don't ask, do nothing; don't seek, don't perform, don't intend. *Simply accept the fact that you are accepted*. Which of these eight italicized words is the most important? The event of these words happens just any way it chooses, with absolutely no strings, except one, accepting the all determining *fact* of our existence: that we are accepted.

> If that happens to us, we experience grace. After such an experience we may not be better than before, and we may not believe more than before. But everything is transformed. In that moment, grace conquers sin, and reconciliation bridges

the gulf of estrangement. And nothing is demanded of this experience, no religious or moral or intellectual presuppositions, nothing but acceptance.

"If that happens": in our deep sense of separation, sometimes something happens that gets said to us that we are accepted, and all we have to do is accept that fact. We don't have to do that, even. Therefore, it is a decision, either *Yes* or *No*. But if we say *Yes* we experience grace. Tillich adds one more time that nothing we do causes this happening of grace: no religious, moral, or intellectual thoughts or actions. The only thing we can do is *accept the fact that we are accepted*.

Tillich finishes his sermon by saying *after* grace strikes and we accept our acceptance by that whose name we do not know, we can *then* accept the life of other beings and even our own life.

> We experience the grace of being able to accept the life of an-other, even if it be hostile and harmful to us, for, through grace, we know that it belongs to the same Ground to which we be-long, and by which we have been accepted. . . .

> [M]oments [of grace] . . . make us love our life, . . . make us accept ourselves, not in our goodness and self-complacency, but in our certainty of the eternal meaning of our life. . . .

> [S]ometimes it happens that we receive the power to say 'yes' to ourselves, that peace enters into us and makes us whole. . . .

Tillich concludes the sermon by reminding us that grace is built into our lives, that it determines our lives, and that it can conquer separation.

> 'Sin' and 'grace' are strange words; but they are not strange things. . . . They determine our life. They abound within us and in all of life. May grace more abound within us![3]

Tillich in his theological writings says much about sin, grace, and faith, but these few paragraphs illuminate the whole. He spends much of the first and second volumes of his *Systematic Theology* making clear our existential predicament of sin or separation from self, others, and God, or the Ground of Being. "Sin is a universal fact before it becomes an individual act. . . . Therefore, it is impossible to separate sin as fact from sin as act."[4] It is the threat of non-being that determines so much of our lives.

> The attempts of man to resist it ['the demonic power of non-being or transitoriness without the presence of the power of being itself'] are of no avail. Man tries to prolong the small stretch of time given to him; he tries to fill the moment with as many transitory things as possible; . . . he imagines a continuation of his life after the end of his time and an endlessness without eternity. . . .
>
> The breakdown of this resistance in its many forms is . . . despair. It is not the experience of time as such which produces despair. . . . His [a human's] existential unwillingness to accept his temporality makes time a demonic structure of destruction for him.[5]

Tillich goes on to make clear that the threat of non-being in relation to space is, like time, deeply a part of our separation from our Ground of Being. We long for a "final home." Instead we become "pilgrims on earth." This condition of finitude throws us into the "despair of ultimate uprootedness."[6] In time and space we are confronted with the despair that is the "end of our possibilities," being "without hope," "beyond possible healing," which is what Tillich indicates is Kierkegaard's meaning in *The Sickness unto Death*. "The pain of despair is the agony of being responsible for the loss of the meaning of one's existence and of being unable to recover it."[7] We are estranged, separated, in a state of sin, longing for reunion.

Tillich goes on page after page of grounding us in our separation, our sin, before coming to the section on the reality of Jesus as the Christ. Tillich makes sense of the strange myths of the gospel by "deliteralizing" them, a more exact word, he says, than "demythologizing" (Bultmann's term) the myths. Why? We must make clear that we are not doing away with the myths which freight ultimate meaning.[8]

Then Tillich articulates the meaning of the "two central symbols" of "Jesus the Christ as the bearer of the New Being in a special relation to existence." "The first relation of the Christ to existence is his subjection to it [the 'Cross of Christ']; the second relation of Christ to existence is his conquest of it [the 'Resurrection of Christ']."[9] Together these symbols constitute the meaning of the happening of grace, or the event that symbolizes the conquest of New Being in the midst of existence, or the event which brings reunion. We experience the power of New Being that declares us acceptable "in spite of"[10] our being unacceptable in our separation.

> Indeed, there is nothing in man which enables God to accept him. But man must accept just this. He must accept that he is accepted; he must accept acceptance. And the question is how this is possible in spite of the guilt which makes him hostile to God. The traditional answer is 'Because of Christ!'. . . It means that one is drawn into the power of the New Being in Christ, which makes faith possible; that it is the state of unity between God and man, no matter how fragmentarily realized. Accepting that one is accepted is the paradox of salvation, without which there would be no salvation but only despair.[11]

This faith that is made possible by grace, or the power of the New Being in Christ, is "justifying faith," "not a human act, although it happens in man; faith is the work of the divine Spirit, the power which creates the New Being, in the Christ, in individuals, in the church."[12] "Justification is first an objective event and then a subjective event. . . . Justification literally means 'making just,' namely, making man that which he essentially is and from which he is estranged. . . . It is an act of God."[13] "Faith itself is the immediate . . . evidence of the New Being."[14] These are the credentials of Jesus as the Christ: as the New Being he is the act of God and brings grace and faith into existence to overcome our separation and despair.

So Tillich's christology is the event of grace through Jesus the Christ as the New Being, who brings faith and new being to us in the lives we are living.

Reflection

Tillich has been called a philosopher rather than a theologian because his christology is described as "spiritual,"[15] meaning that Jesus the Christ is a symbol, not a historical reality. Not so. We know from above that Tillich means Jesus the Christ to be both an existential and a historical reality, understood in the cross and resurrection, both described by Tillich as historical events and symbols.[16] True, he may not fit into fundamentalists' operating images, yet the following chart gives us perspective on the tradition of grace of which Tillich is a *bona fide* member, especially in relation to *Romans* and the Reformation. He stands in the long line of classical christology, communicating Jesus as the crux of the event of faith. (In the *chart on the following page*, you the reader can fill in your content in the four blanks to test where you stand theologically.)

THE REVOLUTION OF GRACE

EMPHASES:	SIN	JUSTIFICATION	FAITH	SALVATION
OLD TESTAMENT	Disobedient to Covenant	Fulfillment of the Law	Obedience to God	At-one-ment with God
BOOK OF ROMANS	Self-Righteousness	God's Free Grace	Faith in God	New Life in Christ
THE REFORMATION	Idolatrous Faith	By Grace Alone	Faith Only in God's Grace	Eternal Well-Being
TILLICH'S SERMON	Separation from Self/Others/Ground of Being	You Are Accepted	Accept the Fact that You're Accepted	Union with Ground of Being/Others/Self
MY CONTENT				

Tillich's christology can be called a christology of *grace*, but his abundant use of *new being*, reflected below, has intensive and extensive meaning for our age and also honors the Christian tradition of grace, ecumenical dialogue, and universality. (The Roman numerals refer to Tillich's three volumes of *Systematic Theology*.)

1. the eschatological event of the *new being* brings us to decide against "old being" (old reality) and for *new being* (new reality)—*new being* brings the new state of things (II, 97[17])
2. *new being* is a happening in history and in our existence
3. "being" connotes existence is in being
4. "being" connotes the person of Christ
5. *new being* is like Paul's "new creation"
6. *new being* was a hidden presence in those who prepared the way for Jesus (III, 150[18])
7. "being" points to a gift—ontological—not an act of will—moral (II, 125)
8. *new being* is essential being under the condition of existence (II, 119)
9. *new being* points to community (community of the *new being*) as well as individual life (III, 155)
10. *new being* represents the essential unity between God and humans
11. *new being* precedes new acting (II, 79)
12. *new being* is the resurrection of life out of death (NB, 24[19])
13. *new being* is manifest in both space and time, though fragmentarily (III, 140)
14. *new being* is more our idiom than Son of God, Son of Man, Incarnation, etc.
15. *new being*, representing the "Son," consistently interchanges with "ground of being" (Tillich's phrase for "God") and "spiritual presence" (his phrase for "Holy Spirit") and therefore upholds his trinitarian insights
16. *new being* indicates something "new" can happen
17. *new being* honors the mythological and historical
18. *new being* is compatible with regeneration, justification, and sanctification (II, 176-80; III, 221-31)

19. *new being* is process-oriented (II, 231)
20. *new being* is amenable in use to philosophy and studies other than theology, fulfilling Tillich's apologetic mission (I, 50[20])
21. holiness is the working of the *new being* within (III, 167)
22. *new being* holds the paradox of the eternal and temporal, the infinite and the finite (I, 50)
23. *new being* is the paradox of the Christian message (II, 92)
24. *new being* in Jesus as the Christ is our *ultimate concern* (I, 50)
25. "being" connotes metaphysical and logical character (I, 55)
26. "being" has mystical implications when used in relation to God as *being-itself* (I, 55)
27. "new" in connection with "being" connotes creativity (I, 55)
28. *new being* is Jesus' being (I, 136)
29. *new being* in Christ is judgment and promise (II, 92)
30. *new being* connotes the ruler of history (II, 162)
31. the concept of salvation has grown with *new being* (II, 166)
32. participation in *new being* is authentic existence
33. *new being* is secular as well as religious (II, 180)
34. *new being* is the ultimate criterion of all revelatory experiences (III, 128)
35. *new being* is renewal: reconciliation, reunion, and resurrection (NB, 20)
36. resurrection, like *new being*, is the transformation of the "old being" rising out of its death—not the creation of another being (III, 414)
37. *new being* is eternal life now
38. the "*new being* in Jesus as the Christ" is not a "divine-human automaton" (II, 135)
39. faith is the state of being grasped by the *new being* as it is manifest in Jesus as the Christ (III, 131)

His christology is all about *New Being*, rich in facets of meaning. Tillich uses both *new being* and *grace* throughout his works to describe the dynamics of the *Jesus the Christ happening*. Both point to the universal and particular meaning event at the center of life.

CHAPTER 11 NOTES

[1] Paul Tillich, "Autobiographical Reflections," *The Theology of Paul Tillich*, ed. Charles Kegley and Robert Bretall (New York: Macmillan, 1952), p.16.
[2] Paul Tillich, *The Shaking of the Foundations* (New York: Charles Scribner's, 1948); *The New Being* (1955); *The Eternal Now* (1956).
[3] "You Are Accepted," *The Shaking of the Foundations*, pp. 160-63 (no emphasis added).
[4] Paul Tillich, *Systematic Theology*, Vol. II (Chicago: University of Chicago Press, 1957), p. 56.
[5] *Ibid.*, p. 69.
[6] *Ibid.*
[7] Ibid., p. 75.
[8] *Ibid.*, p. 152.
[9] *Ibid.*
[10] *Ibid.*, p. 178.
[11] *Ibid.*, p. 179.
[12] *Ibid.*, p. 178.
[13] *Ibid.*
[14] *Ibid.*, p. 114.
[15] Alister McGrath, *Christian Theology: An Introduction* (1994; Cambridge, MA: Blackwell, 1997), pp. 345-46.
[16] "The Universal Significance of the Event Jesus Christ," *Sytematic Theology*, Vol. II, pp. 150-65.
[17] *Systematic Theology*, Vol. II.
[18] Paul Tillich, *Systematic Theology*, Vol. III (Chicago: University of Chicago Press, 1963).
[19] Paul Tillich, *The New Being* (New York: Charles Scribner's, 1955).
[20] Paul Tillich, *Systematic Theology*, Vol. I (Chicago: University of Chicago Press, 1951).

Section Three:

Dynamics of the Christ Event

12. *The Christ Of History*

JOSEPH W. MATHEWS

*[This essay was first printed in booklet form in the **Image**: **Journal of the Ecumenical Institute**: **Chicago**, Number 7, June 1969.]*

THE EVERYMAN-CHRIST

The need to "make sense" out of our sufferings and actions is deeply human. Apparently men everywhere and in every time have sensed themselves as pilgrims looking for a way to really live in this world. In the language of the poet, EVERYMAN quests after some light, way, truth, door. More or less awarely, he searches for a bread or word of life. He dwells in hope that some tomorrow will bring a delivering power, an illuminating story, some saving event, a final blessedness. When that day comes, so he dreams, then surely in some way the essence of life and the living of it will be different. All peoples have forged signs and symbols of this human characteristic. For the Hebrews of old, one such image was the coming "anointed one," the Messiah, translated into the Greek as the Christ.

This Messianic hope of EVERYMAN is born out of his experience of the limitations of existence. His encounter with the unknowns, ambiguities, sufferings and deaths of this world discloses his insecurity. This primordial anxiety breeds the Messiah image. Watch him, as he is thrown up against his finitude, become a seeker after some truth which will overcome the unbearable incomprehensibles of life. Watch him search, however subtly, for the justification which will alleviate his sense of insignificance. Watch him relentlessly strive for a peace which will somehow blot out his lucid awareness of the tragic dimension of life. One senses in this spectacle a creature vainly striving to rise above his creaturely limits. Finding his givenness burdensome beyond bearing, he dreams of discovering some other kind of a world. Indeed he already has a different world for he literally exists in his present hopes about the future. Thereby he escapes his actual life in the Now. His very meaning is his anticipation that some tomorrow will render his situation quite different. On that day the ultimate key will come clear; the final excuse for his existence will emerge and true contentment will bathe his being. Then shall he truly live, so he imagines, delivered from this present world of uncertainty, unfulfillment and anxiety. Such a life-quest is an experience, I submit, that all of us are quite privy to. Men dwell sometimes very explicitly, most times quite vaguely, in great expectations of that which will relieve them of the necessity of living their given life in the present situation. This great hope, whatever its form, is the CHRIST OF EVERYMAN.

THE JESUS OF NAZARETH

The New Testament age opens with the Jews, like EVERYMAN, expecting the Christ. Of course, they were doing so out of their concrete historical memory. The Christ-quest is always tied to specific life situations. It was into this particular Jewish yearning, around the beginning of the first century, that one Jesus intruded. It might have been, in an abstract sense, Herman of Hebbronville or Jones of Smithville. But it was not. It was this fellow Jesus of Nazareth in Galilee. Very little detail is directly known about this man. But as all of us do, he lived a life and died a death. It was, to be sure, *his* life that he lived and *his* death that he died. This is most important for it was in the midst of these very definite historical occurrences, as they disturbed the hopes of Israel, that the New Testament happening of Christ took place.

Perhaps the core of the issue could be put something like this: a very specific man lived a very specific life and for that specific life, died a very specific death. Somehow in these concretions the deeps of human existence became exposed. A man got born, lived his life, and experienced death even as you and I. Yet there was a plus. Not a metaphysical plus, but what might be termed a plus in specifics. I mean he lived a life essentially like that of anyone else, save he seemed to *really* live his. However one chooses to account for it—special mutations of genes, unusual neurotic tendencies, peculiar environmental influences, unique occurrences of lucidity—is all quite beside my concern at the moment. Here was one who apparently not only lived, but *lived* his living. He appropriated his life as an unqualified gift and bore it as a significant mission. The *givenness* of creaturely living appeared to him to be the very meaning of it. Indeed, he kept saying that what everyone is looking for is very much AT HAND.

EVERYMAN, here in Jewish guise, was understandably disconcerted by the style of this unknown and everyday stranger. The very point is that Jesus collided with the lives of all he encountered. He invaded, broke into, penetrated their worlds, leaving them painfully unsettled. To the proud he seemed humble and they were threatened. If men hated life, he loved it. To those who hung desperately onto living, he appeared nonchalant about it all. If they thought of life as detachment, he was utterly involved. If their living was a bondage, he was too obviously free. Where men were other-directed, he was independent. When they were confidently self-determining, he seemed lost in loyalties. To conservatives he was manifestly revolutionary; he impressed the radicals as a reactionary. Obviously, the life of such a human being would be in jeopardy. When men's lives are audited to the quick, either they must re-do their lives, or destroy the occasion of the audit. Jesus was executed.

Death comes to all men. So it had to come in some fashion to Jesus of Nazareth. The specifics are what concern us. A life that was in some way *really* lived drove men to destroy it. Let this be said again. Precisely because his living somehow exhibited the way life actually is, men felt he had to be removed. Rulers saw him as a danger to society. The hierarchy feared him as a menace to religion. The strange irony here uncovers a tragic inversion in human history. There is yet another important concretion. The man of Galilee embraced death as he embraced life. Call it the slaughter of the innocent or the miscarriage of justice; call it murder or mistake; call it social expediency or the intervention of fate; however, and whatever, he took unto himself his death without malice as a part of the givenness of his life. Not that he sought death. But when it came, and as it came, he died it as significant. In consequence, there was a compounding of disturbance. His dying as his living was disquieting.

In some such fashion did the life and death of an unknown, Jesus of Nazareth, protrude into the history and the hope of Israel, and therefore into the life of EVERYMAN. But this is not yet the end, nor even the finally important aspect of the tale.

THE JESUS-CHRIST-EVENT

In the midst of the happenings surrounding Jesus, some individuals were seized by a radically new possibility for living in this world. Incredible as it was to the many, a few actually raised the question of Christ in connection with Jesus. This moves us to the heart of the matter. To really hear this question is to sense an absolutely unbelievable twist in the Christ symbol. The very life-image of the Jews, their very existence, their very history, was cut to the marrow by the question Is Jesus the Christ? Quite understandably they reacted to it as scandalous. Because it was a scandal, crucial decisions had to be made. Here are the keys to the New Testament Christ-happening: scandal and decision.

The scandal is clearly manifest in the broad picture. The EVERYMAN-CHRIST for the Jews was concretized in the anticipated coming of a mighty king or cosmic figure who would fulfill the corporate dreams of Israel. Patently, such a figure Jesus was not. He came a helpless babe in a feeding trough. He left a pitiful personage on the state gallows. This have to do with Messiah? How ridiculous! Indeed, in the light of the sacred hopes, it was blasphemous.

Now the offense of the Jew is the offense of EVERYMAN. The question about Jesus insinuates an unmitigated revolution in human self-perception. The distressing implication is that life is not in the future, it is in the present; it is not in some other circumstances, it is those at hand; it is not to be sought after, it is already given. Obviously this cuts across the notions to which every man has attached his being. The one who seeks to escape his present situation as meaningless must certainly be outraged by the hint that the final meaning is to receive that very situation. Those who look to tomorrow to solve the riddle will surely feel affronted before the intimation that the ultimate solution is living the Now. This is the elemental scandal in the Jesus question.

The point needs to be underlined. If the self-understanding which broke into history surrounding the living and dying of one Jesus is to be designated by the term "Christ," then very evidently a radical eruption has occurred in history through a complete inversion of the Christ symbol. This is not just an addition to or an alteration of life. The total image of life is disputed. In truth, it is literally turned upside down. That is, the scandal is cataclysmic and universal. Concisely, what we shall call the JESUS-CHRIST mortally assaults the EVERYMAN-CHRIST.

The JESUS-CHRIST fronts man with the awareness that there is no messiah and never will be one, and furthermore, that this very reality is the Messiah. This must not, however, be understood as an intellectual abstraction. It is rather a happening that meets men in the midst of their living. Indeed, the fronting is experienced as death itself. For to receive the JESUS-CHRIST is to put an end to my Christ quest; it is to surrender my very life stance; it means that I must die to my very self. Or better still, my self must die. The threat of the JESUS-CHRIST is now unmasked as the threat of death. The scandal, as experienced, is that I must choose to die.

The drama of this deciding unto death permeates the New Testament. This is certainly to be expected. For decision is a rudimentary component of the New Testament Christ happening and a necessary consequence of the Christ offense. Those seized by the scandal of the Jesus question could not avoid an answer. One way or the other they had to decide. Life decisions are always compelled by the disturbance of life modes. But the choice was not apprehended as just *another* choice. It was understood as the *elemental* one, and this precisely because the above scandal was the ultimate assault upon the world of EVERYMAN. In short, the great and final divide of all human decisions is located in the strange New Testament question Is Jesus the Christ?

The response demanded and the only one that could be demanded was a simple yea or nay. There is no possible third option; no middle ground; no perhaps. Not even a delay is thinkable . For not to decide here is still to decide. At any other point, several alternatives, in principle at least, are offered. Such is not the case here. The scandal is either embraced or it is rejected. Though repudiation has a thousand faces, yes, a thousand times a thousand times, all are but some form of re-entrenchment in the EVERYMAN-CHRIST. This extreme dimension becomes clearer when one remembers that for the New Testament people the Christ decision was transparently an election for or against life itself. The negative answer was at bottom a rejection of human existence as it is constituted. The acknowledgement of the scandal, on the other hand, is a full and free affirmation of the significance of the creaturehood of man. When the human situation is nakedly exposed there are but two choices: to affirm life or to negate it.

Perhaps it appears incredible that such fathomless deeps of man and history are caught up in so very concrete a decision. Yet this is exactly the way things are in this dimension of existence. As the search for meaning is always concrete, so necessarily is the offense to this meaning historically rooted. And therefore the ensuing decision must likewise be grounded in the very particular. Though at base the New Testament men were deciding about their own stance and destiny, yet, because Jesus was the occasion of the question, externally it took the form of deciding about him: Is Jesus the Christ? What do you say? Is your CHRIST, JESUS-CHRIST? or the EVERYMAN-CHRIST?

One final concern before the summation. The JESUS-CHRIST-EVENT has been depicted at one and the same time as both death and life. This draws together the entire twist. It is unmistakably plain that the early Christians conceived of and experienced this happening as the very fullness of life. They sensed after themselves as the blind who now see, as the deaf who have been given to hear, the bound set free, the maimed made whole, the dead men who are alive. The death involved in encompassing the scandal was discovered to be life itself. There is no addition here, no subtle way out. Any addendum would be a cancellation of the event. The choice to give up our illusions and false hopes and hiding places is the death of choosing the scandal. This very death is life, they insisted. To die is to live. To use their figures, it is like being born all over again. It is like the healing of a mortal illness. It is like being forgiven a big lie at the heart of our being. It is like a resurrection from a tomb.

The dying to the life-quest becomes itself the very bread of life.

Surrender of the demand for final truth becomes quite the truth about things. Capitulation to the secret that there is no way out becomes the very door and way to being. This is the end of the road of self-understanding. There is no beyond it. There is no need. For one can now freely live in his negations, learn in his perpetual ignorance and walk in all his given creatureliness. In brief, the decision to die is at the same time an election to life. The JESUS-CHRIST is life abundant. As it was in the beginning, is now and ever shall be.

Now to the recapitulation: the JESUS-CHRIST is an historical event. It is a radical revolution in the interior history of men proceeding from an absolute reversal in human self-understanding. Originally occasioned by Jesus of Nazareth, it is first of all the experience of an offense. This offense is grounded in an actual disaffirmation of our creaturely phantasms which issues in a new possibility of living our bestowed existence as a great benefaction. It is, secondly, the decision to receive the offense and embrace the ensuing possibility as our own. This entails a dying to ourselves as defined by our mirages, which very death is experienced as the very life we were mistakenly searching for. Such is the radical transfiguration of the JESUS-CHRIST-EVENT.

The early Christians' pronouncement of it contained an inseparable promise and demand. The demand is to die. That this very dying is life is the promise.

THE CHRISTIAN STORY

Our task is not finished. Any serious dialogue on the Christ symbol must of necessity consider the Christian story, so-called. In and through the JESUS-CHRIST-EVENT an historical community broke into time. The church and the event are actually but two sides of one historical occurrence. Those to whom the event happened constituted the church. Like every historical people the church forged a life-apologue or meaning story by which it communicated to itself and to others that the event which created it was rooted in ultimacy. What we have termed the Christian story became, therefore, along with the event and the church, an integral component of the total historical complex.

The cosmic tale has a universal and definitive agency. Both the social body and the comprising individuals are contingent upon it. As insinuated above, it is the vehicle by which the interior history is transcendently grounded, comprehensively appropriated and significantly communicated. To say it again, it freights the universal dimension to self-understandings and life missions. In fact, all intentional being and doing, all self-conscious existence is finally interwoven with one or another cosmic-meaning drama.

Such stories are conspicuously penetrated by the relative and arbitrary: not in their inner meaning but in their form. Yet once the story is devised, there is a certain absolute quality about even the form. In principle, the detail could have been quite different at its creation. And any time thereafter its basic intent can be expressed in other ways. But once the original dramaturgy is complete, that production is the prototype. It remains prototypal as long as the historical community remains. The early Christians formulated their classical tale out of the relative stuff of their specific Hebrew memory, the unique worldviews of their time, and whatever figures emerged from the collective unconscious. It was a work of expansive conception and consummate artistry. Through it the church continued to grasp for themselves and transmit to others the finality of what had occurred in their midst. This is to say, it endured as irreplaceable.

The story is a strange metamorphic tale of two symbols: the cross and the empty tomb. These basic New Testament emblems pervade the drama from the beginning to the end. The truth of the matter is they play the stellar role. Uncommon and fantastic as it may sound, the leading character of the Christian story is none other than the biform symbol, cross and open sepulcher, indicating and embodying the reality of the crucifixion that is resurrection, the death that is life. To say it another way, the principle player is the meaning-word that man may dare to be fully human, living freely among the uncertainties, ambiguities and anxieties of creaturehood, in gratitude, concern and creativity. The hero, in brief, is not Jesus, but the JESUS-CHRIST-EVENT.

In brief synopsis, the story develops as a dramatic extravaganza in three sweeping acts executed on two stage levels. It opens on the upper stage representing the cosmic, universal, transcendent dimension of life. It moves next to the historical, temporal, human level on the lower stage. Finally, in the third act the movement returns once more to the cosmic gallery. Each of the three acts is a spectacle in itself. Yet all are bound together into one majestic movement by two transitional scenes between the acts.

The time and place of act one is the beginning of the beginnings. Exciting awesomeness is the overarching mood. The JESUS-CHRIST-EVENT, disguised as a most curious lamb which is alive though dead, is the principle figure on stage. Here, before the foundations of the world, a slain lamb is sitting very much alive on the very throne of thrones alongside the creator. Indeed the lamb is portrayed as the creator himself calling all things into being. Without him no thing that comes to be comes to be. Passing to the third and final act of the play, the scene is very much the same. It is again on the cosmic level with the slain lamb occupying stage center. The difference is that it is now the ending of the endings. All things have passed away. The lamb, alive-while-dead, is once more seated on the throne. This time he is playing the role of the unconditional judge presiding over the finale of history. In sober awe all things come forth to account and no thing is judged save by the judgment of the lamb.

Embracing the middle act are two transitional scenes. Their theatric function is that of getting the lamb on and off the historical stage where the second act is performed. The entrance into temporality of the JESUS-CHRIST-EVENT figure cannot of course be like any other entry. Heralded by angelic hosts, he arrives born of a virgin. If the play were being composed today the advent might well have been by way of a space rocket fired out of nowhere. In this case, the lamb imagery conceivably would be replaced by that of a strange little creature from beyond the time-space continuum. The important point is that the cosmic figure invades history on a mighty mission. When the mission is accomplished he departs the temporal, not of course as others do, but through ascending in an effulgence of glory again to the upper level.

In the second act, the interest is in the cosmic mission. The central character is still the JESUS-CHRIST-EVENT. Camouflaged in the first and last act as the slain lamb, it is here disguised as a man. In this double concealment the cosmic figure submits to the ordeal of finitude. He meets and straightforwardly engages the twin forces of death and the devil: that is, the temptation to illusion and the anxiety of creatureliness which drives us into the clutches of illusion. He engages the forces of EVERYMAN-CHRIST and destroys their power by boldly withstanding their subtlest wiles. He enters the very den of death and emerges from the grave the unchallenged conqueror. In a mighty invasion the JESUS-CHRIST-EVENT has overcome the hosts of the foe on the plains of history, pushed to the fortified place and bound the strong man, leading humanity forth from its bondage and slavery unto the glorious freedom of life. The sign and power of the cross and empty tomb are engraved for all time upon the fact of history. Cosmic permission to live has been epiphanied. Mission accomplished, the lamb returns to that realm from whence he came, the manifest victor to rule as sovereign lord and only judge forever and forever. What a play!

It must be underscored that this drama is in no sense a web of metaphysical statements. Nor is it an aggregate of religious doctrines to be believed. It is a story. Its task is to hold before the reader, in a comprehensive, precise, and constraining fashion, the stance of life. One is moved therefore not to ask whether the dramatic images correspond to "objective realities," but whether the life meaning they embody corresponds to the way life comes to us as persons.

When it is received as the truth-story it is, the axial point is quite plain. Though the point is singular, it peradventure ought to be put several ways. First of all, the JESUS-CHRIST is presented not as just a way of life, but the final and only way. The story announces both the cosmic permission and the cosmic requirement to live after this style. Second, it is clear in the play that the JESUS-CHRIST is the way real life has always been from the very beginning of human existence, and will always be to the very ending. Third, the JESUS-CHRIST is a removal of the false veils we have drawn over life as it is. It is in no wise a superimposition upon life. The transfiguration is a restoration, not a novelty. Lastly, the JESUS-CHRIST tells us nothing we do not somehow know. The meaning of being human is that we were constituted to be human. This is what we were given to be. This alone shall be our judge.

The compendium is this: the JESUS-CHRIST IS LORD in every sense of the word. Every man, it is plain, bows his knee to some life image. Before one or another self-understanding under the general canopy of the EVERYMAN-CHRIST, he utters the submissive word: My Lord.

The early church was quite clear about this. She was also transparent concerning the location of her own obeisance and confession of allegiance. Her earliest creedal formula, JESUS-CHRIST IS LORD, is an abbreviation of the whole cosmic tale. It is at once a subjective decision and an objective state of affairs. The story of the cosmic Christ—his pre- and post-existence, his virgin birth and ascension to heaven, his historical life, death and resurrection—are all signs and symbols of this lordship.

In all of this the primitive church was calling upon herself and all men everywhere to live boldly in the JESUS-CHRIST, confidently sure that this is the way things are, ever have been and ever will be. There is but one objective, everlasting, unchanging life truth, namely, the living of life as a gift is the meaning of living life. Put it liturgically: the JESUS-CHRIST IS LORD.

THE ESCHATOLOGICAL HERO

Intimately related to the Christian story, yet not synonymous with it, is still another component of the Christ construct. It is the image created by the primitive Christians of a hero of faith or a cultic exemplar. The hero was first etched upon the common memory of the community. In time he became universally public as the central literary figure in the Four Gospels. One must not be misled here. This cultic man is not Jesus of Nazareth. Nor is he the cosmic figure sketched above. Neither is he simply a representation of what we have termed the JESUS-CHRIST happening. One must rather say that the Christian paragon is a masterfully artistic combination of them all.

Every historical community has its cultic figures. They are the models of the corporate self-understanding in the collective imagination. Such representations inform the liturgical dramas through which the group recollects who it is. They are the "universal" categories which provide the everyday common sense. They are the generalized other in the conscience that prompts and judges action. They are the master signs through which the active and passive emotions are usefully illuminated. In sum: the archetypal persons are the keys of concretion in the corporate worship dramas, the corporate life styles and the corporate practical wisdoms.

It is most understandable, then, that the early church was inspired to create such a hero. His paradoxical nature has already been indicated. He eats and weeps and experiences deep struggles of the spirit. Yet he also withers trees with a glance, does disappearing feats and quite actually rises from the grave on page twenty-five or so of the record. Succinctly, the Christian hero is the JESUS-CHRIST-EVENT embodied at the same time in both the temporal Jesus and the cosmic lamb.

This complex of paradoxes needs a closer look. To begin with, the hero is a man of this world, plus or minus nothing. He was born and he died. In between, he is portrayed as experiencing life's gamut of joys and sorrows, failures and successes, knowns and unknowns. Furthermore, he struggles, as humans must, to assume his posture toward his creatureliness. The stance he embodies, however, is not that of the EVERYMAN. He elects to live entirely within the JESUS-CHRIST faith, deciding and acting only in the style of the death that is life. The Christian prototype, to employ a formula, is in the first instance the historical-JESUS-CHRIST-man.

The other pole of the hero's individuality is likewise a fusion. In this case, the ingredients, like those in the Christian story, are the cosmic dimension and the JESUS-CHRIST-EVENT. This is the figure that stills storms, turns water to wine, casts out demons, and raises up dead men. He signifies the wholly other, the utterly absolute, being in itself. Use any symbol of ultimacy, the beginning and the end, the first and the last, he is it. At the same moment, he is the JESUS-CHRIST-EVENT that takes place in time. His own death and resurrection are presented as the master sign. The wonders he performs and the oracles he utters are likewise symbols of the Christ happening. Actually, his total existence is an unbroken nexus of signs pointing to crucifixion that is the resurrection. In terms of our schemata, the archetypal hero is the cosmic-JESUS-CHRIST-figure as well as the historical-JESUS-CHRIST-man.

The picture is still not complete. The whole emerges only after the polarities in the two formulae are totally amalgamated into one. A diagrammatic statement of this amalgamation would look something like this: the cosmic-historical-JESUS-CHRIST-man-figure. Authentic human existence and ultimate cosmic significance coalesce in the

JESUS-CHRIST EVENT. Here is the bare skeleton on which was shaped the most remarkable personality in the literature of any people. The paradoxes are made to completely cohere in the characterization of that strange personage who moves through the New Testament Gospels. It is a work of consummate artistry. In one paragraph he moves from the very human business of dispersing crowds and enjoying a moment alone to his stroll across the lake. Wonder-filling as this is, the reader is not surprised. There is no jarring. The player is exactly in character, so to speak.

In literary flesh and blood, the gospel hero is first and last a man of mission. Being and doing are consolidated in him. His single-minded vocation is exhibited in a two-fold activity of living life genuinely, authentically—as a man of faith in the midst of the world—and announcing to all others the possibility of such living. This is patent in both poles of his individualization: cosmic and historical. To use our earlier figure, he walks freely out across the anxious, uncertain, ambiguous waters of life. At the same time, he beckons others to do likewise. On the temporal side, the same pattern is discernible. With utter intentionality, the hero lives as the free man. He humbly opens himself to what is given; gratefully receives himself in what is given; and benevolently involves himself on behalf of what is given. He is liberated to be thankful for life; to love this world of neighbors; to be directed toward the future. This is to say, he is free to live life. And while he is busy living, he simultaneously declares to those about who have ears to hear the good news that they too can live in the freedom of the JESUS-CHRIST-EVENT.

Within the cultus, the name of the hero came to be Jesus Christ. This is frequently abbreviated just to Christ. And sometimes, perhaps more of the time, he is simply called Jesus. This is the Jesus of piety. To caution once more, he is not Jesus of Nazareth, but rather Jesus of the holy literature, the Jesus of the liturgical experience, the Jesus of the common life. As such he is the most vividly alive, the most finally significant, the most always present personality in the existence of the cultus. There are, of course, a host of other companions who live in the collective memory. Jesus Christ is the primordial one. The many titles bestowed upon him are indicative of this: Lord of Lords, King of Kings,

Son of Man, Son of God. No designation or mark of honor is too high or high enough to articulate his status for the people who bear his name. This raises a question about the adequacy of the term "cultic hero." The representational Jesus very obviously is the cultic or prototypal figure of the people who live in the CHRIST-EVENT. Yet the church knew him to be more: not just the cultic hero but the final or eschatological hero. That is, he represents the way things are for all men. He is the paragon of man as Man.

This eschatological hero is then the portraiture of what human living actually is. He is an unqualified delineation of the human style of life. He is a model of faith-filled living. A model is a design of the way things are. It is a construct of the manner in which things are understood to function. In dealing with subjects rather than objects, as in the case at hand, where the model is a personage, perhaps the "exemplar" would be a more fitting term. The Christ hero is a model or exemplar of what is going on where unmitigated human living is taking place.

The terms "ideal" and "example" have been intentionally avoided for fear of distracting connotations. To be sure, since a model is necessarily a totally unbroken and unfragmented representation, it might be labeled "ideal." But it is not ideal in the sense of disclosing some ought-world of precepts and virtue through which we can escape our humanity. It is not ideal in the sense of some moral goal toward which men strive for the sake of meaning and significance. All this would be merely a subtle form of the EVERYMAN-CHRIST that builds illusions about the human situation in seeking for truth, perfection and peace.

The Jesus model is the JESUS-CHRIST made flesh. It is a dramaturgical embodiment of that life stance or posture. To follow in the steps of the representational Jesus is not to imitate his words or reproduce his deeds. It is to be and do as a free man in our concretion as he depicted this stance in the concretions of his role. It is to walk out across the uncertain, ambiguous, anxious deeps of my life in gratitude, humility and compassion, with the sure confidence that this very walking is the meaning of life. The Exemplar is an ever present indicative word in the memory of a people, that to live is to live in the Christ event, and an ever present imperative word that continually calls them to it. In this sense, it guides their thoughts and deeds, their words and feelings. It is the context in which and out of which they forge their concrete actions.

The New Testament writers think of their Jesus hero as the pioneer who blazes the way; the elder brother who goes on before; the first fruit of a mighty harvest to be reaped. The followers then see themselves as the second wave of explorers, the younger brother, the latter harvest, yet as embodying the same life, traveling on the same way, participating in the same mission. As he lived his life as the meaning of his life, and announced the cosmic permission for all men thus to live, so the church understands that she can and must go and do likewise. As Luther said, the Christians are to be little Christs.

13. Joseph Mathews: Christology of the Jesus-Christ-Event

Every situation you find yourself in, until the day nobody finds you anymore, calls for a Gautama. You cannot sit around and wait for a Jesus. You must become a Jesus. This is your commission, your assignment, to be Jesus in history. . . .

I had a chance to love the Aboriginal people in Australia. I wrote a bit of poetry, terrible poetry, but it spoke to them about the meaning of their past, including the brutality of the white man. It painted a new possibility for the future of black people across the world. It laid out the meaning of the present in terms of their real demands. That's what I mean by divine love. That's all Jesus did. He opened the future, made new the past, and filled the present full of meaning. And that's our vocation.

—Joseph W. Mathews, *Transparent Being*[1]

In one sense, *The Christ of History* pulls together all we have read of the previous nine theologians—but much more. Joseph Wesley Mathews certainly stands on the shoulders of many of the first nine theologians, especially Kierkegaard, Bultmann, H. Richard Niebuhr (his professor), and Tillich—needless to say, a profound mix. (All three borrowed from Kierkegaard as well as from each other, though they disagreed strongly at times.) Mathews had private and public theological dialogues with Schubert Ogden at Southern Methodist University, where they were both professors. As the first-among-equals of the Ecumenical Institute: Chicago and the Order: Ecumenical, he led us in a depth study of Gogarten's *Christ the Crisis* and introduced us to Segundo's writings. (He would have appreciated Sobrino and Perrin as well—it's a shame he and Perrin did not know each other, especially since they both lived in Chicago and died within a year of each other.) What drew him to these writers was their commitment to make sense of faith out of the understanding of life's dynamics. He appreciated that they created their theologies and christologies in the heart of the human predicament rather than in some nether world of dogma or some ancient world of the two-story universe (*cosmic* and *historical*, according to Mathews). He was a revolutionary churchman who was pushing the limits of his and our self-understandings till the day he died in 1977, relentlessly trying to articulate and communicate what the two thousand years of Christianity had to do with the meaning and mission of authentic self-hood and global community.

Many years before Mathews wrote *The Christ of History*, he entered World War II as a chaplain in the Pacific. Neither he nor the soldiers he ministered to knew what the finality of death would do to a human being. They went in depending on their own strength, seemingly invincible and immortal as young men. When death came to their comrades-in-arms, the crisis fundamentally changed them all. They cried out to know the meaning of what was happening to them. Abstract theology and denominational trappings made little difference in those circumstances. The young chaplain came to know that he was ill equipped theologically to deal with their crises and his own. He entered graduate school to find some answers. Out of this experience came his passion to enable his contemporaries to be sustained by radical faith.

He became obsessed with Jesus the Christ as the all-determining event of common universal existence. One gets a sense of this in this unpublished note entitled "The Christ Event Universal":

> All cultures and histories 'knew' of the Other, the Way, depth consciousness. The Christ event was a part of all of this 'knowing.' It disclosed the white-hot center of the 'know.' That core was the awareness that we don't have to strive to *be* but that we already *are*. The past is approved, the future is open, all is good, and I am significant. This is the ground of faith, the beginning of love, and the essence of hope.
>
> In the above sense all societies have had their own testament in the combination of external happening and internal awareness. This combination came together in certain individuals and was articulated (significantly or insignificantly) to the nations.

The 'Messiah' (depth) awareness, this salvific occurrence, shed significance upon dead or dim, hidden or unde-
veloped awareness in all societies. 'Why callest thou me good.
There is none good but the Father,' who is love, the sovereign
of history, the creator of all that is. However, 'the Father and I
are one.' 'When I go I will send the final Spirit, which
proceedeth both from the Father and the Son'—the preface of
God himself, the proto-thereness and meaning.

The Christ of History, more than any other writing, helps us to
get hold of Mathews' Christian self-understanding, although it continued
to evolve dramatically over the next eight years of his life.[2] From it we
can describe his as the ***christology of the Jesus-Christ-Event***. I have
read *The Christ of History* dozens of times and find a new insight at
each reading. I have taught from it and have seen lives begin the
transformative process as a result of its power of articulation? Why
does it continue to speak to the deeps of human lives after thirty years?
It speaks to the truth of the human experience in the context of the
dynamics of the Jesus-Christ-Event.

In section one, he possibly borrowed the "Everyman-Christ"
concept from Kierkegaard's journal: "Every Christian has had his *earthly
Messiah*," "the expectation of a *worldly Messiah*," "dreams of wealth
. . . , of a happy marriage, of success in some particular career."[3] He
could have borrowed the concept of "illusion" (section two) from Freud,
though with a different context and meaning. And he probably borrowed
the concept of the "Jesus-Christ-Event" (section three) from Bultmann,
as most theologians of the 20th century have. But *The Christian Story*
(four) and *The Eschatological Hero* (five) sections are not as easily
attributable, not in the epochal and yet historical manner in which
Mathews deals with these sections. He honors the tradition and
transforms it "by pulling the sock inside out," the type of down-to-earth
expression he enjoyed using. He enables us to transpose the second-
and third-story (i.e., heaven and hell) of the three-story worldview of the
New Testament into a post-Einsteinian, one-story worldview. He does
this and more in sections one through three: he *grounds* (makes
experientially obvious) the concepts of *The Everyman-Christ, The Jesus
of Nazareth*, and *The Jesus-Christ-Event* in ways Kierkegaard

and Bultmann do not.

In section one, ***THE EVERYMAN CHRIST***, he uses a litany of words and phrases of existential limitation: *unknowns, ambiguities, sufferings, deaths of this world, insecurity, primordial anxiety, finitude, unbearable imcomprehensibles, sense of insignificance, awareness of the tragic dimension, uncertainty, and unfulfillment* to point to our natural reasons for longing. Then he uses another bigger list of words and phrases for our "deeply human life-quest": *make sense, really live, light, way, truth, door, bread, word of life, illuminating story, saving event, final blessedness, essence of life, living of life, alleviating justification, peace, rising above, other kind of world, escape actual life, meaning, different tomorrow, ultimate key, final excuse, true contentment, truly live,* and *great expectations.* Next come summary words and phrases for this second list: *anointed one, the Messiah, Christ, human characteristics, Messiah image, dreams, present hopes about the future, delivered from the present world, life-quest, relieve us of the necessity of living, great hope,* and *the CHRIST OF EVERYMAN.* Put all this together in three paragraphs and we get the kaleidoscopic picture of our natural human condition. Is this picture true or false? Ask anyone, any time, any place. If they're honest they will say, "Sure, I live in that great hope."

Therefore, the stage is set for section two, ***THE JESUS OF NAZARETH***. Jesus is not the one who shows up to deliver our natural heart's desire. Mathews upsets many fundamentalists and traditionalists here, who will say, "Jesus was not like that. He was the Son of God." What was Jesus like? He "collided with, encountered, invaded, broke into, and penetrated" established patterns of individual and social reality. Mathews liked to use the image of a hatpin bursting a balloon in regard to Jesus' *bursting the illusions* (*"Everyman Christs"*) of those he contacted, delivering them back to reality. How did Jesus do this? With his human *authenticity*: he really lived his life, up to and through his death, in which he manifested the "tragic inversion"—dying can also be significant. Or Mathews would say Jesus embodied the truth of human existence. Yet, these five paragraphs do not seem nearly adequate to talk about Jesus of Nazareth. They are not. So Mathews goes on with Jesus of Nazareth in the tapestry of the next sections.

In section three, ***THE JESUS-CHRIST-EVENT***, Mathews gets to the heart of the historical Jesus and the Christ of faith by the amalgamation JESUS-CHRIST-EVENT.

> [T]he JESUS-CHRIST is an historical event. It is a radical revolution in the interior history of men proceeding from an absolute reversal in human self-understanding. Originally occasioned by Jesus of Nazareth, it is first of all the experience of an offense. This offense is grounded in an actual disaffirmation of our creaturely phantasms which issues in a new possibility of living our bestowed existence as a great benefaction. It is, secondly, the decision to receive the offense and embrace the ensuing possibility as our own. This entails a dying to ourselves as defined by our mirages, which very death is experienced as the very life we were mistakenly searching for. Such is the radical transfiguration of the JESUS-CHRIST-EVENT.
>
> The early Christians' pronouncement of it contained an inseparable promise and demand. The demand is to die. That this very dying is life is the promise.[4]

The dynamics of the Jesus-Christ-Event[5]—or the "radical revolution in the interior history of men [humans] proceeding from an absolute reversal in human self-understanding"—is as follows. Like a life-changing event occasioned by Jesus of Nazareth, some historical event happens in my life and bursts my operating illusion of who I am. This event is, first of all, an offense which is grounded in "an actual disaffirmation of [my] creaturely phantasms" or "mirages"—an illusion. I see my life just as it is, in the raw, "which issues in a new possibility of living [my] bestowed existence as a great benefaction." Out of this indicative/imperative comes the second dynamic, the decision "to receive the offense" of my assaulted self-understanding and to say *Yes* to my real life. This entails the experience of the death of the old self, living in its illusion. By embracing this death, new life begins as I understand that my life, as given, is what I was really searching for all along.

The question we must ask ourselves about the Jesus-Christ-Event dynamics is Are they true to life? Do the Jesus-Christ-Event dynamics come out of life[6] or are they a superimposition upon *the way life is* in reality? That is the question Mathews is always asking. This is his hermeneutical question, the key to his interpretation of the gospel truth. Why in the world would God create *the way life is* in the beginning —as perfectly Good—and then come along and create another set of life dynamics for the Christian Gospel? What is life really like? Look at the New Testament. Look at Jesus of Nazareth. Why did they call him the Christ? Because he elucidated[7] the final reality of God and *the way life is*. Jesus is the Christ because he transparentizes the authentic life and because he brings the final reality to view. Jesus is the Christ because he slays our illusions and reintroduces us to *the way life is* and to our lives as they really are. Jesus is the Christ because he reveals to us the truth that every situation in which we find ourselves is not bad but one that affords us the opportunity to decide to embrace it the way it is. Jesus is the Christ because he will not allow us to live the lie of the *false-Christs* (a Chapter 3 imbalance) or the Everyman Christ—he will not let us have life the way we think we want it to be. Jesus is the Christ because he will not let us live the "good life" of this world but calls us to live the Good Life that God has given us to live. Jesus is the Christ because he will not let us go without constantly bringing us to re-decide to live in reality rather than in a false reality. Jesus invites us home, to live in God's reality rather than our often illusory "reality."

For Mathews, Jesus is the Christ because he is always reuniting us to God's good creation. If we are in Christ we are in the Father. We are in the Father because of Jesus; therefore, we call him the Christ. This is the way Mathews did christology, from life. He is a Christian existentialist, meaning he believed that existence is the way it has always been, the good creation of God. Jesus came to reunite us to our real lives as they are—sinfully broken. When this paradoxical event happens to us and we decide to be who we are, without illusion, then we are given back—even resurrected to—the glory of our existence in our brokenness. This is why we declare Jesus to be the Christ.

Mathews continues to push the edge of christology in the following quotes. If authentic life does not allow us to live out of our illusions, what does this lead us to say about the life-dynamic of the Messiah?

> The JESUS-CHRIST fronts man with the awareness that there is no messiah and never will be one, and furthermore, that this

very reality is the Messiah. . . . [T]he fronting is experienced
as death itself. For to receive the JESUS-CHRIST is to put an
end to my [false, Everyman] Christ quest.[8]

Mathews is saying the Messiah (Jesus-Christ) is not ever what
we are longing for (the Everyman Christ) but keeps reintroducing us to
the real life we have on our hands. The real Messiah comes to us who
are "following every wise man and every star, looking for that which we
will never find and which was never promised." We experience this
authentic Messiah as death to our great longing for a different life than
the one we have. Jesus-Christ mortally assaults our false-Christ,
whatever it is, by saying to us, "Are you looking for the Messiah? Well,
there isn't going to be one and I'm it." We keep being driven to live our
real, God-given lives. This is the "no messiah" Messiah. So we begin
to see that

for the New Testament people the Christ decision was
transparently an election for or against life itself. The negative
answer was at bottom a rejection of human existence as it is
constituted. . . . When the human situation is nakedly exposed
there are but two choices: to affirm life or to negate it.[9]

"The Christ decision was transparently an election for or against
life itself. The negative answer was at bottom a rejection of human
existence as it is constituted." The key word is *transparently*, which
Mathews uses throughout his works, meaning that which is seen through
and thus reveals *human existence as it is constituted*, good as it is created.
The twist here is that we humans are seldom aware of existence as it is
constituted; we cover it up because it is bad to us, essentially, the way it
is. (I am reminded of Mathews' asking the undertaker for a piece of
cloth and alcohol so he could take off all the make-up that the undertaker
had used to cover up the "wonderfully chiseled wrinkles" of his dead
ninety-two-year-old father.[10]) Some dynamic of life must come along
and uncover what we cover up. Jesus delivers to us the decision of all
decisions: Is life—and my life—good or bad the way it is?

The choice to give up our illusions and false hopes and hiding places is . . . [the decision to die]. This very death is life, they insisted. To die is to live. To use their figures, it is like being born all over again. It is like the healing of a mortal illness. It is like being forgiven a big lie at the heart of one's being. It is like a resurrection from a tomb. . . .

Surrender of the demand for final truth becomes quite the truth about things. Capitulation to the secret that there is no way out becomes the very door and way to being. This is the end of the road of self-understanding. . . . For one can now freely live in his negations, learn in his perpetual ignorance and walk in all his given creatureliness. In brief, the decision to die is at the same time an election to life. The JESUS-CHRIST is life abundant. . . .[11]

Mathews' most used phrase for the message of the New Testament is "to die is to live," and all the quotes above represent his way of coming at this ultimate truth of the gospel. The other side of this, or the life-style imperative of this indicative, is what he called the "cruciform principle." "Die your death or it will die you" was his aphorism for the flip-side of the fundamental life decision. What does that look like? (His favorite question.) It looks like the "Jesus-Christ made flesh":

To follow in the steps of the representational Jesus is not to imitate his words or reproduce his deeds. It is to be and do as a free man. . . . It is to walk out across the uncertain, ambiguous, anxious deeps of my life in gratitude, humility and compassion, with the sure confidence that this very walking is the meaning of life. . . . [We] are to be little Christs.[12]

Mathews is pointing to our vocational mission as followers of Jesus. This is what he is saying in the beginning quote: "You must become a Jesus. This is your commission, your assignment, to be Jesus in history." (Elsewhere he has much to say about individual vocation and the corporate vocation of the church.) "In your freedom, get out of your boat and walk on water—be little Christs. Even though you lose your nerve and sink like Peter, get up and go again. That is the glory of life," as Mathews would have said. In one sense, this has to do with vocation, not christology. In another sense, it is what Mathews would say christology is, fundamentally, our stepping into the cruciform life-style along with Jesus. More about this in Chapter 18.

In section four, *THE CHRISTIAN STORY*, Mathews says the church grew out of the Jesus-Christ-Event, made up of those to whom it happened and who received it in the decision of faith. They of course wrote a story of what happened to them, "rooted in ultimacy." So we have in early Christianity 1) the event, 2) the story, and 3) the church, or the "integral historical complex." The hero of the church's story is not Jesus but the Jesus-Christ-Event that brought the storytellers to new life in the midst of their same old lives. We go through three acts, of course. Mathews reminds us that the story is not "a web of metaphysical statements," not "an aggregate of religious doctrines to be believed," but is a story that is to hold before us meaningful life images. If we believe it as the story of our lives, then the Jesus-Christ becomes our Lord, meaning "the living of life as a gift is the meaning of living life."[13]

In the final section, *THE ESCHATOLOGICAL HERO*, Mathews writes that "this cultic man" is not Jesus of Nazareth, not the cosmic figure of the Story, nor the Jesus-Christ happening or event, but is the "masterful artistic combination of them all." He is "the cosmic-historical-JESUS-CHRIST-man-figure. Authentic human existence and ultimate cosmic significance coalesce in the JESUS-CHRIST-EVENT."[14]

> It is a work of consummate artistry. In one paragraph he moves from the very human business of dispersing crowds and enjoying a moment alone to his stroll across the lake. Wonder-filling as this is, the reader is not surprised. There is no jarring. The player is exactly in character, so to speak.
>
> In literary flesh and blood, the gospel hero is first and last a man of mission. Being and doing are consolidated in him. His single-minded vocation is exhibited in a two-fold activity of living life genuinely, authentically—as a man of faith in the midst of the world—and announcing to all others the possibility of such living. This is patent in both poles of his individualization: cosmic and historical. . . . [H]e is free to live life.

> And while he is busy living, he simultaneously declares to those
> about, who have ears to hear the good news, that they too can
> live in the freedom of the JESUS-CHRIST-EVENT. . . .
> Yet the church knew him to be more: not just the cultic hero
> but the final or eschatalogical hero. That is, he represents the
> way things are for all men.[15]

Mathews dramatized the self-understanding of the Jesus-Christ-Event in all its complexity in the simple liturgical way Jesus did it, by the breaking of bread and the spilling out of wine, with the admonition that "We can feast on the brokenness and the spilled-out-ness of life—and of our lives. This is the life we have. These are the lives we have. Let us give thanks for *the way life is*. In the name of Jesus the Christ our Lord. ***Amen*.**"

One more question, Why does Mathews call his writing *The Christ of History*? He wrote it during the time of great debate over the historical Jesus and the Christ of faith (Kähler's polarity) going on between the Bultmannians, the post-Bultmannians, the second quest for the historical Jesus, and the imminent rise of groups like the Jesus Seminar. For him the point was neither the historical Jesus nor the Christ of faith, but the Jesus-Christ-Event that has always happened in history and brings us to a conscious experience of faith, pending our decisive response. For Mathews, then, why not transform the stuck-in-the-rut, polarized, two-dimensional debate and get to the heart of the matter, the Jesus-Christ-Event. Therefore, he chose the *The Christ of History* title, by which he meant "the Jesus-Christ-Event of history." He even included us who are commissioned to be *little Christs* in history. As Mathews says on page 114, all is part of "the total historical complex."

CHAPTER 13 NOTES

[1] Summer Research Assembly, Chicago, 1972.

[2] Mathews and the Order: Ecumenical have gone further by talking about the dynamics of the "contentless Word" and devising secular-religious methods that allow Christians and non-Christians to understand the dynamics of life, i.e., the method of the typology of the states of being of human consciousness, which allows a re-mythologizing about the way life is for all peoples in whatever tradition or culture.

[3] *A Kierkegaard Anthology*, ed. by Robert Bretall (Princeton: Princeton University Press, 1936; New York: Random House [The Modern Library], 1946), p. 9.

[4] Joseph W. Mathews, "The Christ of History," this book, pp. 113-14.

[5] Mathews and the Ecumenical Institute: Chicago helped to formulate courses for clergy and laity. One such course, Religious Studies I (RS-I) contains the "Jesus-Christ-Event Lecture" with the following outline: A. *The Christ Event Situation*: 1. The Mundane Event; 2. The Personal Intrusion; 3. The Defense of Self; 4. The Radical Decision. B. *The Christ Event Word*: 1. All Is Good (Creation); 2. All Is Received (Self); 3. All Is Approved (Past); 4. All Is Possible (Future). C. *The Christ Event Dynamic*: 1. The Seizure of Possibility; 2. The Offense of Vulnerability; 3. The Decision of Radicality; 4. The Experience of Death. D. *The Christ Event Story*: 1. The Scandal of Jesus; 2. The Significance of Christ; 3. The Confessional Lord; 4. The Story of My Life.

[6] Mathews led the Order: Ecumenical in studying *The Image*, by Kenneth Boulding, who employs a secular, non-religious manner as he articulates the process of image transformation. What became clear for Mathews and company was that behavior changes (Boulding even uses the analogy of "conversion") when one's operating image is altered by a powerful new message, and leaves one with the decision to accept or reject the message; however, our resistance to a new message is strong. The "aha!" was a secular articulation of life dynamics similar to the Christian articulation of the dynamics of the Christ Event: when that life-changing event happens to a person, Mathews said, the "contentless Word" or "contentless Christ-Event" has happened.

[7] Mathews often used the phrase "final reality" to point to God, and "lucidity" to point to the Jesus-Christ-event.

[8] "The Christ of History," this book, p. 112.

[9] *Ibid.*, pp. 112-13.

[10] Joseph W. Mathews, "The Time My Father Died," *i.e.* (bimonthly newsletter of the Ecumenical Institute: Chicago), reprinted in *Motive*. "And I began the restoration. As the powder, the rouge, the lipstick disappeared, the stranger grew older. He never recovered the look of his ninety-two years but in the end the man in the coffin became my Papa."

[11] "The Christ of History," this book, pp. 113-14.

[12] *Ibid.*, p. 121.

[13] *Ibid.*, p. 118.

[14] *Ibid.*, pp. 119-20.

[15] *Ibid.*, pp. 120-21.

14. The Christ Event in Life and Art

Encounter is that event in which the self is confronted by the necessity for decision, the necessity for a decision which will affect one's self-understanding. For self-understanding is achieved, lost, modified or developed by the decisions which are forced upon one by those encounters which are a necessary part of being-in-the-world. To use our own terms, these encounters can be brutal—Auschwitz, the assassinations in America—or they can be gentle—love of a mother, the making of a friend. They can be from the past—the challenge of the self-understanding revealed in the teaching of Jesus or the deeds and words of Abraham Lincoln—or they can come from the future—the necessity of providing for retirement or of facing loneliness after the loss of a loved one. The one thing they all have in common is that necessity for decision which will further shape that self-understanding which makes a man what he is in his own personal, existential being-in-the-world.
—Norman Perrin[1]

When we begin to ground what we mean by the Christ event, the personal stories we tell in conversation or writing and the ones we witness in movies, plays, or on television are among the best modes we have. One of my colleagues, Gene Marshall, has given me permission to quote what he experienced as a Christ event, using the image of the *actively defiant self* in Kierkegaard's *The Sickness Unto Death*, one of his favorite pieces of literature.

I experienced something of my own defiance a few years ago when I chose to take some therapy. I did not take therapy because I was non-functional. I was exploring the sort of help I believe all of us need badly in these times of such great demand for increased consciousness. Nevertheless, doing this was frightening. I had played the role of teacher and the teacher of teachers for many years; so to put myself in the position of being a student, an humble learner about enigmas in my own life—well, something in me revolted against the humiliation of being in this position. That was only the beginning. I knew I had weaknesses in my abilities to be an emotional person, to be a warm person, to be honest with myself and others about what I was feeling. But I did not know the extent of it. Nor did I know the manner I was using to remain weak in that part of my life. My defiant self, as I was soon to learn, did not want to know about this. Gradually my therapist helped me become conscious of how I was using my skills as a thinker and talker to talk my way around my weaknesses as an emotional person. He said I had an advanced case of *feelingless verbosity*. In a word, I could give competent lectures about emotional feeling, but I could not express simple and honest personal things to other human beings. For example, I was reluctant to say things like 'I feel sad,' or 'I feel ashamed,' or even 'I don't know.'

My therapist gave me an exercise to do in our group sessions. I could only talk in five-word sentences. For me this was very difficult to do. In the midst of trying to do it, I became intensely conscious that my old self was DEFIANT against changing and against all the humiliations entailed with learning to be different. My defiant self was saying things like, 'I am a great teacher, a person of wisdom. I am not a child. I am not a person who does not even know how to talk clearly.' I could feel myself getting angry. . . . I could feel myself in terror over giving up my images of strength and beginning to admit my weaknesses and to go to work on them. I knew that the values of a deeper relationship with my wife, my children, and my own body were worth a struggle. But this death of an 'old self' was a price my 'old and defiant me' did not want to pay.

This experience has helped me to clarify anew what it means for me to be committed to Christ. Commitment to Christ means a trust that a life of greater reality is the good life, the wholesome life. Commitment to Christ is also an active passion that results in choices to oppose my own defiant self. Such opposition is, first of all, a simple admission that this defiance is defiance of reality, the very realistic living to which I say I am

committed. Secondly, it is hearing again that deep DAWN-
ING that I, even I, the defiant self, am accepted in spite of my
defiance. Thirdly, I oppose my defiant self by accepting my
acceptance. All three of these aspects of the 'Healing Event'
are simple but forceful 'No's' to acting out my life in the defiant mode. A huge transformation results. No flight from my
defiant self is necessary. Simply the firm 'No' of acknowledging the defiance as defiance, hearing my acceptance, and accepting it defeats my defiant self.

Faced with such firmness, the defiant self simply vanishes,
perhaps to return another day; but for now it quite completely
goes away. The various states of awe I call 'tranquility' flock
around me to celebrate the dying and rebirthing of my perpetually changing me.

Such happenings as this leave me with a fresh understanding . . . of openness to die to whatever I now am and to begin
again on my journey of realistic living, a journey on which my
sense of reality is perpetually expanding along with my
selfhood. Such obedience is commitment to Christ, and commitment to Christ is nothing else than such obedience.[2]

Browsing through my memoir, I quickly checked more than
twenty-five Christ events. I will share one to further illustrate the
dynamical process that happens to every conscious person. This one
goes along with Perrin's quote above: "these encounters can be brutal—
Auschwitz, the assassinations in America."

On a warm November day in 1963, I was sitting in the library
of a large university researching for an exhaustive bibliography of the
tens of works of Robert Browning for my professor, a Browning scholar.
One omission meant failure. All was quiet for several hours until I
heard a commotion at the front desk area of the library, so loud that
those of us hunkered-down all over the library came out to see what was
going on.

The unholy noise was the shocking news of the assassination
attempt on JFK—he was in critical condition. Nobody wanted to talk
about it or hold eye contact. I don't remember whether I packed my

books or not, but I somehow walked home through downtown without getting run over. I was in an honest-to-*God* stupor. What the hell was going on in this nation? I started to seethe. President Kennedy had become a symbol of hope and integrity for me and my generation. And now, O *God*, he lay dying. The awful tragedy was shaking my foundations.

Lynda heard it on the intercom at school where she was teaching, and a teenage boy in her class whispered for all to hear, "I'm glad he got shot!" By the time she got home from school, about a thirty-minute drive, our President was dead. We propped each other up in the apartment as the long day's journey into night began. I wanted to forget what I knew. I wanted to scream at something supposedly in charge of this absurd universe.

The nation and I began to watch TV together. For days I mourned, cried, sighed hard, walked in and out of the apartment, prayed, and tried to make sense out of the assassination, but mostly my life. I picked up the little book *Our Faith*, by Emil Brunner, that had made sense to me in college. He wrote it for me at this time, calling me to faith in that power that is absolutely not this earthly madness, but has called me to do something about it.

"Lynda, studying Old English and doing that Browning bibliography is nonsense in light of what's happening in our country. I'm going to call the Bishop."

Into the conversation the Bishop asked me if I felt called to the ministry again, since I had "lost my calling" at college when he was president there. His question came as an answer for me. He said he would call Emory University and see if they would receive me, starting the January semester. They would indeed.

I called home to share all this with Mama, but Dad answered. I spilled it and added what I hoped would be authority enough for him, that the Bishop had helped get me into seminary. Dad said, "You're a fool!" and handed the phone to Mama. I remember well those words said so long ago. He wanted me to be a professor, not a minister. Lynda concurred.

A couple of days later I told the head of the English Department that I was leaving the university to enroll in seminary. "Damn!" he reacted, for his department would lose its three-year matching NDEA grant money from the government. I was receiving mixed signals about my calling. Nevertheless, within six weeks we had moved to Atlanta, where I attended and graduated from seminary.

Since then I have come to understand JFK's assassination as a Christ event in my life. This external event set loose an internal crisis in my life, experienced as a vocational calling. I had a decision to make for sure: to stay where I was or go to prepare for my new calling. Against formidable odds I chose the later. Said another way, I perceived JFK's assassination as judgment upon our nation and my life. I was chasing the prestige and security of a college professorship. The assassination event questioned that direction as an authentic one for me under the circumstances. I felt I must do something directly about the spirit malaise in our nation, and seminary seemed the will of *God* for me at that time. I felt I could do no other than obey this calling, whatever the consequences. Was I absolutely sure I was doing the right thing? Of course not, but I observed, judged, weighed up, decided, and acted, using Bonhoeffer's model of the free deed.

As I came to later understand, this is the model Bonhoeffer himself used as he decided it was the will of God for him to turn from the pacifism of the Sermon on the Mount and to enter into a clandestine assassination attempt upon the life of Hitler, which failed, and for which he was arrested and later hanged by the SS just before the liberators came.

> The responsible man acts in the freedom of his own self, without the support of men, circumstances, or principles. . . . The proof of his freedom is the fact that nothing can answer for him, nothing can exonerate him, except his own deed and his own self. . . . The action of the responsible man is performed in the obligation which alone gives freedom and which gives entire freedom, the obligation to God and to our neighbor as they confront us in Jesus Christ. At the same time it is performed wholly within the domain of relativity, wholly in the twilight. . . . Precisely in this respect responsible action is a free venture; it is not justified by any law; it is performed without any claim to a valid self-justification, and therefore also without any claim to an ultimate valid knowledge of good and evil. Good, as what is responsible, is performed in ignorance

of good and in the surrender to God of the deed which has become necessary and which is nevertheless, or for that very reason, free; for it is God who sees the heart, who weighs up the deed, and who directs the course of history.

With this there is disclosed to us a deep secret of history in general. The man who acts in the freedom of his own most personal responsibility is precisely the man who sees his action finally committed to the guidance of God. The free deed knows itself in the end as the deed of God; the decision knows itself as guidance; the free venture knows itself as divine necessity.[3]

When I think of the free deed, I am reminded of the movie, *Requiem for a Heavyweight*, which we in the Ecumenical Institute showed at RS-I seminars as a reflective exercise for the participants to discern the life-dynamics of God, Christ, Holy Spirit, and Church.[4] In this Rod Serling black and white film, Anthony Quinn plays Luis "Mountain" Rivera, a super proud, punch-drunk boxer who fought 111 fights and was ranked number five in the world; Jackie Gleason plays Maish, his manager for seventeen years; and Mickey Rooney plays Army, his trainer for seventeen years. They are family, Maish like a father and Army like a mother to the champ. Julie Harris plays Miss Grace Miller, the employment counselor who tries to help Mountain get a job, and more.

Early on we find out that Maish secretively bets all the "family's" money that Mountain will not go past four rounds against young Cassius Clay—instead he goes seven and is knocked out—since he can't make any money betting on him to win anymore. Maish also tipped the mob-like leader, Ma Greeny, to put a "bundle" on the fourth round. By going seven, Mountain has put Maish's life in danger, for he can't pay. Worse, the doctor visits the locker room after the fight to announce that Mountain must quit, never fight again because of eye damage: "He had no business being in there, Maish. Are you hungry?" As this gets through to Mountain, he asks the biggest question of his thirty-seven years, "So what do I do now?"

Grace Miller, the liberal and not unattractive spinster, enters Mountain's life to save him. Instead, she fills him with illusions: that he could be a boys' camp counselor—he goes off at the memory of a fight and uncontrollably reenacts the punches—and that he could be her boyfriend. She sets an appointment for him with the camp owners, but Maish knowingly gets Mountain drunk. He makes a real punch-drunk scene and blows the interview before it even begins. After he runs in fear of rejection, she comes looking for him at his slum bedroom to help him redecide about the interview. At this weak moment in his life and still a little drunk, Mountain is led on—at least not resisted by Miss Miller—until he throws her on his bed, to which she recoils and pushes him off. It is all over. No job, no girlfriend. Only an ex-fighter who is further devastated by her seeming mercies.

As Miss Miller hurries from the scene, Maish encounters her on the steps and says, "Go out and find yourself another charity." She slaps him and cringes in unbelief that she does. Maish continues, "You want to help him. Don't con him. Don't tell him he can be a camp counselor in a boys' camp. He's been chasing ghosts all his life, the champion's belt, a pretty girl, maybe twenty-four hours without an ache in his body." Through tears she says, "I just thought the next thing he wanted I might be able to give him." She is pitiful as she leaves.

But further humiliation awaits Mountain. Maish is desperately trying to make money to save his own life. After the fiasco with Grace Miller, Mountain has run out of options. Maish manipulates Mountain, out of guilt, to do something for his manager of seventeen years. Mountain finally consents to be in a wrestling match. In the locker room of St. Christopher's Arena he sits with his Indian wig and costume on and begs,

"Maish, don't make me. Don't ask me to play a clown."

Maish retorts, "My life is on the line. You cross me and I'm dead."

The horrible secret comes out.

Mountain in disbelief asks, "Maish, you bet against me? Why, Maish?"

Maish replies with head down, "You're not a winner any more. Only one thing left, make money from a loser."

Mountain, coming up off the bench, "For seventeen years I'm not ashamed of one single round. Now you make me ashamed." He starts undressing.

Enter Ma Greeny, who is expecting Mountain to wrestle so she can get her money back; she sees Mountain about to "take a walk."

She says, "Maish, darling, take a good look at yourself in the mirror. Where do you want it, here or in the alley?"

The wrestling promoter, Perelli, says, "Yeah, make it nice and slow."

Mountain gets the big picture, stops and says to Perelli, "Pay that lady off."

Perelli seizes the opportunity, "Eight matches and an option for sixteen more?"

Mountain, in a transformed state now as he starts putting his costume back on, mumbles, "Sure, sure."

He freely puts on the black wig with long braids, the skimpy Indian cover for his loins, picks up the rest of his garb, looks straight ahead as he marches past Maish, who is kneeling and reaching for him to beg for forgiveness. Mountain slams the door on the way up the aisle to the ring. Army chases after him in tears.

At the raucous jeering of the crowd, Chief "Mountain" Rivera steps into the ring—his gaze still straight ahead—puts on his headdress and starts his dance as he lifts his tomahawk. He has become the clown and prepares to "take his first dive."

From the time he heard Ma Greeny's "here or in the alley," he became his own man, living out of his own decision, not Maish's or Miss Miller's. Tragic, some would say. Nevertheless, we see a transformed "Mountain" Rivera paying for Maish's life, the "father" who betrayed him.

Reflection

Is this a religious movie? Where are Christ events in the movie? Where was the Christ event(s) in the movie that brought Mountain to reality and released him to authenticity? What is the transforming *process* of the Christ event?

I am also reminded of Steven Spielberg, who knows much about life-changing events in his movies, *Shindler's List, Amistad,* and *Saving Private Ryan.*

Yesterday afternoon I saw George C. Scott play Scrooge and witnessed a life transformed through the event of a three-part dream.

And last night we watched the Hallmark Christmas Special, *Grace and Glorie,* when the dying Grace asks Glorie—who was preparing for suicide—to get it all out about her son's dying in her arms last year, at age eight, in a car wreck. "Life is what connected you and your son, not death. You can't hold on to his death and try to escape your life." Glorie's life was transformed as she was encountered by the life and word of a dying woman, Grace.

The arts are about the eventfulness of our lives. Good art reflects life's transforming dynamics in a powerful way, even releasing us to pick up our lives anew.

The Christ event can happen most any way in our everyday lives. This *Christmas greeting* shows how:

"The Word became flesh and lived among us"

And still does. Incarnation happens in the most unexpected places. Perhaps in the Phnom Penh newspaper boy badgering you to take a paper from him and not from the ten others crowding around the hotel entrance as you came out. It isn't so much his pitiful plight as a homeless, orphaned street child subject to who knows what in the way of social abuse, but rather his mischievous twinkle that bubbled through his torrent of broken English.

"From me. Here. Me. Remember me? You Promised. Get mine. Only 1200 riel. . . ."

Not exactly the babe-in-a-manger, but certainly a powerful young self in ignoble circumstances.

His address was highly personal. He may have also pursued

other hotel occupants, but this time it was very personal. An audit to the quick, as you wonder what gives you the right to be the one with advantages that he will never even conceive. Gratitude for your status would be contemptibly arrogant; identification with his plight, hopelessly naïve. In the vast distance between us lies sheer Mystery, bridged only by the twinkle as if we both know something deep about life that neither of us can fathom.

Maybe being thrown up against the unfathomable is what Christmas celebrates. In those moments of confrontation with sheer Mystery, there is sometimes a faint echo of "Gloria in excelsis deo," as if the angels are telling you something, and you have the chance again to appreciate life as it is.

Merry Christmas from

Ann & John Epps

As Good As it Gets, recipient of seven Academy Award nominations in 1997, flashes on the screen life-changing events happening every which way. A modern Scrooge, Melvin Udall (Jack Nicholson), hates dogs, homosexuals, Jews, African-Americans, women, and cracks in the sidewalk. His homosexual neighbor across the hall, Simon (Greg Kinnear), loves his little dog, Verdell, more than anything. Carol Connelly (Helen Hunt) is a single-parent of a nine-year-old son, Spencer or Spence, who has some unknown asthma-related disease. As she nurses him and runs him back and forth to the emergency room, her life is frantically full. All in all, three very broken people.

On the productive side, Melvin is just finishing his sixty-second novel; Simon is a rising artist; and Carol is the best waitress in a yuppie restaurant in Manhattan, where she is the only one who will wait on Melvin, the most cantankerous neurotic in Manhattan—an everyday customer who has to have his same table, and with unmentionable verbal abuse will run off anyone sitting there.

After Simon has been beaten up within an inch of his life by thieves, Frank (Cuba Gooding, Jr.), Simon's African-American agent, screams in Melvin's face, "You will keep his dog!" while Simon is hospitalized for weeks. Melvin had just thrown the little dog down a many-flights garbage chute days earlier for peeing in front of his door in the hallway. Little Verdell wins Melvin's heart, occasioning a big crack in his absolutely closed and neurotically fixed universe. When Simon returns and wants Verdell back, Melvin cries ("Over an ugly dog!" he says as he wipes his eyes).

The klutz, Melvin, who earlier in the restaurant verbally abuses Carol in reference to her sick boy and receives the tongue lashing of the movie in return, lets the air out of Carol's life by paying his publisher's husband-doctor to make a house call and begin to cure Carol's son Spencer's problem. Carol, because of an unexpected event that takes away her life's significance, is left with a life that is so un-full that she begins thinking of someone, a man, to fill it. With that, her failures of the past in this regard flood her and leave her in a puddle of self-pity. Yet something is conceived in her in this event as she frantically writes a thank-you letter to Melvin, saying, "What you did changed my life. You have done more for my mom, myself, and son than anyone ever has. We remember you in our prayers."

Melvin asks Carol to go with him to drive his homosexual neighbor, Simon, south of Baltimore to his parents—his father told him to never come back—to ask them for money: after his beating he goes broke and loses his secretary, agent, housekeeper, apartment, upcoming show, friends, the affection of his dog, and most of all his motivation to paint. On the trip, in a swanky restaurant, Carol threatens a compliment out of Melvin: "You make me want to be a better man." Carol moves over to kiss him as the first physical sign of their romance. Then Melvin puts his foot plus leg in his mouth again in a comment about her dress, and instead of the first beautiful date either has had in ages, she stalks out in a rage. She goes back to Simon's room and continues to reawaken his life-urge through mercies shown toward him, and with them comes his motivation to paint again. He decides to pick up his life and not even ask his parents for help.

After returning to New York, Carol tells Melvin, "I don't want to know you anymore. All you do is make me feel bad about myself."

Taking Simon into his apartment until he can get on his feet—first the dog, now the homosexual master—to which Simon says, "Thank you, Melvin. You overwhelm me. I love you." Melvin gives him an awkward pat on the shoulder. Carol calls to apologize, to which Melvin replies, "I should have danced with you" at the restaurant. He hangs up and tells Simon, "I'm dying here." Simon gets Melvin clear: you love Carol. "Go over there tonight . . . now!" (About 4 o'clock in the morning.)

Melvin stumbles up the stairs of her modest apartment and stammers and mutters until she realizes that he's really her boyfriend. Given courage, he invites her to walk down the street for a sweet roll. On the way he dodges all the sidewalk cracks. He mumbles as he tries to tell her what he feels for her, but finally erupts, "I may be the only one on earth who knows that you are the most amazing woman alive. Is that someone bad to be around?" She is absolutely affirmed and they grab each other for one big awkward kiss, and then another that is more like it. He steps on a crack, but looks at it as if to say, "So?"

In this movie, aptly named *As Good As It Gets* (Melvin runs through his ex-psychiatrist's waiting room asking the half-dozen broken souls waiting to be healed, "What if this is as good as it gets?"), we witness event after event in the lives of three people like us in many ways. The events come in the command to keep an unwanted dog; in the wiped-out and mercied-back-together life of Simon; in the crazy way in which Carol's son is cured and she becomes a self-pitier. Sometimes the event is a word ("You will keep this dog!"), sometimes a hug (Carol in answer to Melvin's question to Simon, "Did you have sex with her?": "What we had was better than sex. We held each other."), and sometimes an apologetic deed (Melvin's sending the doctor to see Spence). Together there are blows, abusive words, tender strokes, a necessary deed, and volcanic affirmations. Either through smashing the old or gently beckoning the new, resurrection happens in the lives of Melvin, Simon, and Carol in their real life situations, which are "as good as it gets!"

Reflection

Was this a religious movie? Did people face up to reality as events happened? Were they reunited to others, themselves, and to the ground of being? Were lives changed and conversion decisions made?

Did they begin to care for each other authentically? If so, how would you begin to talk about where you saw the Jesus-Christ-Event happening? What other name would you give the movie? (*Redemption Runs Through It* is my second choice.)

Chapter Reflection

The Christ event is a dynamic that has always been happening in the lives of human beings. It is not the possession of the Christian religion or church but is the possession of all, shared through the good creation, releasing possibility for new life. The Christ event is an encounter that changes lives and makes them whole.

Again, to quote Perrin, "The one thing they all [the encounter events] have in common is that necessity for decision which will further shape that self-understanding which makes a man what he is in his own personal, existential being-in-the-world." And again to quote Marshall,

> Such happenings as this leave me with a fresh understanding . . . of openness to die to whatever I now am and to begin again on my journey of realistic living, a journey on which my sense of reality is perpetually expanding, along with my selfhood.

Such are Christ event happenings that change lives.

CHAPTER 14 NOTES

[1] Norman Perrin, *The Promise of Bultmann* (Philadelphia: Fortress, 1969), p. 29.
[2] Gene W. Marshall, "Commitment to Christ" (Texas: unpublished, 1984), pp. 3-4.
[3] Dietrich Bonhoeffer, "Freedom," *Ethics* (1955; New York: Macmillan, 1965), pp. 248-49.
[4] The Religious Studies I (RS-I) seminar, taught by the Ecumenical Institute: Chicago, has these four dynamics: I am enthralled (God section); I am accepted (Christ section); I am freed (Spirit section); I am sent (Church section).

Section Four:

Rethinking
My Christology

15. Theological Rebalancing of Christology

> It would seem to be apodictically [expressing necessary truth]
> inherent in Christian faith—*a priori* so far as faith is decisional
> commitment, *a posteriori* so far as it is gracious experience—
> that, praise God, there is this integral saving reality: our Lord
> Jesus Christ. Without it, as Barth so well saw, trying to piece
> together Scripture, tradition, reason, and experience is a
> hopeless effort to reglue Humpty-Dumpty. . . . [T]here is a
> very weighty theological agenda confronting . . . the whole
> church in our time.
>
> —Durwood Foster[1]

What is the current debate on christology? The church celebrated
the 1500th anniversary of the Council of Chalcedon (451 C.E.) in 1951,
at which time the Roman Catholic Church really entered the current
christology debate. Its leading theologians found the statement of
Chalcedon inappropriate in three ways: 1) it takes for granted Jesus'
divinity; 2) it tends to leave out Jesus' life, death, and resurrection; and
3) it suggests to our imaginations a "mythological figure far from one
who, in his humanity, is 'like us in all things except sin.'"[2] Why did it
take us so long to begin to begin to get clear about this?

Both Protestant and Catholic theologians were making the turn
by mid-century:

> In 1953 Ernst Käsemann reacted against Rudolf Bultmann's
> position by arguing that a New Quest for the historical Jesus
> was legitimate, necessary, and possible. Three years later the
> first response to Käsemann's call appeared with Günther
> Bornkamm's slender but enormously influential *Jesus of
> Nazareth*. Within two decades Roman Catholic scholars had
> joined the movement; in 1974 the Flemish theologian Edward

Schillebeeckx published a massive and encyclopedic synthesis of biblical scholarship entitled *Jesus: An Experiment in Christology*. The movement reached a watershed of sorts when, in 1985, in his book *Jesus and Judaism,*[3] E. P. Sanders [now at Duke University] offered a critical review of the New Quest to that point in some ways similar to Albert Schweitzer's critique of his predecessors in the Old Quest.[4]

At the same time this contemporary religious debate is evolving, globally we are entering a new phase:

The myth of scientific progress that Comte proposed as modern culture's substitute for the biblical narrative has itself encountered . . . suspicion of late. Progress that creates a consumer society, that fosters an international market in high-tech instruments of human destruction, and that is not far from destroying the organic systems that make our planet habitable has proven highly ambiguous. With this recognition, some would say, our culture is shifting into a *post-modern* phase.[5]

In this regard, over 100 million have been killed in the wars of the 20th century—*the war century*. Some say the spirit of Hitler is a stronger influence in our world than the Spirit of Christ. I was shocked when my son, who was finishing a two-year teaching stint in Indonesia, said he was scared to come back to the USA, afraid he would be accosted or even shot on our city streets. Why are the computer programs so slowly coming that will guard against other Chernobyl meltdowns? "Progress" is indeed calling our planet's life into question, and *vice versa*. In this post-modern age we experience our vulnerability and responsibility as never before as human beings.

Within this context—in a time of epochal transition—what do we mean by christology? Will its meaning keep changing? Yes, because it is connected to our interpretations of Jesus the Christ. However, the final reality to which Jesus Christ points will not change. There is a wide spectrum of christologies, to say the least. Roy Zuck says, "Jesus Christ is central, and He alone is to be worshiped! He is the object of every Christian's worship because He is God."[6] Contrast this with Bultmann's very critical essay in 1951, challenging the World Council of Churches' statement that the Council "is composed of churches which acknowledge Jesus Christ as God."[7]   Zuck and WCC: Jesus is God. Bultmann and probably all ten theologians we have reflected upon: Jesus is not God. If Jesus is not God, then how do we talk about christology? Zuck is in the classic company of the creeds. Bultmann is in the classic company of Paul (who was the earliest writer in the New Testament), John (the last gospel writer), and the 20th century experience of vulnerable existence. Who is right? and How do we know?

Harvey Cox says, "When asking the question Who was Jesus? we must expect different answers because only part of the response can come from history. The other part comes from the heart of the person answering the question. The query is both historical and personal, so the answers will be as well."[8] Can we therefore say that everybody is right? We can, but there are potentially damaging theological imbalances in the christologies of theologians and the mass of Christians. Why then try to rebalance them? In past history, imbalanced christologies have led to bloody warring. Further, imbalanced christologies have pushed millions of would-be Christians out the door or not attracted them in the door of the Christian tradition.

Why does Jesus the Christ not make sense today to growing numbers of serious people? Although most Americans surveyed say they believe in *God*, most would not be able to communicate who *God* is for them in a way that would make sense. And if I asked the same people to explain what they mean by "Jesus is the Christ," they would not be able to make sense of that either, which means they are un-thought-through on their christology, or they think they have not been encountered by this reality. If I asked them Is Jesus *God*? they would probably split 50-50. If I asked them why they answered as they did, most would not know what to say.

We have considered and reflected on the heart of the christologies of ten theologians. Admittedly, this group is my personal choice, hardly a comparative analysis of those representing the spectrum of christological thought. I picked theologians who have spoken to me in my search for a christology that makes sense. I hope they will make sense to the enlightened agnostics and serious Christians who read this book.

Let us take a "Christ image evaluation" to see what makes sense to us after reading the preceding chapters. (Hopefully, you did this evaluation before you read the first chapter.)

Christ Image Evaluation

*Answer **T** (true) or **F** (false)*. (There are no trick questions.)
1. Jesus was 100 percent divine.
2. Jesus was 100 percent human.
3. Jesus was 50 percent divine, 50 percent human.
4. Jesus lived historically.
5. Jesus is a mythological figure.
6. Jesus lives universally today.
7. Jesus was a Jewish layman.
8. Jesus is God.
9. Jesus was crucified.
10. Jesus is my personal Savior.
11. Jesus was resurrected.
12. Jesus and the Father are one.
13. Jesus had faith in God.
14. We have faith in Jesus.
15. We have the faith of Jesus in God.
16. Jesus atoned for the sins of the world.
17. I go along with the christology of the Councils of Nicaea and Chalcedon.
18. Jesus is the only revelation of God.
19. "Jesus Christ" means Jesus is the Messiah.
20. Jesus is the Christ because he was without sin.
21. I have experienced the Jesus Christ event.
22. The Jesus Christ event is not complete without my decision of faith.
    Finish the Statements:
23. A false Christ for me is_____.
24. Jesus is the Christ for me because_____.
25. The phrase that best describes my christology is_____.

Journey Questions: When did you first do this evaluation? What answers have changed? Which answers surprised you this time? Have you grown in your understanding of Jesus as the Christ? Do you sense that your answers really make a difference? Are you a Christian? How do you know?

Let us summarize the christologies of the ten theologians and then begin to reflect on how their christologies rebalance christology in general and ours in particular. The *chart* on the next two pages holds the emphases of 1. Sin (what for them is sin), 2. Jesus as the Christ (the

ELEVEN CHRISTOLOGIES

THEOLOGIAN	Christology of:	1. Sin	2. Jesus as the Christ	3. Key to Faith
OGDEN	Re-Presentation	Faith in False gods	Jesus as Re-Presentation of God	Human Experience of the Event
BULTMANN	The Word	The Old World of Willfulness	Jesus as Word of God	Eschatological Event Calls for Decision
NIEBUHR	Radical Faith	Corrupted Faith	Radical Faith *of* Jesus	Reconstructed Faith through J.X. Happening
SOBRINO & SEGUNDO	Anthropology	Following Our Way	Faith *of* Jesus	Following Faith of Jesus

GOGARTEN	Faithful Obedience	Responsibility *to* the World	Event of Jesus' Faithful Obedience	Re-Expression of Jesus' Faith
PERRIN	Risen Lord	Slave to the World	Experience of the Risen Lord	Faith-Image of Jesus
KIERKEGAARD	Radical Existentialist Meaning	Unwilling to be the Self	Paradox of Revelation/ Contemporaneous with Christ	Grounding Oneself Transparently in the Power that Constitutes
TILLICH	New Being	Separation	Jesus as the New Being	Accept the Fact You're Accepted
MATHEWS	Jesus-Christ-Event	Illusion of Everyman Christ	Jesus as "No Messiah" Messiah	Offense of Event
Note: I include the current edge of my christology below and will explain in Chapters 16-19.				
COCK	Transparent Event	Existential Despair	Transrational Grace	Presence of Other World

key to their christologies), and 3. their Keys to Faith.

Reflecting on these ten christologies, the following gestalt emerges.

1. All ten are struggling to articulate christology in the post-Nicaea and post–Chalcedon worldview of the authentic humanity of Jesus, a historical person.
2. Theirs are "christologies from below" which do not *assume* Jesus' divinity but indicate our relationship with the divine reality in life, through faith.
3. All ten are Christian existentialists, asking the question of human meaning to be found in our existence rather than beyond it, i.e., metaphysically.
4. Jesus is not God for any of the ten.
5. They base their christologies on the life-changing event initiated by Jesus—the event then and now.
6. Most of them believe Jesus had faith in God, as we can.
7. For them "sin" is not a moral category—first of all—but an existential one, i.e., separation.
8. *Christology* has to do with *our* relationship with God, not Jesus' equality with God.
9. Jesus as the Christ is a re-presentation and revelation of God.
10. For them, Jesus occasions and catalyzes our decision for faith in God.

Existentially, christology begins at the point of our sin, our condition of separation, illusion, corrupted faith, self-will, or our human dis-ease. This is where we live; this is the state of our existence. Who will deliver us from ourselves to our authentic selves of faithful obedience to God? We certainly cannot. An outside event or encounter initiates the process of salvation from our sin.

Historically, where does christology begin? seems to be a most significant question. Does it begin with the historical Jesus, with the New Testament accounts of him, or with the early tradition accounts of him? Willi Marxsen informs us here. He says in essence that christology began when Jesus initiated faith in the first believer.[9] He goes on, with the help of Gehard Ebeling, to explain this.

> *Faith* is always connected here [in the healing miracles] to an
> *event.* The event, in turn, is connected to *Jesus.* Jesus expects
> faith or requires faith or attributes the event to faith. . . .
>
> The person who believes is the one who is helpless, who
> cannot help himself, who has reason (as the stories of the heal-
> ing clearly show) for despair in the face of the overwhelming
> power of sickness, whose very existence has been shaken—
> *and* the one who now (as a believer, in the accomplishment of
> faith) allows God to act, allows that to happen which only God
> is able to do.
>
> This faith arises in the encounter with Jesus; it is connected
> . . . with the activity of Jesus. It is a faith awakened by Jesus.
> Its immediacy is revealed itself in the fact that faith is com-
> pletely undogmatic. It is not oriented to some *concept of God.*
> No confession of faith was required of the pagans who were
> healed. Indeed, they apparently did not even know what hap-
> pened to them. . . .
>
> Both [the call to faith in the activity of Jesus and the concrete
> proximity of God] supplement one another. . . . In the en-
> counter with Jesus, therefore, God is no longer the distant God,
> but rather the One who is presently active. His nearness oc-
> curs in faith. In this sense, Jesus was understood by the primi-
> tive community as the initiator of faith.
>
> *The stories of healing are therefore basically not stories of
> healing at all. Rather, they are exemplary stories for the power
> of faith which is awakened through Jesus.* . . . What the heal-
> ing is intended to show is that which faith, that which believ-
> ing, is able to do—to show what happens where faith is present,
> and indeed a faith whose initiator is Jesus. . . .
>
> [The] relationship is . . . a double one. The first unites the
> person who is ill with Jesus and awakens faith. The second
> unites the ill person who has come to faith through Jesus with
> God. . . . The relationship to Jesus is the basis of the relation-
> ship to God. . . .
>
> That does not yet mean that he has also thereby become the
> object of faith. He is proclaimed as the originator of faith.[10]

An intuitive summary of Marxsen's points reminds us of what

the previous ten theologians have been saying about christology:

- Faith is connected to an event.
- The event is connected to Jesus.
- The event depends upon faith.
- The person who believes desperately needs faith.
- Our faith allows God to act fully in our lives.
- The act of Jesus is to call us to faith in God, to awaken faith in God.
- Faith is undogmatic, meaning we do not have to believe or confesss any set of beliefs.
- Those experiencing the event did not know what had happened to them.
- God becomes near in faith.
- Jesus initiates faith through life's encounter with us.
- We are united with Jesus and therefore united with God.
- Jesus is not the object of faith,[11] God is.
- Jesus is the originator of faith.

No one knows who was the first believer or when the first encounter between Jesus and a believer happened; but the historical consensus is *It did happen.* This is the *crux of christology: one comes to faith in **God** through Jesus.* Let us simply say that christology began with all those who came to faith through their encounter with Jesus. If so, three things are clear: 1) christology comes in an existential encounter; 2) christology cannot happen without the faith of the believer; and 3) christology is faith in the power that constitutes faith. I say this secularly to emphasize its universality, which includes its timelessness. Abraham benefited from the same christology as the man by the Sheep Pool in Jerusalem, and as Paul, Augustine, Luther, Wesley, and as you and I. Was (and is) Jesus present, and therefore *God*? Assuredly. How do we know? Because of "the way life is." Life's dynamics have not and will not change. One comes to faith in *God* the same way he or she always has. The christological dynamic is ever the same and universally true.

Does one have to believe a certain way? No. Does one have to be a certain kind of disciple? No. Does one have to live during the time of Jesus and near Nazareth? No. Does one have to be baptized afterwards and join a church? No. There are no conditions upon this *faith in God* through the encounter with Jesus. Only that one has faith and embodies it. Could this event have happened to Jesus? Yes. Can it happen to a young Jewish lady named Etty Hillesum (hardly a "victim" of the Holocaust but a woman of unbelievable faith who was exterminated at Auschwitz)? Yes. Can it happen to an un-churched woman like Mary in Asheville (who lived her faith immodestly in spite of her completely amputated legs, leaving her body a trunk to be leaned against a bedboard)? Yes. Can it happen to a Buddhist or Muslim? Yes. Can this event happen to an atheist or agnostic like Camus? Yes. Could it have happened to a caveman? Yes. An alien. I don't know. Anyone who is up against these dynamics of life can be encountered by the Jesus the Christ dynamic in life and be brought to faith in *God*, if he or she but chooses for life as it is constituted—graced to the core.

Where does this leave us? The ***Jesus-Christ-Event*** is *historical*, backwards and forwards. It is *universal* in the most inclusive and expansive sense. It is *ecumenical* and *inter-faith* in the deepest sense. It is *pluralistic*. It is *religious*. It is *secular*. It is *existential*. It is *unconditional*. It is *ultimate*. It puts us in touch with "holy reality," a phrase of Ernst Troeltsch.

In the happening of the Jesus-Christ-Event we realize that Jesus is the Christ, that the Messiah has come, and the blissful Buddha has taken over from the wrathful Buddha. In its happening all prophecy of the fullness of life is come and human life is fulfilled, though still broken, sinful human life. Meaning is let loose and received. All relationships, all time, all space are experienced as holy, because we are reunited to our ground of being, to others, and to ourselves. Do we know what happened? Not really. Do we know the name of the power in this happening? No, but we give it names. Do we need to do anything? Only this, accept the fact that we are accepted. Will we soon fall out of this sense of fulfillment? Of course. Will we forget what happened to us? No. Will it happen again? Definitely, but we may not receive it. Is this "the way life is"? Yes, this is gracious existence, made possible by the Jesus-Christ-Event.

This event is grounded in the historical Jesus, in the proclaimed Jesus of the New Testament and early church, in the Christian tradition, and most of all in life as *God* has constituted it—else Jesus, the New Testament, and the Christian tradition would not have known what they were talking about. No person or group can possess this event. Impossible, for it is *a happening*, not a dogma, not a ritual, not a moral principle. We do not have to believe a certain way to be saved or be a part of a particular body; we do not have to go through a certain ritual to be saved; we do not have to do certain deeds to be saved. *We are saved but do not know it, or know it and have not said **Yes** to the fact.* Like the religious that Jesus spurned, any religion, denomination, or sect today that thinks it has salvation wrapped up, guess what. Jesus would say, "Get out of the way of *God's* gracious activity." Let us not become a part of the imbalance of christology. Let us not block the door to *God's* saved and chosen ones—all his children.

Out of the Jesus the Christ event comes unfettered and unbrokered[12] wholeness: freedom, vocation, discipleship, mission, compassion, community, peace, and meaning. All that is required of this experience is faith, accepting and obeying the all-determining fact of our existence—grace. Where sin does abound, grace does all the more abound. If Jesus originates and initiates all this, surely he is the Christ.

CHAPTER 15 NOTES

[1] Durwood Foster, "Wesleyan Theology: Heritage and Task," *Wesleyan Theology Today: A Bicentennial Theological Consultation*, ed. by Theodore Runyon (Nashville: Kingswood Books, 1985), p. 34.
[2] William P. Loewe, *The College Student's Introduction to Christology* (Collegeville, MN: Liturgical Press, 1996), p.9.
[3] E. P. Sanders, *Jesus and Judaism* (Philadelphia: Fortress, 1985). I question Sander's book being the watershed since Schweitzer, however solid his research may be. I appreciate his categories for New Testament claims about Jesus: I. Certain or virtually certain; II. Highly probable; III. Probable; IV. Possible; V. Conceivable; and VI. Incredible. If every New Testament scholar "had the guts" to fill out that list in a couple of pages as Sanders does in this book (pp. 326-27), laypersons would be less tyrannized by the literalistic pronouncements of fundamentalism.
[4] *Ibid.*, p. 40.
[5] *Ibid.*, p. 12 (emphasis added).

[6] Roy B. Zuck, editor, *Vital Christology Issues: Examining Contemporary and Classic Concerns* (Grand Rapids, Kregel Resources, 1997), p. 7.

[7] John Macquarrie, "Christology in Dialogue with Existentialism," *Christology in Dialogue*, ed. by Robert F. Berkey and Sarah A. Edwards (Cleveland: Pilgrim Press, 1993), pp. 269-274.

[8] Harvey Cox, *Our Religions*, ed. by Arvind Sharma (San Francisco: Harper, 1993), p. 366.

[9] Willi Marxsen, *The Beginnings of Christology: A Study in Its Problems*, trans. Paul J. Achtemeier (Philadelphia: Fortress Press, 1969), pp. 21, 54.

[10] *Ibid.*, pp. 52-56 (emphasis added).

[11] *Ibid.*, p. 69: "It was not faith *in* Jesus, as it seems to me the material quite clearly indicates, but rather it was the faith awakened by Jesus. Men who have come to faith through Jesus, and that means those who have been placed in the eschatological relationship, proclaim what part Jesus, in his words and his deeds, had in that event. That could clearly have happened before Easter. Even if we do not have a single actual illustration of that, it is hardly conceivable that it did not happen." This is a radical statement: faith through Jesus is not dependent upon the cross and resurrection, even.

Marxsen clarifies another point of christology in these quotes: *the faith and love of Jesus do not save us.* Jesus saves us by calling us to faith in the God of grace and love, by awakening us to faith in God through what we have been calling the Christ event. This frees us from trying to gain our salvation by having to walk *in his steps* of faith and love. Needless to say, we cannot even historically verify Jesus' faith and love, except through the *story* of the New Testament, which we have said is subjectively biased to the faith of the believer then and now. Further, we cannot even accurately measure our own faith and love at this or any moment in our lives. Therefore, the Christ event which addresses our lives, which awakens us and calls us to faith in God, happens in the events of our lives, through the Spirit of Christ. This was what Jesus was about in the New Testament *story*, encountering others with the decision for faith in God through his words and deeds. The Bible, including the New Testament, is a *story book*, full of *stories* about the God-human relationship, full of the essential truth about our lives, but not always factually true. Are the *stories* about Jesus true? Absolutely. Factually true? Often not. Is there enough truth there for faith? Without a doubt, when that truth addresses our lives and calls us to a decision of faith in God.

[12] John Dominic Crossan's word, meaning to me that which has no middleman.

16. John Cock: Christology of the Transparent Event
—*Part One*

I *see skies of blue*
and clouds of white—
the bright, blessed day,
the dark, sacred night—
and I think to myself,
What a wonderful world!
—Sung by Louis Armstrong,
Good Morning, Vietnam[1]

The Evolution of My Christology

Declaring one's christology is awesome. Is this really what I believe? How can I ever fathom the mystery of christology? Does this make sense to anyone else? Will it change? What will the 2000 years of tradition say? How will those outside the church respond? What will the enlightened agnostic say? Does anyone care? What does this mean for my self-understanding (including my self-embodiment)?

From early age every Christian has a christology. As Chapter 1 describes, my formative christology was very traditional. College shook and somewhat shattered the Jesus-image I took there with me. My christology during the intervening years until the assassination of JFK was dysfunctional, or at least on hold. Seminary and years in the local church stimulated and nurtured a rational/ethical christology practiced earnestly in the piety of small-group fellowship. When my wife and I read about and attended two religious studies seminars with the Ecumenical Institute: Chicago, my christology underwent revolution. Grace struck. Freedom rang. Radical discipleship called. We responded by selling almost all and joining in covenant with that family order for over sixteen years, living with the poor all over the world in urban ghettos and villages of the third world. Outsiders would describe the Order: Ecumenical's christology as Christian existentialist; it was that, and much more.

The following complex of christological meaning is apropos for the Order: Ecumenical period of my journey. John Knox lists seven component meanings of the Christ event.[2] A Christ event complex of meaning makes sense to me, although Knox's and my components are different. When I say "I believe in Jesus Christ," these eleven components point to the composite meaning I am giving to that christological name. If I had to say it in summary form, it would be the event of grace—including revelation, decision, and deed. Is it any wonder that christology is hard to communicate, e.g., Knox's seven components, my eleven, and whatever your number is?

My Christological Complex of Meaning

1. the *words of Jesus*, emphasizing his obsession with the Kingdom of *God*
2. the *deeds of Jesus*, manifesting his love for *God* and Neighbor (captial "N" designates more than person next door)
3. the *faith of Jesus*, responding to his Father's graciousness
4. the *cross of Jesus*, representing his faithful obedience unto abandonment and death
5. the *resurrection of Jesus*, representing his Father's faithfulness even in death
6. the *event in the lives of his followers*, building the tradition through word and deed
7. the *presentation about Jesus*, including witness, testament, ritual, and art
8. the *event in our lives*, gracing us and calling us to faith
9. *our response to that event*, accepting our acceptance (first response)
10. *our deed of faith*, manifesting our love for *God* and Neighbor (second response)
11. *our covenant community of faith*, vowing discipleship and common sustenance

We are describing a rather comprehensive faith-image when we declare our christology. "Simply accept Jesus Christ into your heart" and "Simply accept the fact that you are accepted" are hardly simplistic christological understandings. They are complex meaning hubs that defy fully satisfying explanation. As I said in the Prologue, we will never fathom what we mean by "Jesus is the Christ," yet if this is the entry into the meaning of *God* and life, we are driven to the task of creating and re-creating our christologies.

  I use the categories of Chapter 15 to chart the evolution of my christology:

THE EVOLUTION OF MY CHRISTOLOGY

Category / Time	Christology	Sin	Jesus as the Christ	Key to Faith
0-18 Years	Traditional	Sins	Jesus is God	Accept Jesus into My Heart
College+ Years		Dysfunctional Christology		
Seminary+ Years	Rational	Injustice	Exemplar/ Man For Others	Small-Group Fellowship
O:E Years	New Possibility	Illusion of "The Way Life Is"	Christ Event	Accept the Fact You're Accepted
Current Edge	Transparent Event	Existential Despair	Transrational Grace	Presence of Other World

The *current edge* does not mean that I have outgrown the previous christology arrived at during my Order: Ecumenical years. Hardly. Better said, that christology has been deepened over the past fifteen years and especially during the last nine.

My Christology of the Transparent[4] Event

My evolving christology has a new name, the *christology of the transparent event.* The word *transparent* is rich in meaning, coming from "to show through"; "fine or sheer enough to be seen through," "revealing," "capable of transmitting light," "translucent," "readily understood," "true"; sometimes the connotation of "lighted from the inside"; in computer usage, "interchangeable." These are the connotations I will use.

Last night, clouds covered the winter moon. Then, as I looked, the clouds parted, leaving a misty haze over the moon. As I watched some more, a wide circle of yellow surrounded the moon, with many inner-circles of whiter rings, giving it a glorious aura. I saw the moon transparently. (It occurred to me that I probably always see the moon transparently, through some tiny particles of dust at least.) What was not visible at first because of clouds was later revealed to the eye of this beholder because the lit moon shown through a transparent, misty haze. It was an event of magnificence.

The transparent event happens: what was not apparent suddenly shows through—is revealed. This is always an event of lesser or greater magnificence. Transparent events sustain and miraculously enliven our human lives, through consciousness. Let us recall a few illustrations of the millions of transparent events that make up our lives. One gazes at a flickering candle flame and encounters the transparent truth that light shines in darkness eternally. One watches an ant colony do its work and sees through transparently to corporate effectiveness. One reads the Psalms and transparently becomes David railing at the Lord. One holds a new baby and encounters the transparent event of joy, always present but seldom experienced. I watch the movie *Judgment at Nuremberg* and see clips of bulldozers pushing thousands of naked bodies into mass graves for gassed Jews; that clip goes transparent to the slaughter of the tribe and I experience righteous rage. I sing a simple love song and discover that I'm singing it to all that is. I see the African Children's Choir. They go transparent to all the African children who die before they reach age fourteen. I look at the Earthrise and see through to my home. I hold the hand of my dying mother, whose last words are, "John, I love you!"—I see through to the reality of love.

In a real sense, all of this is looking at life and all creation as Shakespeare knew: "All the world's a stage"; not only are we actors but also the audience, seeing what is going on, and sometimes—when the transparent event happens—what is *really* going on. In the Order: Ecumenical we followed Joseph Mathews' art form methodology, developed out of a professor's insights.[5] One observes a work of art and discusses objective, reflective, and interpretive reactions to it, be it a movie, a painting, music, a poem, a play, literature, etc. (That is how I filtered the movies in Chapter 14.) This method allows one to contemplate life and creation. A three-way conversation takes place among *art form*, *creator*, and *oneself* as the viewer or listener.

Martin Heidegger understood this dynamic of art, especially in his later period. He saw that truth comes through the events of existence, that what really *Is* gives itself to be known by us. (This is also what Heidegger means by "the clearing within which Being presents itself,"[6] always and only through what is in existence: another way to talk about the transparent event, or Being revealing itself.[7]) When we see through to what really *Is*, in that grace event—beyond our willing and doing—we begin to see the holy dimension of life.[8] The function of the art form method is to set us up to receive the giving by what really *Is*, to see through transparently and to name it as it *Is*, holy—full of fascination and sometimes fear. Therefore, for me, the role of the artist is to make us aware of the awesomeness of life. The use of the art form method is to help us focus on, reflect upon, and interpret life in the earnest hope that we will be given to see what really *Is*.

This depth dynamic of human life and creation as a work of art—given to be seen through—is at the heart of what I mean by the transparent event, and likewise what I mean by the Jesus-Christ-event. When Being presents itself in the clearing, or when we are given to see through[9] to what really *Is*, we have been encountered by the transparent Christ event.

What really *Is* is revealed to us and we are given the eyes to see.

We see what really *Is* and name it all sorts of religious names depending on the tradition we're standing in at the time: I AM; YHWH; ABBA; VERY GOD OF VERY GOD. Or when this event happens, we use holy expletives: HOLY, HOLY, HOLY; HALLELUIA; MY LORD; OH JESUS; AMEN. When this happens, we understand eventfulness, newness, blind-but-now-I-see-ness. We understand what Moses understood seeing the burning bush and holy ground, and why he hid his face, "for he was afraid to look at God" (Exodus 3: 2-6).

We understand what AWE is. We understand what the first ones saw when they called Jesus the CHRIST, or what St. John said Jesus said, "The Father and I are one" (10: 30); and (14: 9) "Anyone who has seen me has seen the Father. Then how can you say, 'Show us the Father'?" We understand that we have been given to see the MYSTERY of life, which is always in charge of this existence, because THOU art incarnate in existence as THOU wilt, lo here and lo there, showing us THY PRESENCE WITH US transparently through the events of life. "You are the CHRIST, the Son of the LIVING GOD." And who revealed this to Peter? Jesus said, "Flesh and blood has not revealed this to you"—not anything of this world, not the church, not historical accounts of Jesus, not your theology—but "my FATHER who is in heaven" (Matt. 16: 15-17). Who revealed it to us? The HOLY MYSTERY, whom we call GOD, the ONE to whom Jesus is transparent event. We experience the event and then try to name the holy one we met there—like Jacob did at Bethel. Sometimes at such epiphanous moments a religion is born in the numinous encounter with the holy.[10]

Being given to see transparently to the center of what *Is* in the stuff of life—in nothing special and in everything in particular—points to the understanding that each piece of creation is transparent to meaning, or just beneath the surface of each piece of reality is meaning. Or meaning is everywhere in the event we are transparently given to see through. Just as Ken Wilber talks about holons of reality and that each holon is subsumed in the next higher holon or the next holon up, we can talk about the transparency of reality and that each holon can be seen through transparently. There is meaning all the way up and meaning *all the way down,*[11] one might say. Or there is no top or no bottom to reality.[12]

To recapitulate, this mundane, stuff-of-life event happens to us, revealing awe and wonder. We are given to see clearly what *Is*. We feel compelled to name what is happenning, to interpret it. If the event opens us up in the deeps of our lives, we walk away knowing that we will not be the same. We internalize the happening, rehearsing it many times over. It leaves us with a depth resolve, either to call to remembrance, to bow in worship, to walk humbly with the One, to witness to its power, to show compassion for creation, the Neighbor. When this happens, we have completed the event (as I talk about in the eleven components above): the event is complete in the embodiment of a faith relationship with the One and the Neighbor.

The fuller life method, going beyond the steps of the art form method, is

> Focus
> Reflect
> Interpret
> Internalize
> Resolve
> Symbolize
> Embody

Or to use another scenario of the dynamics of the profound transparent event,

- An external event happens . . .
- which occasions an interior crisis . . .
- which sometimes opens us up to the reality of *the way life is* . . .
- which leaves us with the possibility to elect or reject human existence as it is constituted.

These methods and dynamics are built out of and upon the transparent eventfulness in existence; therefore, we call them *life methods*, methods that mirror the dynamics of life. This is what we mean by *the way life is* (TWLI)—not to be equated with "God," but with that which "God made," if one chooses to say it that way. If one's christology does not mirror *the way life is*, then it is suspect relative to its reality, to say the very least. There are too many christologies built upon our doing something or knowing something that do not reflect *the way life is*, i.e., a christology of works. I am espousing a christology of grace, built upon the event of the Mysterious Other, whom some call *God*, the One revealed to us in Jesus as the Christ. An authentic christology is built upon the hermeneutic of grace (Chapter 7), on the event of grace, on what has been given to see, on the graciousness of *the way life is*. This christology leads to enlivening awe. The christology of works is built upon egoic willing and doing, which leads to human pride and stoic burnout—both leading to despair.

Jesus and the Transparent Event of Grace

I have been writing about what is true for every person, regardless. Every person is given to see through transparently to the center of what *Is*, to the Final Mystery, to GOD—if only "through a glass darkly" (I Cor. 13: 12). Jesus occasioned a new and utterly radical interpretation of this seeing through. First, what he was given to see[13] was his Father, the Gracious One, reigning at the heart of gracious existence. In his seeing he became at one with the Father through grace: "I and the Father are one." That experience was the profundity of his life, the all-determining fact of his existence. He obsessively lived at one with his Father (*Abba*) in faith, word, and deed. Second, Jesus was given to be seen through transparently to reveal the Father, the Gracious One, reigning at the heart of gracious existence: "Anyone who has seen me has seen the Father. Then how can you say, 'Show us the Father'?"

His followers told the story of his cruciformity that was given to be seen through as the all-determining grace that is at the center of what *Is*, and believing that, they called him the Christ: transparent to the One who reigns as the Giver of Grace at the center of gracious existence. When they were really given to see Jesus, they did not see him but the One who reigns as the Giver of Grace at the center of gracious existence. They did not see the window but saw through the window to what it was transparent to, Graciousness itself. Jesus was and is the window, the transparent event of GOD. Thus he was and is what he was sent to be. As his followers, we too are to be seen through, to reveal the Gracious One.

Let the above paragraphs of poetry—for all christology is poetry—be our paradigm of transparency as far as Jesus is concerned. Jesus is transparent to Grace itself: to the all-determining fact that *the way life is* is eternally gracious for every person and for all creation. And like unto it, Jesus is transparent to a life of grace: life lived in grace is the life-style of gracious cruciformity on behalf of creation. Jesus' cruciform embodiment of grace was his mission, pure and simple. Did he accomplish it? Billions would say so. Billions would say not. Billions would say they don't know.

Was he the unique—one and only—transparent event of *God*? No. If not the only one transparent to grace, was he the most grace-conscious human in existence? For me, yes, without qualification. He was and is the quintessence of grace in human form. Will fundamentalists say I do not know Jesus as the Christ, meaning maybe I don't know him as they do? I know him as the Christ as I say above in my witness. *God* will judge me and them, out of the graciousness of Jesus the Christ, the very transparency to Being itself.

Who was the first transparency? Let me say what I believe another way:

> *1ˢᵗ Transparency*: From the beginning, Abraham (as representative human) was given to see through and was seen through
> *2ⁿᵈ Transparency*: Jesus was given to see through and was seen through
> *3ʳᵈ Transparency*: the Tradition of "little Christs" (his followers) were/are given to see through Jesus as the Christ and were/are themselves seen through
> *4ᵗʰ Transparency*: like the **1ˢᵗ**, any piece of creation is given to be seen through and can be seen through, world without end

Just in case someone still does not understand me, there is only one transparency with four or more manifestations; and as far as I am concerned, Jesus is the first-among-others.

But you ask, What then is the reason for taking Jesus to Muslims, Buddhists, Hindu, etc.? Let me say, I won't and we shouldn't, for out of my understanding of christology, Graciousness and the Transparent Event are the quintessence of any tradition—including the secular, non-religious "religious" tradition of our day—dispensing grace without qualification. Will I try to publish my self-understanding abroad? Of course, and whosoever will can dialogue with it out of her or his self-understanding.

Every person has a "christology" in the sense I am talking about, Christian or not. What they choose to call the transparent event of life is their choice. All I care about proclaiming is the truth that grace is the all-determining, transparent event for all human beings.

This is authentic evangelism: say it over and over and over, as Frost wrote, "till we answer from within. The thousandth time may prove the charm." Let us experience the Transparent Event of Grace, interpret it, internalize it, and embody it, as Paul wrote, that "grace may more abound," for "God's act [event] of grace is out of all proportion . . . [to our sin that] is vastly exceeded by the . . . gift that came to so many by the grace of the one man, Jesus Christ" (Rom. 5: 15-16).

As Louis sings of the Transparent Event—changing the words the least bit—

> *I see skies of blue*
> *and clouds of white—*
> *the bright, blessed day,*
> *the dark, sacred night—*
> *and I'm given to see,*
> **What a wonderful life!**

I am also reminded of the movie written by, directed by, and starring Roberto Benigni (several 1999 *Oscars*), the outrageous man who sees and proclaims *Life Is Beautiful*, even in a Nazi death camp.

CHAPTER 16 NOTES

[1] (George Weiss and Bob Thiele) Harold Square Music, Inc. on behalf of Range Road Music, Inc. and Quartet Music, Inc. (ASCAP).

[2] John Knox, *Jesus: Lord and Christ* (New York: Harper, 1958), p. 217.

[3] TWLI: *the way life is*. Used by the Order as a contemporary equivalent of Augustine's "that which is."

[4] *Transparentness* is the noun form of *transparent*. *Transparency* has a different and more narrow meaning, though I will use this word later on once I have established the use of *transparent*. These uses are more precise than using *transparent* as an adjective modifying christology, which can be misunderstood. I like the related words *transpicuous,* "see through" and *transpadane* ("see across"), a word Joseph Mathews used to relate

interchangeably the religions through his transparentized understanding of reality via the transparent and therefore contentless dynamic of the Christ event.

[5] *The Art of Focused Conversation*: *100 Ways to Access Group Wisdom in the Workplace*, gen. ed. R. Brian Stanfield (Toronto: ICA Canada, 1997), p. 2.

[6] Wilber often uses this image of the "clearing."

[7] Tillich says, "the . . . experience of the holy is mediated by some piece of finite reality. Everything can become a medium of revelation, a bearer of divine power. 'Everything' not only includes all things in nature and culture, in soul and history; it also includes principles, categories, essences, and values." Paul Tillich, *Biblical Religion and the Search for Ultimate Reality* (Chicago: University of Chicago, 1955), pp. 22-3.

[8] These reflections on Heidegger come through Thomas K. Carr's review, "Only a God Can Save Us" (Internet: *First Things* 55, August/September 1995: 57-62), on John Macquarrie's lectures and book, *Heidegger and Christianity*: *The Hensley Henson Lectures 1993-94* (London: Continuum, 1994).

[9] I will use this phrase, *we are given to see through,* to designate the gracious initiation of life rather than our initiating the seeing through. The event of seeing through transparently is beyond our control.

[10] In the Order: Ecumenical we studied and were guided by Rudolf Otto's, *The Idea of the Holy* (1923; New York: Oxford University, 1965). He, along with H. R. Niebuhr and Bultmann, pointed us to the development of methods to understand the reality of the Other Word in the midst of This World (this World is transparent to the Other World). We will look at these methods in Chapter 18.

[11] Ken Wilber uses this phrase.

[12] Ken Wilber talks about *holons* in his tome *Sex, Ecology, Spirituality*: *The Spirit of Evoltuion* (Boston: Shambhala, 1995) and in *A Brief History of Everything* (Boston: Shambhala, 1996). I have tinkered around with word formations such as *trans-paron, parnythons, parons, sheerons, depthons, windons*: meaning there is no bottom to reality; each reality is transparent to the next level down; every reality is given to be seen through.

[13] Some of my colleagues call this Jesus' experience of the "Christ event." Rightly so.

17. Interior Qualities of the Event: *Transrational Spirituality*—Part Two

Dawns the World

Tune: *Glorious Things of Thee Are Spoken*

Dawns the world of *aweful wonder*, chained to my contingency,
All protection torn asunder, shame and weakness wounding me;
Then there groans a re-creation, born anew, within recast,
In unfolding transformation pains a passion unsurpassed.

Dawns the world of *deep awareness*, self-transcending liberty,
Shaping self and world in boldness, sign for all humanity;
Then in lonely free creation, with no map of good or ill,
I decide in obligation, I surrender all my will.

Dawns the world of *deep compassion*, yoked to life's strange harmony,
Unrelenting in my mission, doomed to die for history;
Bearing every time's long hour, every human agony,
I am strangely filled with power, wondrous deeds are done through me.

Dawns the world of *joyful living*, shocked by truth's absurdity,
Earthly hopes and dreams forsaking, I am blessed with victory;
And in raptured self-denying, dancing in the arms of strife,
I perceive in final dying bleeds the glorious, endless life.[1]

*****

And yet, and yet: how to refer to this always already Emptiness [or Spirit]? What words could a fish use to refer to water? How could you point out water to a fish? Drenched in it, never apart from it, upheld by it—what are we to do? Splash water in its face?[2]

—Ken Wilber

As I describe the interior qualities of the transparent event of my christology, I will lean on Joseph Mathews, the Order: Ecumenical, and Ken Wilber to inform us about *transrational spirituality*. Let me review again my current edge of christology from Chapter 16:

Category / Time	Christology	Sin	Jesus as the Christ	Key to Faith
Current Edge	Transparent Event	Existential Despair	Transrational Grace	Presence of Other World

In this chapter, I describe the last three categories of the chart: sin of existential despair, the transrational stage of grace, and the presence of the Other World in This World as the key to faith.

Wilber bases his transpersonal psychology (*spirituality* is a more apt word) upon three stages of consciousness evolution: from prepersonal to personal to transpersonal. He uses other sets of words interchangeably with these: from prerational to rational to *transrational*; from subconscious to self-conscious to super-conscious; from id to ego to God.[3] There are several transitions between these stages, and this is where I want to begin, with the existential transition[4] to the transrational or transpersonal stage. The existential worldview points to the integration of the body and mind, or biosphere and noosphere.[5] We will get to this later, but first let us get a big whiff of existentialism.

The Sin of Existential Despair

Reminiscent of Kierkegaard, who pointed to despair as sin (Chapter 10), I want to talk about the sin of existential despair. In a recent *New York Times* review entitled "Zombies—For the characters in these stories, existential dread permeates life in the Twin Cities," Paul Baumann critiques *How the Dead Live*: "Too many characters are sacrificed to an assumed faith in life's futility. With his acute ear for the emptiness of so much of modern American aspiration, [Alvin] Greenberg captures the truncated words and lives of a society deprived of spiritual oxygen."[6] The 20th century hallmark of existentialism is not dead by any means as we enter the 21st century.

Wilber gets at the heart of existentialism, both its gift and its contradiction, in the question and answer format of *A Brief History of Everything*. First its contradiction:

> *Q*: But there is such a grim atmosphere in these existential writers.
> *Ken Wilber*: Yes, this is classically the home of existential dread, despair, angst, fear and trembling, sickness unto death. . . . [B]ecause existentialists recognize no sphere of consciousness higher than this, they are stuck with the existential worldview. . . . Why, by all standards, this [existential] self ought to be smiling all the time. But more often than not, it is not smiling. It is profoundly unhappy. It is integrated and autonomous, and miserable . . . in a hemorrhage of despair.[7]

Elsewhere, Wilber writes of the consolations that are gone for the existential self, setting it up for the leap into the transrational, which is the context of its gift:

> It [the existential self] can no longer tranquilize itself with the trivial. From the depths, it cries out to gods no longer there. . . . Its very agony is worth a trillion happy magics and a million believing myths, and yet its only consolation is its unrelenting pain—a pain, a dread, an emptiness that feels beyond the comforts and distractions of the body, the persona, the ego, looks bravely into the face of the Void, and can no longer explain away either the Mystery or the Terror. It is a soul that is much too awake. It is a soul on the brink of the transpersonal [transrational].[8]

So what is sin here? It is fundamentally believing that the spirit dimension of life is gone with the magic and mythological distortion religions have made of existence, that finally authentic existence has only to do with body, mind, and will. There is the material, the rational, and the decisional: the will to decide—the crown jewel of existentialism—to take a relationship to one's despair and endure it nobly by oneself. If stuck here, one is hemorrhaging in despair, the despair of being separated from the reality of *the way life is*, for TWLI is far more than my ego's cut-off vision of reality. Existential sin is living as though existence is graceless rather than gracious.

When my first grandchild was born, I experienced the truth of what I am saying and wrote it in a Christmas poem:

> *The mystery of the messiah comes*
> * into our world anew in the birth of a baby,*
> *   whoever it belongs to,*
> *   whatever gender, nationality, color, or religion.*
>
> *It comes to us who think we do not want it or need it.*
> *It comes to us hardened cynics who have given up*
> * on new life ever happening to us again.*
> *It comes to us who think we have learned to live with separa-*
> * tion and have given up on reunion.*
> *It comes to us who have shunned religion;*
> * yet, it rattles us with deep religious rumblings.*
> *It comes to us who are following every wise man and every*
> * star, looking for that which we will never find*
> *   and which was never promised.*
>
> *The mystery of the messiah comes as it wills,*
> * where it wills,*
> * when it wills.*
> *Sometimes it wills to come in the form of a child.*
>
> *The Messiah has come.*
> *Be ready or not for its coming again.*[9]

In my cynicism and existential despair, I was broadsided by the wonder of new birth and reunion. I was opened up to *the way life is* in a fuller dimension, in a dimension I had come to believe was only for those bound to the religion of magic and mythology. I realized my sin of buying into the myth of flatland, the worldview that body, mind, and will is all there is. Again I had become blind to the depth dimension of the Spirit that explodes the limited vision of flatland.

Transrational Grace/Presence of the Other World

Thankfully, existentialism is also vulnerable to the event of transrational grace. This is why Wilber's poetry is helpful to me. He is articulating the biggest context I know[10] concerning the journey of Spirit—the journey of consciousness that is the signature of every person; and he writes as if he knows whereof he speaks. Like a spirit guide should, he offers us a vision beyond the one we have at the moment, thus freeing us to rise above our crippling reductionism of *the way life is*. The role of releasing the captives springs eternal: the blind see, the lame walk, and the despairing dance with a smile in their being as they cuddle the messiah baby.

I began to describe transrational grace in Chapter 16. Here let us begin to look at spirituality in the midst of this world. As many have been turned off by the other worldliness of Christianity, especially over the past two to three hundred years during the rise of atheistic empiricism and existentialism, we have ended up spiritually bankrupt. Life comes to us as flat and arid, in the vicinity of "wasteland." Life seems uneventful. We do not see much meaning; we do not experience our experience as fulfilling, or we interpret life as not worth much; we have a corrupted faith and therefore a limited commitment. Spirituality has become too much the property of the other-worldly fundamentalists and the ethereal new-agers, further turning us others off. This has to stop. Spirituality is not other-worldly and is not the property of anyone, but is the birthright of all. The masses must rediscover that Spirit is in this-one-and-only-world, not in some other world above or beyond this one.

Since the 17th century Cartesian paradigm, and before with the Greeks, this dualistic notion has led to the great split between matter and spirit—object/subject split. Matter has captured the domain of the real world for us since. Magic, mythology, and spirituality are not of this world and are thrown out with religion when it is cast off by the Enlightenment. The separation of matter from Spirit began when we as the Western civilization, at least, and as individuals rebelled against the tyranny of institutional religion and its other-worldly dogmas, i.e., heaven. Either be religious or not, secularism was urging as it won the day with its non-religious, one-story understanding of existence, which is absolutely true and absolutely false. It is true that this is the life we

have—for sure—between birth and death, the time of consciousness. It
is absolutely *not* true that Spirit is separate from this life we have between
birth and death. Let's say it radically: our lives between birth and death
are the only domain of the Spirit. Spirit is only in this world. The other
world is in the midst of this world. This is *our* reality. This is *the way
life is.* Salvation is now. The kingdom of *God* is here and now, for sure,
but we don't know and don't need to know what it shall be, except that
we can trust it.[11]

Joseph Mathews and the Order: Ecumenical in 1972, through
the development of a context and practical constructs, began to give
flesh to the self-understanding that the Other World is in This World.
The *Other World Charts* map four major breakthroughs of consciousness
in the 20th century, experienced in sixty-four states of being that every
person is more or less aware of during the human journey.[12] The crux of
this understanding is the realization of radical incarnation: Spirit is present
in this existence. Another way to say incarnation is to say the Jesus the
Christ event, or the transparent event, reveals Spirit at the heart of life.
Further, the Reformation of the 16th century and the Wesley movement
of the 18th century were clear that the coupled doctrines of justification
and sanctification talk about the life of faith events: faith events keep
happening from birth to death, or Spirit is always already present, as
Wilber would say it.[13]

Mathews gave a contextual speech in 1972 about the presence
of the *Other World.*[14] The following comments from the speech
summarize his early thoughts on the subject.

> • When you talk about the Other World, you are dealing with
> the ordinary secular world and secular human consciousness.
> • The Other World is the world beyond reason that reason it-
> self points to.
> • In our time we have succeeded in a rather admirable way in
> destroying the two-story [or three-story] universe.
> • We have gotten rid of metaphysics, which was related to the
> second-story universe.
> • The new metaphysics: we grasp living on one plane, but we
> have experienced the transparency of that plane itself. . . . In
> this transparency, in which there is one world, or one plane,

the transparency of that plane is the new metaphysics.
• A state of being, a state of awareness, a state of consciousness is the most objective reality that one ever experiences.
• Those of us who have come down hard on the existential
pole, on freedom and decision, were always taking for granted
the [transparent] understanding of humanness in the midst of
which that decision was made.[15]
• A state of being is made up of an image [the Big Think], an
accompanying affection [the Primordial Feel], and a pre-
decisional resolve [the Indicative Resolve].
• Mythology is the frame whereby man has held his experience of the Other World. The mythologies of the past are gone.
They no longer communicate to us. . . . Probably the biggest
contradiction in our time is the absence of an adequate
mythology whereby we have a roadmap over and through the
terrain, the topography, of the Other World.
• The Topography of the Other World in the midst of This
World: I. *The Land of Mystery*; II. *The River of Consciousness*; III. *The Mountain of Care*; IV. *The Sea of Tranquillity*.
• The last arena we call 'The Sea of Tranquillity.' I rather like
that. It dawned on me when the astronauts were walking on
the moon, that when you stand on the moon, the earth is 'up
there.' I always knew heaven was 'up there.' But when you
are on the moon, 'up there' points exactly to this life here,
where the Other World is. I want to go there one of these days
and see, just to be sure that the Other World is right here.
• Actually, in the Other World there is only one state of being,
not four. For where *consciousness* is, there is the *mystery*,
there is the world on your back [*care*], and there is the peace
[*tranquillity*] that passes reason's capacity to grasp it as peace.
• I pause a moment to remind you that because the Other World
is beyond the realm of good and evil, it is in the ontological
and not in the moral.
• In the Other World there is only the indicative. When you
talk about the Mountain of Care, or picking up the burden of
all mankind, you are not talking about something that says
you ought to do it. The indicative is that the one who lives in
the Other World *has* the world on his shoulders. When you
live before the Mystery, the world *is* yours.
• You could have drawn the road map a million different ways

with different poetry. We have delineated four arenas which we think broke loose in our century. . . . You understand there is nothing new at all in what we are doing. What is actually going on is a translation from one language to another.
• What is life all about? The poetry that you build is the secret to the new mythology that will enable mankind to find its way to swim [and not drown], if you please, in the rivers of radical consciousness and become human.

Mathews was passionate about the self-understanding and methods that would allow any person to walk in the fullest awareness that Spirit is the center of our lives. The spirituality I am talking about is not ancient, medieval, or modern, but part of the emerging post-modern worldview. That's why the term *transrationality*, abstract as it sounds, is my choice and not some conventional term everyone thinks he or she has an understanding of and dismisses out of hand. Let's load up this word.

Transrational Grace is pointing to the understanding of the transparent event of grace, or the Christ event, which has no particular content (*contentless—universal* would be another way to say it).[16] Transrationality has no special message but describes a dynamic of *the way life is* for everyone. This is not to say that I have to give up my tradition—again, including the secular tradition. Of course not. At the bottom of one's tradition is the contentless, transparent event of grace, or transrational grace. It is grace that transcends and underlies one's tradition; it is the property of none and the birthright of all; it is the truth about life to which all religious understandings and methods are transparent. So, transrational grace is transparent, eventful, contentless, universal, dynamic, and secular. Transrational grace, through the transparent Christ event, is at the heart of *that which is*.

Again, how does grace work? As far as my christology is concerned, grace does not directly unite me with *God*. No, grace comes to me in an event in the midst of This World and calls for my response. To quote Tillich from Chapter 11,

> Sometimes at that moment a wave of light breaks into our darkness, and it is as though a voice were saying:

'You are accepted. You are accepted, accepted by that which
is greater than you, and the name of which you do not know.
Do not ask for the name now; perhaps you will find it later.
Do not do anything now; perhaps later you will do much.
Do not seek for anything; do not perform anything; do
not intend anything. Simply accept the fact that you are
accepted!'

If that happens to us, we experience grace. After such an experience we may not be better than before, and we may not
believe more than before. But everything is transformed
[transrationalized]. . . . And nothing is demanded of this experience, no religious or moral or intellectual presuppositions,
nothing but acceptance.

This transrational event happens "sometimes" to every person,
to transparentize or transform one's human existence. It may come as
"a wave of light" or "a voice." What was before still is, but really *IS* at
the moment of grace. The Other World is revealed in This World. When
this happens in the Christian tradition, Jesus becomes the Christ, revealing
his Father, to whom we are united when grace strikes, when life is
transparentized, transrationalized, when the Other World is present.[17]

And what does this do to sin? Tillich says, in semi-religious
parlance, "In that moment, grace conquers sin, and reconciliation bridges
the gulf of estrangement." Speaking transrationally, our sense of the
separate-self[18] is experienced as "at one"[19] with what is: with the ground
of being, with the other (all creation), and with oneself. One experiences
Spirit at the heart of existence, that grace reunites all that is separate.
Our existential despair, dread, and sickness unto death are transformed:
we have been given and decided to embrace a new relationship with all
that is, including our existential despair. Does our despair go away?
Maybe momentarily. Does it *reign* over our lives as before? No, not if
we "accept the fact that we are accepted by that which is greater." We
are transformed into the victoriously despairing ones, dancing with a
smile in our being.

As I wrote in Chapter 13, reflecting on Mathews' christology,
the "no messiah Messiah" has come. That means grace is setting us
straight with *the way life is*:

The question we must ask ourselves about the Jesus-Christ-Event dynamics is Are they true to life? Do the Jesus-Christ-Event dynamics come out of life or are they a superimposition upon the way life is in reality? That is the question Mathews is always asking. This is his hermeneutical question, if you will, the key to his interpretation of the gospel truth. Why in the world would God create the way life is in the beginning— as perfectly Good—and then come along and create another set of life dynamics for the Christian gospel? What is life really like?

'The Christ decision was transparently an election for or against life itself. The negative answer was at bottom a rejection of human existence as it is constituted.' The key word is 'transparently,' which Mathews uses throughout his works, meaning that which is seen through and thus reveals 'human existence as it is constituted,' good as it is created. The twist here is that we humans are seldom aware of existence as it is constituted; we cover it up because it is bad to us, essentially, the way it is. . . . Some dynamic of life must come along and uncover what we cover up. Jesus delivers to us the decision of all decisions, Is life—and our life—good or bad the way it is?

These two paragraphs are as secular and contentless in meaning as can be. The transparent Jesus-Christ-Event has always been talking about the same life dynamics as the true life dynamics—the way life really is. Our life of living in the sin of existential despair is transparentized through the event of grace. We are given to see that we have become victims to the illusion that Spirit is *not* at the heart of existence. Grace happens and reveals to us our rejection of life and our lives as constituted. This rejection is the essence of our despair. Grace both reveals our rejection of life to us for what it is and accepts us as the despairing ones we are, giving us the possibility of being decisive in Spirit, giving us the possibility to see life as it really is and making a new decision to elect life and our lives as constituted.

Grace is to have the possibility to decide; faith is to decide (not by grace alone [direct union] or faith alone [works righteousness], but by grace-through-faith). Some say, "I am what God makes me." I say, I am who I choose to be as I live in the transparent presence of grace. When I accept my acceptance, transformation is the result: my identity is no longer the separated self but the reunited self.

When grace happens, I have experienced what Wilber points to as the transrational or the transpersonal or the superconscious. He talks about the gift of the existential self as being free from body/mind, beyond the personal/rational reductions of always seeing God and Spirit in *my* image, and present primarily to serve my ego needs. The personal is the second stage of development in which most fundamentalists and traditional Christians are stuck. So existentialism rises above the personal reductionism of idolatry but gets stuck in its own reductionism of grace-less-ness.

Although I have not run the same gamut of spiritual practices as Ken Wilber, I share his worldview, as reflected in his "seamless union of transcendental and empirical, other-worldly and this-worldly. For the higher levels themselves are not *above* the natural or empirical or objective, they are *within* the natural and empirical and objective."[20] His understanding of the *always already presence of Spirit* is much kin to my understanding of the transparently revealed or transrational grace. The following comments come from his "Always Already" chapter in *The Eye of Spirit* and reinforce what I have been saying.

- There is . . . nothing but Spirit in all directions, and not a grain of sand, not a speck of dust, is more or less Spirit than any other. . . . [T]here is no place where Spirit is not. . . . But there is no space lacking, and there is no space more full. There is only Spirit.
- The Great Search presumes the loss of God . . . the mistaken belief that God is not present . . . and thus totally obscures the reality of God's ever-present Presence. . . . The greater the Great Search, the more I can deny God. . . . But the effort to stop the Great Search is itself more of the Great Search. . . . It will not do to say that Spirit is present but I don't realize it. That would require the Great Search. . . . [S]eeking misses the present.
- You and I are already convinced that there are things that we need to do in order to realize Spirit. We feel that there are places that Spirit is not (namely, in me), and we are going to

correct this state of affairs. . . . [N]ondual meditation makes use of that fact and engages us in the Great Search in a particular and somewhat sneaky fashion.

• The Great Search is the search for an ultimate experience, a fabulous vision, a paradise of pleasure, unendingly good time, a powerful insight—a search for God, a search for Goddess, a search for Spirit—but Spirit is not an object.

• [O]ur awareness is clouded with some form of avoidance. . . . [W]e want to run away from it, or run after it, or we want to change it, alter it, hate it, love it, loathe it, or in some way agitate to get ourselves into, or out of, it . . . the agitation of the separate-self.

• Somehow, no matter what your state, you are immersed fully in everything you need for perfect enlightenment. . . . One hundred percent of Spirit is in your perception right now. . . . [T]he trick, as it were, is to recognize this ever-present state of affairs, and not to engineer a future state in which Spirit will announce itself.

• [A]bsolute reality and the relative world are 'not-two.'

• Spirit is the only thing that has never been absent.[21]

One can see the affinity between Wilber's worldview, Mathews', and mine. Spirit is shot through all that is. This is the essential truth about life. The Other World is in This World, or it is not anywhere. Those who go searching for anything other than what they are already given are playing a game with life. We are talking about the interior dynamics and qualities of a symbol system that is transparent to *the way life is*. We are reinterpreting established symbol systems out of our understanding of their dynamic essence.

In dialogue with a colleague recently, he said, "Maybe when you make a symbol system transparent to life, you lose the symbol system. If you want the richness of Christianity, you have to decide to live within the symbols. That gave me a different way of looking at fundamentalism. They hold onto the symbol system." I replied,

> *Reinterpreting the symbol system* has been going on in our tradition throughout its history, beginning with the Gospel writers and especially St. John, to Augustine, to Luther, to Eckhart, to St. Teresa and St. John of the Cross, to Kierkegaard,

to Bultmann, to de Chardin/Berry, to Tillich/Niebuhr/O:E.

Granted, in O:E we have been split: part of us offer the consensus to decouple from the symbol system, which has gone on for 2000 years. To reinterpret or not? That is the question. Religious Studies-I and The Other World in This World honor the tension and are transformative.

Fundamentalism is hardly the alternative, though they would want us to think so. I'd rather use the transpersonal understanding of Wilber, as one example, to help reinterpret the symbol system (as Bultmann used Heidegger).

I have no other place to start than from my tradition. Any tradition can go transparent to the universal, and all must. We will hardly invent a new one out of the blue or out of some grand gestalt. Let the bottom be blown out of the one you're given. Human beings will have a symbol system, so why not be an agent of enlivening reinterpretation, hopefully?

William Abraham fashions the following paragraph to depict "Liberal Protestants" within the United Methodist dialogue on doctrine. I take it he thinks he is pointing to a problem. I do not think so, except to say that his use of the word *liberal* here is hardly apt—the word *Protestants* by itself would do just fine. His paragraph represents a creative theological climate and makes me proud to be a Protestant. In part, it reminds me of Tillich's definition of the "Protestant principle."

If you believe that Christian doctrine is essentially an attempt to capture dimensions of human experience that defy precise expression in language because of personal and cultural limitations, then the truth about God, the human condition, salvation, and the like can never be adequately posited once and for all; on the contrary, the church must express ever and anew its experience of the divine as mediated through Jesus Christ. The church becomes a kind of eternal seminar whose standard texts keep changing and whose conversation never ends. In these circumstances, pluralism is an inescapable feature of the church's life. Pluralism effectively prevents the emergence of Christian doctrinal confession, that is, agreed Christian conviction and truth; and it creates the psychological and social conditions for constant self-criticism and review.[22]

I want to say *Amen* to Brother Abraham's insight into the truth about God, the human condition, salvation, *et cetera*. True, the church at its best is expressing "anew its experience of the divine as mediated through Jesus Christ." That's what this book is about, hopefully. Will there ever be certainty? Absolutely not. Therefore, I can absolutely live by faith.

I am *wagering*, to use Pascal's word, that the Christian symbol system is transparent to *the way life is*, that TWLI is centered in graciousness, and that this is what Jesus was given to see, breathe, preach, live, and die for—and that this self-understanding will be what keeps his tradition alive in Spirit. We can trust the way life is created and that which keeps it gracious. We can trust the reality that we have been given to see. We rely on the divine mercy Jesus reveals. As H. R. Niebuhr says, "He [Jesus] discerned the divine mercy and relied upon it."[23] In the movie *The Gospel According to St. Matthew*, Jesus lives his starkly real life in the Other World that is only in This World, and makes his concrete decisions out of that self-understanding.[24] He was given to see that the whole of *the way life is* is full of grace and ultimately worthy of a life of thanksgiving and radical faith—the hallmarks of his new tradition. When we are given to look through Jesus, we praise and trust the One I call *God*. Through the miracle of the transparent event of Jesus the Christ we see and give thanks for the way our existence is, and we trust it as gracious.

CHAPTER 17 NOTES

[1] Lyrics by colleagues of the Order: Ecumenical, 1972.
[2] Ken Wilber, *Sex, Ecology, Spirituality*, Notes, p. 705.
[3] *Op. cit.*, p. 92.
[4] *Op. cit.*, p. 186. He uses the word *centaur(ic)* (half human/half horse) or the phrase *vision-logic* to point to the same reality as the *existential*.
[5] *Ibid.*, p. 187.
[6] *New York Times* (Internet Book Review, Dec. 20, 1998), *How the Dead Live: Stories*, Alvin Greenberg (St. Paul: Graywolf Press, 1998).
[7] *A Brief History of Everything*, pp. 194-96.
[8] *Sex, Ecology, Spirituality*, p. 264.
[9] John Cock, *Called To Be*, "The Mystery of a Child," p. 217.

[10] Through his "four quadrant" model or his articulation of "I/We/It," Wilber has one mega-context—and new paradigm—for understanding reality. It is revolutionary in scope. Read his *The Marriage of Sense and Soul* to appreciate its significance in a condensed form.

[11] Matthew Fox and Rupert Sheldrake, *Natural Grace* (New York: Doubleday, 1997). I like Fox's image of the ultimate recycling project: "In some way *we* get recycled, it seems to me, into the pool of being," p. 156 (emphasis added).

[12] My colleagues Jon and Maureen Jenkins have pulled these Order: Ecumenical research methods and constructs together into the book *The Other World . . . In The Midst of Our World* (Brussels: ICA, 1985; Gröningen, NL: Imaginal Training, 1997).

[13] Ken Wilber, "Always Already: The Brilliant Clarity of Ever-Present Awareness," *The Eye of Spirit: An Integral Vision for a World Gone Slightly Mad* (Boston: Shambhala, 1998).

[14] Joseph Mathews made his speech in Chicago at the beginning of the Research Assembly Lecture Series, July 3, 1972, on "The Recovery of the Other World."

[15] Mathews goes on to quote Tillich here to further make his point: "Tillich is a good example. Those of you who know his *Systematic Theology* know that he begins with the ontological situation and then moves to the interpretation of Christ, which is the existential for Tillich. Tillich himself made the case that when you talk about the essence of a person being the kind of essence that creates its own essence, the first use of the word 'essence' in that sentence is dealing with the ontological. . . . [O]ne could not even make the decision that determines his selfhood if he did not already have a montage in his being through which he looked at reality."

[16] Mathews says transparency and universality, in the sense of relation to all, are inseparable.

[17] Mathews said in a speech in the summer of 1973 that "the Other World is the world of transparency."

[18] Wilber's hyphenated phrase.

[19] "At one with Being" is *union* in Tillich's language, but is it what Wilber means by ***union***? When he says "a great liberation, rebirth, metanoia, or enlightenment on the soul fortunate enough to be immersed in that extraordinary union, a union that is the ground, the goal, the source, and the salvation of the entire world" [*The Marriage of Sense and Soul: Integrating Science and Religion* (New York: Random House, 1998), p. 168], is he saying the same as Tillich? We know that Wilber's spiritual practices are mystical and anticipate "direct union" with the ground of being. Tillich's articulation of union with the ground of being emphasizes one's decisional response to

the event of grace—union presupposes faith. In reality, when the transparent event happens, Spirit shows itself (is seen/experienced) in the world of existence.

[20] *The Marriage of Sense and Soul*, p. 196.

[21] *The Eye of Spirit*, pp. 281-96. I agree with Wilber's quotes. I struggle to go all the way with his "ever-present Seer" or "I am the Eye of Spirit." This is too mystical for me at this time. I understand "I am consciousness" in a different way than he does. We share the same paradigm of Spirit presence but not the same mode/experience of appropriation of Spirit.

[22] William J. Abraham, "United Methodists at the End of the Mainline" (Internet: *First Things* 84, June/July 1998: 28). Dr. Abraham is the Albert C. Outler Professor of Wesley Studies at Perkins School of Theology of Southern Methodist University.

[23] H. R. Niebuhr, "The Responsibility of the Church for Society," *The Gospel, the Church and the World*, ed. Kenneth Scott Latourette (New York: Harper & Brothers, 1946).

[24] The 1972 speech.

18. Exterior Signs of the Event: *Transestablished Style*
—Part Three

Many people in Jesus' religious world were considered sinners by profession (prostitutes, shepherds, toll gatherers). They could not do restitution since they could never find all those they had sinned against, and anyway, there was seldom a way to pay back. So Jesus just declares the playing field level for everyone. He does not wait for sinners to repent, become respectable and do works of restoration. Everything is reversed: You are forgiven; now you can repent! God loves you; now you can lift your eyes to God! The enmity is over. You were enemies and yet God accepts you! There is nothing you must do to earn this. You need only accept it.
—Walter Wink, "Excuse Me"[1]

Both through his words and deeds Jesus lived the transestablished life, a life of radical faith in *God's* grace and love, to the point that Jesus is transparent to that grace and love—when you image Jesus, you image the grace and love of *God*. Wink gives us a practical and external example of Jesus' style that has revolutionized the world. I cannot think of a greater historical paradigm shift than "You and all others are already forgiven. There is nothing you must do to earn this. Only accept it." Jesus was the very embodiment of this Word about life. He is the foundation of what I mean by transestablished style.

When I talked about transrational spirituality in the last chapter, I emphasized the self-understanding of Spirit at the heart of life (Part Two), occasioned and made clear by the transparent event of grace (Part One). Out of this self-understanding comes the indicative, transestablished style (Part Three). If I were a football coach, I would call it the "3-T christology": transparent, transrational, transestablished. Again, I wish to load up somewhat empty words with meaning rather than try to communicate through loaded words.

The Big Context

As I referred to Ken Wilber's big context for Spirit in Part Two, I wish to use Fr. Thomas Berry's big context for describing the Neighbor in this chapter. Thomas Berry, influenced by Teilhard de Chardin, gives us in *Befriending the Earth: A Theology of Reconciliation Between Humans and the Earth* a good overview of his prophecy [numbers in parentheses denote the page numbers of the above book; numbers in brackets denote the page numbers of the book *Thomas Berry and the New Cosmology*; my comments are woven in between]. Berry has become one of the leading prophets of the universe community, by which he means the one primary sacred community (16)[2] the communion of all things (16) to which everything belongs and is elected (17), not just humans—in other words, God's chosen universe, not just God's chosen people. There is no separate human community (43), and therefore human history is but a small part of earth history (5), which is a small part of universe history, which is a small part of the history of God,[3] as a theologian might say. As Mathews says, "you emerged from the universe, creation, humanity (not family, race, nation, etc.) and [therefore] you belong to the all."[4] In this context, these lines from Max Ehrmann's poem *Desiderata* (1927) make sense, "You are a child of the universe no less than the trees and the stars; you have the right to be here."

What would this universe understanding do to our politics? We would move from democracy to biocracy (42), shifting from human rights to creational rights (60). All life forms must be represented in our parliaments, congresses, and constitutions, if any of us is going to survive (42). What would this understanding do to our economics? Human technologies would be replenishing earth technologies rather than destroying them, for if nature goes into deficit we all do [6].[5] We cannot begin to imagine the cost of purifying the waters and the atmosphere. "Pay later" is a sinful economy in the context of sustaining the life of the universe.

God is not going to save the planet if we decide to destroy it (46), unless one believes with the man I was talking with recently who reads in his Bible that God will never allow the earth to pass away. Most of us act that way. Why is it none of the major religions has shown any effective responsibility for the fate of the earth (9)? If Christianity is to survive, it must bring about a reinterpretation of all its teaching within the context of the universe (74). But we are still overly concerned with personal salvation (75), and Christian personal salvation at that.

Berry believes our western Christianity has not done well dealing with suicide, the homicide in our streets and homes, not to mention the genocide of 6,000,000 Jews—and virtually whole ethnic groups and regional populations in the last decades. How in God's name will we deal with biocide (the murder of nature) and geocide (the murder of the earth) if they are not even in our screen [12] or in our prayers? Christianity goes ballistic over right doctrine and right sex, excommunicating, defrocking, and splitting off. Who will excommunicate and defrock those who murder the earth? Certainly not church councils, bishops, or the Pope. Our morality is sinful.

The personal self is precious for sure, but no more so than the family self, the earth self, the universe self (135). We in the West have to re-brainwash the multi-self to the big reality if we want the earth to last for our progeny. We humans are the beings in whom the universe reflects on itself (14). We are the ones therefore who are the self-conscious stewards of all. This is the uniquely human role, to vision and implement the care systems for the universe, and especially the earth—even if that is a bit reduced. And what is the big answer for Berry? Sacrifice, *on behalf of,* makes the universe of 15 billion years possible (134). People are effective to the extent to which they enter the sacrificial mode (135) of the universe. The whole cosmos is in the salvation process (56).

Thomas Berry is talking about loving the Neighbor with a capital "N," as H. R. Niebuhr might say. Who is my Neighbor? The universe, earth, and humanity (all those who ever were, the soon-to-be 6 billion present inhabitants, and all those who will ever be). What does it mean to love the Neighbor? To sacrificially live on their behalf. Is this the same as loving God? No. The Mysterious Other meets us in the midst

of all this, but is not all this. Jesus said one cannot love God and hate
and kill the Neighbor. The first and second commandments are our big
context for transestablished style.

Establishment, Dis-establishment, and Trans-establishment

In the Order: Ecumenical we tried to get hold of the dynamics
of change by talking about the opposing forces of the establishment and
the dis-establishment, and how the trans-establishment deeply honors
both and enables their transformation and reconciliation with each other.

Who is the pro-establishment or *establishment*? At all levels
they are the bankers, lawyers, elected representatives, bishops, business
leaders—the leadership of civilization. They are good men and women
in that they preserve the structures of civilization. There would be no
society without the establishment, who establish law and order and
maintain the status quo. They are pillars of civilization.

The *dis-establishment* at its best is the prophetic dynamic in
society. They are the ones that call the establishment into question, i.e.,
protesters, Green Peace, Sierra Club, unions. They are that creative
dynamic that never lets the establishment rest easy in its power. They
are eternally calling for change, demanding that those who have been
left out be let in.

The *trans-establishment* is both and neither. It's as though
they have their periscopes up, seeing above the heads of the rest. They
are "in but not of" the establishment and dis-establishment. They see
the gifts and the perversions of both. They are out to catalyze authentic
transformation of both to allow authentic reconciliation to happen
between both. As Paul writes, "a new order has begun. All this has
been the work of God. He has reconciled us to himself through Christ,
and has enlisted us in this ministry of reconciliation" (2 Cor: 5:17-18).

For example, in the church some will say any call for reform is
too radical and will dismiss it out of hand. Others will say the reform
suggested is not radical enough, just shuffling chairs on the Titanic.
This latter group might list the following astute contradiction titles and
then diminish their insights with unrealistic demands.

•*Unimaginative and selfish leadership*. They would demand that a Lee

Iacocca type work a 120-hour week for room and board.

•*Worldly bureaucracy*. They would demand dismantling it.

•*Puny ecumenical thrust*. They would demand that the churches move beyond their Christian Gospel hang-up and become a part of a pan-religious organization, with new creeds and liturgies.

•*Undisciplined membership*. They would demand discipline equivalent to the "desert fathers."

•*Un-Christian mission*. They would demand that the churches sell all their assets and give the money to the poor.[6]

Ordinarily, people who think this way are dis-establishment. They bulldoze our consciousness and what is established, as did many prophets in the Old Testament.

On the other side is the establishment or pro-establishment. They have held the denominations and churches together, in spite of all odds, for 2000 years. They have sustained tens of thousands of churches and approaching two billion members (Roman Catholics claim one billion) and the tradition on which they stand.

Yet, within that awesome tradition, the churches would have surely stagnated without the reformers, or the trans-establishment. The Protestant Calvin and the Roman Catholic Pope John XXIII are this type. They have authentically intended to re-form and trans-form the existing church, not raze it. The trans-establishment reformer thanks God for what is, as a part of the good creation, and blesses it with his prayerful and sacrificial action. The church is transformed—at least for a time—not destroyed.

Exemplars of the Transestablished Style

Where does this style come from? It comes from Jesus, among others. Where did his radical freedom come from? From his radical faith in his Father's grace and love. What was he free from? Jesus was free from always having to do his own will. He was free from conforming to the norms of this world, the values of this world, the rules of this world, the claims of his family, the rules of his religion. He was free from the need for status, from having to be somebody. It's scary to be that free. He was not bound to anyone, anything, any institution. He was in bondage to nothing, slave to none and servant of all. He was free to be open to all, to show compassion for all neighbors. He demonstrated that the freer one is, the more obligated. This is radical freedom, the kind that changes what it touches. No one could tell him what to do or say or think. We would probably say with the political and religious leaders of his time, "He is too free. Either he buckles under or else." Jesus was put to death for being his *God*-given freedom.

The point is, everyone has this *God*-given freedom. We are as free as Jesus came to show us we are, if we but choose our freedom. If we but choose. The consequences of this freedom are frightening: deciding for oneself in each and every situation what to do, after observing, judging, and weighing up what needs to be done. Always asking what is the necessary deed, always asking what is the will of *God*, and if not receiving a sure revelation of the will of God, deciding for oneself and doing it. Then rendering up the decision and deed and moving on to the next one, thanking *God* for the mercy to live life in such awesome freedom. This is best illustrated in the scriptures when Jesus said, "You cannot take my life from me, but I can give it."

He walked freely out over the "anxious, uncertain, ambiguous waters of life" and beckons us to step out on the waves of life with him. Now, what would that look like, to walk on water? To fulfill the prophecy of Jesus and do the great things he was doing? Where do we glimpse such freedom taking place right before our eyes? And what would it look like for us to be part of that freedom as caring members of the universe? The Christian tradition is all about catalyzing freedom, the transestablished freedom of Jesus.

As I watched on television the 1999 service celebrating the anniversary of Martin Luther King, Jr.—his would-have-been 70th birthday—from Ebenezer Baptist Church in Atlanta, a great confluence of transestablished style was swirling in my consciousness. We watched as John Hume—who had already won the 1998 Nobel Peace Prize jointly with David Trimble, the two key architects of peace in Northern Ireland— accepted the MLK Peace Prize, saying the example set by the slain civil rights leader laid the groundwork for peace in Northern Ireland. "Fate decreed that I would not only be inspired by Dr. King but would find myself facing a challenge like Dr. King faced."[7] Following was a sermon by South Africa's Archbishop Desmond Tutu, who was a past recipient of the MLK Peace Prize. He talked of the influence of MLK on his life as we remembered all that Tutu has done to bring reconciliation in South Africa, most lately accepting the assignment from Nelson Mandela to lead in the Truth and Reconciliation Commission. He said, "There is no future without forgiveness."[8] (Besides Hume and Trimble, MLK, Tutu, and Mandela received the Nobel Peace Prize. Others of note in this transestablished tradition who received the Peace Prize are Albert Schweitzer, Dag Hammarskjöld, Mother Teresa, Elie Wiesel, and the Dalai Lama.)

This swirl brought to mind Mahatma Gandhi (who unbelievably has been overlooked for the Nobel Peace Prize), who influenced MLK. So there I sat, seeing the visible evidence of the transestablished style of Gandhi, MLK, Tutu/Mandela, Hume/Trimble, all of whom have done nothing more in my lifetime than free India/UK, free the USA, free South Africa, and free Ireland/UK. That's all. Although there have also been tens of millions killed in wars during my lifetime, I do have hope because of what these few have done for the many.

Just recall those transestablished scenes of the past half-century. Gandhi repeatedly put his frail body on the line and brought the British Empire to its knees. Dietrich Bonhoeffer was hanged in a concentration camp by the Nazis because he tried to assassinate Hitler—just a Lutheran pastor who decided Hitler's death was the will of God. Martin Luther King, Jr., gave himself freely to change the law of the land to guarantee freedom in the land of the free. Mother Teresa stalked the earth setting up structures to care for the dying on the streets, whether in Calcutta or the USA. These dared to act out the freedom of Jesus. They are the transestablished, if not saints.

Anyone who embodies the freedom of Jesus revolutionizes time and space and relationships. Rosa Parks did it by not going to the back of the bus in Montgomery. A simple deed. A courageous deed. As it turned out, a revolutionary deed. Who is qualified for such a deed? Just from the examples given, Black, White, Brown, Tan; Asian, African, Middle-Eastern, European, American; educated and uneducated; rich and poor; male and female; conservative and liberal; young and old; Christian and non-Christian. Anybody can embody the freedom of Jesus and change the situation around them, that is, if the person is up to the threat of death or willing to take the consequences for doing what he or she thinks is the will of *God*. Freedom is scary but real. Freedom is given to all *God's* children to choose to embody.

Some Marks of the Transestablished Style

Reflecting on the list of exemplars above, what are the marks of the transestablished style? Notice, we are going from empirical, fleshly demonstrations of such style to reflective qualities—from the bottom up.

Commandeered by the All. Called, vocated, assigned: these are the words that describe the entry into the transestablished style, usually through some triggering event.

Radical self-understanding. The transestablished one only bows before the *God* above all gods. He or she loves the universe the way it is given, its past, present, and future. Not obedient to the gods of this world, he or she is free to care for all.

Radical faith. Obsessive faith in the One flows in service to the universal Neighbor. The faith of the transestablished one signifies a change from faith in this world to faith in the One of all goodness and grace in the midst of this world.

Gives up certainty. The transestablished one gives up certainty. For example, one gives up his or her "Christian bigotry"[9]—or any religious bigotry[10]—to live on behalf of the pluriform world. There is the promise of full life but no certainty of it, as well as no security, and usually no reward or applause until after death, if at all.

Decisive in Spirit. As Kierkegaard indicates, the person of Spirit is hardly wishy-washy, but lives willing only one thing. Mathews says, "to be absolutely free is to be absolutely committed"—free for the universal Neighbor. Faith and freedom are not accomplishments but decisive responses to what is given.

Does the Free Deed. The transestablished style is that of

observe, judge, weigh up, decide, and act—out of Berry's universal context and Jesus' freedom. Finally, one renders the deed up to history, never knowing for sure if it is the true or right deed.

Turns matter into spirit. Relentlessly the transestablished one sees that nothing is hopeless, that every situation and every piece of creation is full of possibility. What is given is what is good, with all the mysteriousness of that fact.

Ready at a moment's notice. The transestablished one represents the detached style of simple living that leaves one ready to move out to do anything, anywhere, when called, without the obsessive attachment to worldly goods and relationships that tie one down. Mother Teresa only had two outfits and a Bible.

Reconciles the establishment and the dis-establishment. Forgives, honors, begs the pardon of, pays restitution to, repents on behalf of, and bows to the ever-present Spirit in every situation, out of the understanding that there is no victory unless all win.

Directed at the underlying contradiction. The transestablished one has decided to give his or her primary energy to that which holds the most enslaved. That contradiction in our time is the disparity between those who have and those who have not. A glaring example: the combined wealth of the world's richest 225 people = $1 trillion; combined annual income of the world's poorest 2.5 billion people = $1 trillion.[11] What would Jesus do?

Cruciformity. As Berry says, we are effective to the extent to which we enter the sacrificial mode of the universe. Cruciformity is that decisional human style, knowing that the truth about life is not to save up life but to give life; and "not renunciation but expenditure."[12]

Sign of the Kingdom. The transestablished one lives the will of the commissioning One to the extent that he or she seems guided by the One and appears transparent to the One, thus manifesting the Kingdom on Earth. (Only sometimes the world sees this reality and gives peace prizes to acknowledge it.)

Creates the New Decalogue. The transestablished one catalyzes
the new order that sometimes eventuates in new laws of humanness,
sometimes manifest in new laws of the land, as in N. Ireland-UK, South
Africa, India, and the USA.

Dietrich Bonhoeffer in his *Ethics* gives us his radical self-
understanding that led him to embody the transestablished style:

> The master and the servant, while preserving the relationships
> of obedience, can and should answer for each other in free
> responsibility.
> The ultimate reason for this lies in that relation of men to
> God which is realized in Jesus Christ. Jesus stands before God
> as the one who is both obedient and free. As the obedient one
> He does His Father's will in blind compliance with the law
> which is commanded Him, and as the free one He acquiesces
> in God's will out of His own most personal knowledge, with
> open eyes and a joyous heart; he recreates this will, as it were,
> out of Himself.
> Obedience without freedom is slavery; freedom without obe-
> dience is arbitrary self-will. Obedience restrains freedom; and
> freedom ennobles obedience. Obedience binds the creature to
> the Creator, and freedom enables the creature to stand before
> the Creator as one who is made in His image. Obedience shows
> man that he must allow himself to be told what is good and
> what God requires of him (Micah 6:8); and liberty enables
> him to do good himself. Obedience knows what is good and
> does it, and freedom dares to act, and abandons to God the
> judgement of good and evil. Obedience follows blindly and
> freedom has open eyes. Obedience acts without questioning
> and freedom asks what is the purpose. Obedience has its hands
> tied and freedom is creative. In obedience man adheres to the
> decalogue and in freedom man creates new decalogues (Luther).
> . . . [The responsible person] finds justification neither in his
> obligation nor in his freedom but solely in Him who has put
> him in this (humanly impossible) situation and who requires
> this deed of him. The responsible man delivers up himself
> and his deed to God.[13]

The transestablished one is a changed person who changes history. Whether in Rosa Parks or Mahatma Gandhi, the transestablished style is that without which life is not changed for the good of all. This is a radical morality, far beyond the concern of one's personal salvation. My salvation is commingled with universal salvation.

Summary

Transestablished style is the external sign of the internal qualities of transrational grace; both are triggered by *God's* transparent event through Jesus the Christ—or we can talk about a 1st and 2nd conversion. All begins when we are given to see transparently the heart of Spirit, that the Other World is only in This World, and that it is full of grace and glory. This world eternally goes transparent to the graciousness of *God*. And those who operate out of this radical self-understanding— the universal worldview and Jesus' freedom—are the transestablished ones, even the ones who become transparent to the same graciousness as Jesus—Luther even been called *little Christs*.

CHAPTER 18 NOTES

[1] Walter Wink, "Excuse Me" (*Christian Century,* October 20, 1998); the author of *When the Powers Fall: Reconciliation in the Healing of the Nations* (Fortress), from which this article is adapted.
[2] Thomas Berry with Thomas Clarke, *Befriending the Earth: A Theology of Reconciliation Between Humans and the Earth*, ed. Stephen Dunn and Anne Lonergan (1991; Mystic, Conn.: Twenty-Third Publications, 1992), page numbers within parentheses.
[3] Karen Armstrong, *A History of God* (New York: HarperCollins, 1994).
[4] Joseph Mathews, "The Happening of Transparency," speech given at the 1973 Summer Council of the Order: Ecumenical in Chicago.
[5] *Thomas Berry and the New Cosmology*, ed. Anne Lonergan and Caroline Richards (1987; Mystic, Conn.: Twenty-Third Publications, 1991), page numbers within brackets. (On April 17, 1999, we were present as Fr. Thomas Berry inaugurated Nelson and Elaine Stover's "Universe Story Walk," a half-mile narrated pathway through the woods adjoining their house in Greensboro, North Carolina—a narration that commemorates key evolutionary points along the journey of the past fifteen billion years.)

[6] John Cock, *Called To Be*, pp. 163.

[7] In 1993, amid considerable controversy and hostility, especially from unionists, John Hume declared he did not care "two balls of roasted snow" about all the criticism he faced. This is the stuff of the transestablished style.

[8] Nobel Peace Prize Laureates Conference, University of Virginia, November 6, 1998, C-SPAN2.

[9] One of Mathews' oft spoken phrases.

[10] Nobel Prize laureate Soyinka said, "I believe that there is no greater force [than religion] that exists today for tearing apart humanity." Speech on Founders' Day Convocation at Wake Forest University, February 3, 1999 (*Winston Salem Journal*, p. B 1).

[11] "Matters of Scale: Spending Priorities," *World Watch Magazine* (Jan/ Feb 1999).

[12] Mathews, Summer 1973 speech. He went on to say, "no mortifying the flesh. It is investment of flesh and the creating of other flesh." John Epps e-mailed me recently: "the point is not to save and actualise my potential, but to expend it fully—getting nailed" for something worth my life.

[13] Dietrich Bonhoeffer, "Freedom," *Ethics* (1955; New York: Macmillan, 1965), pp. 252-53 (emphases added).

Section Five:

Christ Image
Re-creation

19. Christ Image Re-creation

This, my comrades, is our new Asceticism, our Spiritual Exercises!

God cries to my heart: 'Save me!'

God cries to men, to animals, to plants, to matter: 'Save me!'

Listen to your heart and follow him. . . .

Love matter. God clings to it tooth and nail, and fights. Fight with him.

Die every day. Be born every day. Deny everything you have every day. The superior virtue is not to be free but to fight for freedom.

Do not condescend to ask: 'Shall we conquer? Shall we be conquered?' Fight on!

So may the enterprise of the Universe, for an ephemeral moment, for as long as you are alive, become your own enterprise. This, Comrades, is our new Decalogue.

—Nikos Kazantzakis, ***The Saviors of God***[1]

Some would have us think that if we start tinkering with our *Christ image* (my word for *christology* from here on), we are heretical. Re-creating one's Christ image has been going on in the Christian tradition throughout its history, beginning with Paul and the gospel writers. Each was grasped by the oral witness about Jesus the Christ and was compelled to pull it through his own interpretation of reality. That's why not one of the christologies of the New Testament writers is the same. Ever since, Christians have been interpreting *Jesus the Christ*—therefore reinterpreting—the symbol system of the tradition. Has the symbol system changed consequently? Of course. Has christology changed? Of course. Is there such a thing as orthodoxy? Not really. There are many who would claim there is and that they are its spokespersons, i.e., some Roman Catholics, fundamentalists, and scholars of many stripes.

But what we all know is that there is not special knowledge given to some. In this sense we are all *agnostic*: having no special knowledge of truth or of the divine. We are all human with finite knowledge, building symbol systems as best we can over the aeons— out over the abyss as Kazantzakis would say. I inherit my symbol system (or fundamental presuppositions, if you prefer) and do one of my deepest human activities: I make the symbol system my own, modifying it accordingly. What is crucial in this process is that my symbol system makes sense to me. If not, it has no power and becomes a millstone around my neck.

I have no problem admitting that I do not share the christology of Matthew, Mark, Luke, the Gnostics, of those at the Councils of Nicaea and Chalcedon, the Roman Catholics, the Greek Orthodox, the Calvinists, the traditionalists, the liberals, the conservatives, the fundamentalists, the mystics—and many others. My christology is unique and so is yours. It is the most crucial part of our symbol system, especially if we have been a Christian, or are still a Christian. If our christology is defunct, so is our Christian symbol system. We have choices: either get it together or declare for the symbol system we are really operating out of; or we could research another symbol system. That's fine, but we must live whatever symbol system we choose, with integrity. Either re-create our christology or self-consciously choose another symbol system.

I get tired of those who would lead us to believe that the fundamentalists or the Roman Catholics, for example, reign over orthodox christology, and everyone outside their sway is heretical. Not so. *God* only knows who is right—none, finally. To ask which christology is right is the wrong question. To ask which empowers is the right question. Does my christology empower me? If not, why not? Do I want to give it all up, or do I want to be empowered by it anew? These are the questions of those who are searching to make sense of Jesus the Christ.

Do we want to decouple from the Christian symbol system or to radicalize for ourselves that symbol system which has gone on for 2000 years? It's a matter of interpretation and reinterpretation, as Bultmann helped us clearly see. He picked out a non-Christian philosopher's methodology to help freight and authenticate his own christology. Heidegger's method of existentialism made sense to Bultmann. Not the content, but the method. Bultmann added Heidegger's wheels under his own engine of christology. The result has had great effect for our century of Christians.

Likewise, I can decide to take the method of, say, Ken Wilber, a Buddhist transpersonalist, to help freight my christology. We can choose any guide or method we like. That is why I laid out ten christologies, plus my own, as possible help for our christologies. Not just any christology, but one that makes sense, that I can live out of with integrity. Those other ten do make sense to me. Yet we cannot jump totally into any of their Christ images. Each developed his own christology to walk around in. So must we. That's the way it always has been. What a plethora of christologies in the 2000 years of Christianity. Better to pick a few as models and let them guide our own. After a time we will discover that our christology is ours, and at some point we will understand that we are operating in the confluence of the great Christian tradition. In any case, we will not be heretical. We will be able to stand before the church—either literally or in our heart—and say with integrity, "I really do believe Jesus is the Christ."

None of us has any place to start except within our own tradition. But it's not ours until we make it ours. We can hardly invent a new Christ image at this point in the tradition. It would hardly be new, if we do comprehensive research. But we can authenticate our own tradition: we can radicalize our Christ image and make it our own by re-creating it, always asking the question, Is it transparent to ultimate reality as we know it?

And if we don't? All human beings have some kind of a symbol system, be it self-conscious or not. Is it delivering? Does it make sense out of our life experience? Does it empower our living, filling us with meaning and purpose, reuniting us with the mystery, depth, and greatness of our existence?

A bigger question still, Will my new Christ image assist the universe in this epoch of history? If it's needed for that reason, and we all know it is, what better reason than that? Much better for the universal than for our own personal deliverance.

> *So may the enterprise of the Universe, for an ephemeral moment, for as long as you are alive, become your own enterprise. This . . . is our new Decalogue.*

During this section of the book we will participate in exercises that will hopefully prepare us to articulate our credos. *Exercise 1* will put us in touch with our interior councils that guide our lives. *Exercise 2* will put us in touch with those followers of Jesus who have been our primary exemplars. In *Exercise 3*, we will list those life events and decisions that have sustained the pattern of who we are. In *Exercise 4*, we will do a review of christologies or Christ images of the eleven theologians studied in Sections Two through Four, in preparation for writing our own credos in *Exercise 5*.

There will be no right answers in these exercises, only what is our authentic answer at this time, what makes sense to our life experience as we consider our journey in dialogue with some of the thinking of the tradition of those who have seen Jesus as the Christ. We will become interpreters of all this in order to articulate what is the axial symbol of our life, what for us is at the heart of our self-understanding. We are on a uniquely human adventure.

CHAPTER 19 NOTE

[1] Nikos Kazantzakis, *The Saviors of God: Spiritual Exercises*, tr. Kimon Friar (New York: Simon & Schuster, 1960), p. 118.

20. Who is Religious and/or Christian?

Kierkegaard talks about the *Religious A* person as one who grasps a relationship with God inwardly, but fails because he or she cannot finally achieve an absolute relationship with the Absolute—there is an infinite qualitative difference. The *Religious B* person, aware of deep sin and disrelation between God and himself or herself, comes into relationship through faith, both a gift of God and an act of will. What Kierkegaard means by what he says here is volumes full. I wish to amplify the meaning of the "religious person," but not directly in dialogue with Kierkegaard's definitions.

My **Religious A person** is one who follows the Christian tradition: baptism, training, worship, prayer, confirmation and belief, faith and commitment, love and mission. This person strives to be Christ-centered. Where all this often fails is in the misunderstanding that one comes into and stays in relationship with *God* through one's striving, for one cannot *achieve* and *sustain* a right relationship with God.

My **Religious B person**, first of all, is one who acts out of the consciousness that life is a gift. Though the situation be inhumane or unfair, one can freely take a creative relationship to it as given. Because possibility is always present, free choice is always present. This person knows there is freedom only because there is possibility, and only this because of grace, though he or she may not use those words. This person comes to spiritual practices and community out of gratitude and the will to rehearse the truth about life that is rooted in the gracious gift of possibility.

Second, this B person loves and suffers over and with creation. If his son suffers, he suffers. If the poor suffer, he suffers. If the ill suffer, he suffers. If water suffers from pollution, he suffers. This person is a suffering servant, out of compassion. On the other hand, if any part of creation is filled with joy, so is she. If her daughter is filled with joy, so is she. If her roses are in bloom, so is she. She rejoices with the lilies of the field, cherishing creation.

My Religious A person in caricature is a "Christian" who attends church regularly, teaches Sunday school, is on the board, on a committee, gives generously to the budget, does a daily devotional reading, visits the sick, goes to funerals, attends church conferences, takes the preacher out to dinner, does not take *God's* name in vain, struggles some with miracles, virgin birth, and bodily resurrection, and has picked out a hymn and a verse or two for his or her own funeral.

My Religious B person in caricature is *not* a "Chrisitian" and does not go to church, Sunday school, or work with a church group. B person is not religious in a formal sense and may even profess to be agnostic. "B" chooses the style of compassion out of grace; chooses to rise above the human separation caused by ideology, race, and class; sees life as a gift and his or her life as an instrument; sacrifices for others and all life on the planet; bands together with a community of those who care and who support each other in mission. In essence, "B" believes that life is sacred and only worthy of a reverent response. In such ways he or she is secular-religious.

The A or B Religious person would equally agree that the likes of Bonhoeffer and Gandhi lived exemplary lives. Both men loved life and held it to be a sacred gift; both operated out of grace, possibility, freedom, and compassion; both became prisoners fighting the oppressors of large segments of humanity, ultimately sacrificing their lives tackling the slaughtering Nazi regime and the suppressive British Empire at that time. One was a devout Christian minister—though controversial; the other was not formally religious, though a devoutly religious person by universal consensus. Both men were exemplary in spirit and mission. Their common mission was to deal with the "poor in spirit," whether rich or poor, Jew or Gentile, friend or jailer.

Were these two men "Christian"? Some would say only Bonhoeffer was, yet others would say he was not because of his attempt on Hitler's life and his later thinking and writings. Almost all would agree with Gandhi when he said he was *not* a Christian, although he had the greatest respect for Jesus and The Sermon on the Mount.

However, the *real* religious question is, "Were the two men consecrated to *God* on behalf of creation?" "Of course" is the unanimous opinion. It would therefore seem to me that to be a consecrated person one does the universally free and loving deed, regardless of creed or no creed. Finally, we are not talking about whether or not Bonhoeffer or Gandhi were Christian, but whether they did the consecrated deed.

Many are "Christian." Few are consecrated.

Reflection

True or False:

1. Jesus was a Christian.
2. Abraham was a Christian.
3. Kierkegaard was a Christian.
4. Gandhi was a Christian.
5. Bonhoeffer was a Christian.
6. I am a Christian.
7. I am Religious A.
8. I am Religious B.
9. I am consecrated.

Exercise 1: My Meditative Council[1]

Each of us has an interior council who guides us, to whom we listen. This is part of what it means to be human. Let us try to make this council more self-concious in this exercise.

1. Who are my 10 council members, dead or alive, who guide me, to whom I listen most? A non-human can be on my council. (These members can have postive or negative influence on me.)

2. I draw a rectangular table (next page) and pencil in the ten around it in this order: four on each side, one at the head and one at the foot.

How many are alive? Who is number 1? Number 2? Who has been on

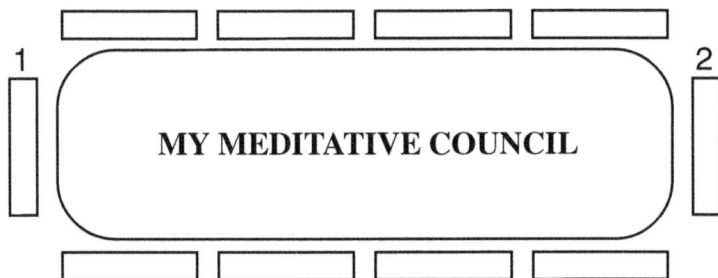

```
┌──────┐  ┌──────┐  ┌──────┐  ┌──────┐
└──────┘  └──────┘  └──────┘  └──────┘
┌──╭─────────────────────────────────╮──┐
1 │  │                                 │  │ 2
  │  │      MY MEDITATIVE COUNCIL      │  │
  │  │                                 │  │
└──╰─────────────────────────────────╯──┘
┌──────┐  ┌──────┐  ┌──────┐  ┌──────┐
└──────┘  └──────┘  └──────┘  └──────┘
```

my council the longest? Who is the newest member? Who is a surprise member? Whom would I like to kick off the council, maybe because that one is a negative influence on my life?

3. How many of them are Christian? "C's." How many are consecrated religious? "R's."

4. Who are the 4 that I listen to most? (Numbers 1-4 beside their names.)

5. What struggle in my life right now are they helping me to deal with? What are they saying to me, especially the four I listen to most? Where am I in making a decision?

6. What are they telling me might be/is my mission in life?

7. How does one put a new member on the council?

8. Is Jesus on my council?

CHAPTER 20 NOTE

[1] This method was devised by the Order: Ecumenical during the early 1970's. I use two questions from Nelson and Elaine Stover's "Here I Stand: A Nine-week Journey Toward Constructing a Theological Position Using a Facilitated Approach," 1998, which I helped to edit.

21. Companions of Jesus

> *Walk by him the man* [Jesus] *and thou comest to God. By him thou goest, to him thou goest. Look not for any way except himself by which to come to him. For if he had not vouchsafed to be the way we should all have gone astray. Therefore he became the way by which thou shouldest come.* **I do not say to thee, seek the way. The way itself is come to thee; arise and walk.** —St. Augustine[1]

How does one come to have faith in *God*, to trust *God*, to be loyal to *God's* cause above all else, to have the faith Jesus had in his Father—to have the faith of Jesus?

Most of my life has been a dialogue with the Christian tradition in my trying authentically to relate to Jesus. When the wife and boys and I joined the family order and worked around the world with Christians, Buddhists, Muslims, and Hindus, my image of Jesus was called into question by the pluralism of religions. I found out, however, that I could not enter the door to faith through the Buddha, Mohammed, or Krishna. I was raised a Christian. Back to Jesus.

I perchance picked up *Faith on Earth*,[2] a book of essays on faith by H. Richard Niebuhr, posthumously published in 1989. In it I found a persuasive articulation of faith in God through Jesus the Christ—good enough that it should be shared. In his chapter "The Reconstruction of Faith" (written about 1950), Niebuhr describes (I) the faith of Jesus in God and (II) the mediating dynamic of Jesus' faith for us. I will paraphrase Niebuhr's thought following these two points.

THE FAITH OF JESUS IN GOD

Jesus' cause was the rule of God, his faith was in the One who thrust him into existence, and his trust was in the Lord of Heaven and Earth, who cares for all and the whole of creation. Jesus' faith in God was personal: he could not be separated from the love of God, for God never forsook him; Jesus was the dearly beloved son, the heir of God. Jesus never counted equality with God, much less claimed to be God, but only trusted God as his Father. Because of his ultimate trust in God, and because of his loyalty to all God's creatures—especially the despised—the establishment profoundly distrusted him.

In a real sense, his radical faith in God and his love for what God loved brought him to his cruel death. Even at the edge of nothingness, however, his was still the cry of faith, "My God. . . ." He was not saved or delivered miraculously. He died as we all die; yet, he died faithfully, commending his spirit into the hands of his Father. He, the betrayed, denied, and forsaken one of faith, was given the name above every name in heaven and earth. He became the personification of faith, the man of complete faith.

THE MEDIATION OF JESUS' FAITH

Jesus' faith reconstructs the broken faith relation between humankind and God, especially of Christians as depicted in our tradition through the betrayal of Judas and the denial of Peter, the reconstructed one in faith upon whom the church was built. The reconstruction process begins as one is introduced to trust in Jesus by people who trusted him, and believed with him in God as Father (here Niebuhr uses "Ground of Being," one of his many phrases of designation for God). These people of trust in Jesus and consequent faith in God are called "companions" of Jesus in faith, and through them Jesus becomes our faith companion. (Segungo [Chapter 7], years later in his *Faith and Ideologies*, talks about Jesus the Christ's being revealed to us in personal and social lives, which he calls "anthropological faith," which precedes "religious faith.")

Sometimes that person who first introduced us to trust in Jesus as a companion in faith in God was a parent, a benefactor, a friend, who by his or her integrity of faith communicated the Christ of faith to us. (Gogarten [Chapter 8] in his *Christ the Crisis* says that it is possible for us to have the faith of Jesus in God. Sobrino [Chapter 7] in his *Christology at the Crossroads* says we are as free to believe in God as Jesus was; and because he demonstrated for us such radical faith, as his companions in faith we too become sons and daughters of God.) Jesus is reflected in the lives of those past and present who through their faith and devotion pray with him, "Abba, Father." Jesus is the focus of the companions of faith. He is the unseen head of the seen companions (company of believers).

Only through these companions and Jesus—a person and figure of historical fact because of their faith in him—are we finally compelled to faith in God. Jesus is not an idea, not superman, not a spirit, not the incarnation of the divine. He was a human who had seemingly superhuman faith in God. Such faith, however, is not a contradiction of the laws of personal existence, but is conceivable. Likewise, we do not doubt when those of his companions tell us of their trust in him and their consequent faith in God. Through the authenticity of the faith of his companions, his existence is manifest and he lives as though he never died, risen in their history through reconstructed faith. One experiences his risen life—even as he or she experiences the brokenness of his betrayed, denied, and forsaken life—and is enabled to appropriate his life and death and resurrection as his or her companion in faith. Such faith allows one to pray with Jesus, "Our Father, who art in heaven, hallowed be thy name." "I believe, help thou mine unbelief."

Jesus founded neither empire nor religious institution, formulated neither doctrine (i.e., trinity) nor formal rites of initiation (i.e., an altar call). He comes to us through the company of the faithful who have allowed us to believe through the authentic demonstration and communication of their faith in God, through Jesus the Christ. Jesus and his companions of faith are ours in order to mediate faith in God.

Reflection

To test Niebuhr, I have to reflect upon my life and answer, Who has brought me to the faith of Jesus? Which companions of Jesus have mediated his faith to me? Answer: many and precious few.

Many have nurtured me in the faith: parents, wife and sons, immediate family, extended family, Sunday school teachers, ministers, youth directors, school teachers and professors, lay people in many congregations, the Order: Ecumenical colleagues, writers such as the Psalmist, Kierkegaard, Niebuhr, Tillich, Bultmann, and Kazantzakis, lives of great people such as Mother Teresa and Gandhi, and saints such as John the Evangelist and Ignatius of Loyola. My life is full of their intimations of faith in *God* through their companionship with the Jesus of faith.

Yet, few have been the companions who have communicated and demonstrated the faith of Jesus so profoundly that I call them my *primary companions* or *mediators of faith*.

I was first awed as a teenager by the faith and prayerful style of Frank Laubach at a week-long retreat near Asheville, North Carolina. His faith was palpable. He was praying without ceasing, closing his eyes as he spoke, conversed, walked, ate, worked. His global mission of "each one teach one" demonstrated that he loved what *God* loved. His intimate relation with *God* through Jesus was compelling. His audacity to call each of us to a life of radical faith and vocation deeply marked me. Most of all, I have never forgotten his presence, his aura of faith. He truly believed. Through him I knew such faith was possible for me.

The second primary mediator of faith for me has been Joseph Wesley Mathews, the co-founder of the Ecumenical Institute and the Order: Ecumenical, the covenant group of faith for my wife, two sons, and me for over sixteen years. More than any other person I have ever known, he wrestled passionately with *God* and the radical faith of Jesus until they blessed him with a fulfilled life of adventurous service. He was of the style of Paul, Benedict, Luther, Ignatius of Loyola, Wesley: all or nothing for the cause of *God*; fanatically obedient to his vision of the will of *God*; a reformer of the company of faith; and a builder of *God's* society. His radical faith has scarred me for life. Because of my years with him, I can never forget that life is about only one thing: being faithful to *God* as I am confronted through the event, faith, and mission of Jesus the Christ.

Two other companions of faith have introduced and re-introduced me to the faith of Jesus: St. Paul and Dietrich Bonhoeffer. The witness of their words and lives has been a constant reflection of the faith of Jesus for me throughout my adult years. Paul's writings, especially *Romans*, have been a beacon, reminding me that life is faith through grace for obedience. Recently the saga of his life of radical faith, played by Sir Anthony Hopkins on film, had a significant impact. Bonhoeffer's writings, especially *The Cost of Discipleship* and *Ethics*, are as pure faith and freedom statements as come from the Jesus tradition. His life of faith, even death like unto that of Jesus, will always indicate that faith in *God* is possible in any situation. His life of faith is imprinted in my being.

So, the Niebuhr model for how we come to the radical faith of Jesus, through his companions in faith, bears out in my experience. Without these few and these many I would not be in touch with the reality of faith, would not know its awesome possibility for me, would not know about the radical *Yes* to life or how to pray "Abba" with Jesus. I humbly say *Yes* to being a part of Jesus' company of faith in *God*.

Exercise 2: Companions of Jesus

1. Using Niebuhr's model, I list at least 8 persons who have most nurtured me in faith. This is a different question than who is on my meditative council, though some of the persons will probably be the same.

2. In addition to persons in #1, I include 2 writers, 2 books, 2 fictional characters that have most nurtured me in the faith?

3. From this list of 14+, I decide who have been the 3-4 primary companions of Jesus for me. If I am not from the Christian tradition, then I list the 3-4 primary *mentors* in faith for me.

4. One has brought me to companionship with Jesus—or my mentor— more than any other? I double circle my *primary mentor*.

5. What are wise sayings of those who are my 3-4 primary companions of Jesus, or my primary mentor? (I write on the next page.)

   a.

   b.

   c.

   d.

6. Writing sentences for each of the 3-4 primary companions of Jesus, I state how he or she has influenced my faith journey.

   a.

   b.

   c.

   d.

7. I write a paragraph to explain how I have come to faith in *God*.

8. I write a paragraph on what I have learned about my faith journey from this exercise?

CHAPTER 21 NOTES

[1]This is the concluding paragraph in H. R. Niebuhr's *The Meaning of Revelation*.

[2] H. Richard Niebuhr, "The Reconstruction of Faith," *Faith on Earth: An Inquiry into the Structure of Human Faith*, ed. Richard R. Niebuhr (New Haven: Yale University, 1989), pp. 83-101.

22. Life Events

A Heartfelt Christmas!
December 1998

I have always struggled with the question Have you accepted Jesus into your heart? It seems simple to say, and makes a whole lot of sense besides, that when my heart is opened to truth, grace, or compassion—by great joy or great pain—then Christ has come into my heart. I think this is what we celebrate at Advent and Christmas, the coming of the Christ into our hearts: "where meek souls [or, better, 'open hearts'] receive him, still the dear Christ enters in,"as the carol goes.

*My heart has been opened so many times to truth, grace, or compassion by an awesome encounter. Whatever the event or revelation, my heart has been awakened, strangely warmed, or blowtorched by the mystery of **God's Word**—hundreds of times:*

- *delivering Christmas baskets to "Colored Hill" as a boy*
- *when I "fell in love" with Lynda*
- *holding a new baby, especially John, Jeremiah, Kaitlyn, and Nolan*
- *seeing the Blue Ridge Mountains after an absence*
- *hearing majestic music, i.e., **Bel Canto** at Christ Church*
- *seeing a great movie, i.e., **Gandhi***
- *reading a great book, i.e., **Grace and Grit** (Ken Wilber)*
- *attending the spirit-filled memorial service of a mentor, Lyn Mathews Edwards*
- *barely escaping a fatal accident in my red VW Bug*
- *when a village or ghetto I worked with picked up its life*
- *when JFK and MLK and RFK were assassinated*

- *when a loved one died, i.e., Pate, Mama Dotte, and Judie*
- *when the life of Billy and Debbie's son tragically ended*
- *learning that the wealth of 225 of the richest in the world = $1 trillion, and that the total annual income of 2.5 billion of the poorest in the world = $1 trillion*
- *reading that over 100 million have been killed in wars of the 20th century*
- *reuniting with tens of old colleagues through the wonder of an e-mail list serve*
- *writing my first book, **Called To Be***

*Yes, I have received Christ into my heart in big ways and small, when I was willing and when I wasn't, consciously and unconsciously, when I was a child and when I became a man. The event of Christ happens as it will: knocking at the door of my heart as benign revelation, crashing in, or gently blowing the door open with tender mercy. Whether I say "I accept Christ into my heart" or not is not all-important. What **is** all-important is that I know that every time my heart is opened, it is by the event of Christ. The meaning of the Incarnation is not **God's** coming into our realm, but **God's** coming into our hearts. That's what we celebrate at Christmas, the fact that the power of **God** has come to us, that the power of Christ has awakened us again, that the power of the Spirit will come into our hearts one way or another eternally.*

*The real **Yes** is acknowledging my open heart, bowing to that Power that opens it, and saying, "Welcome! Come in!"*

Reflect this Christmas on how your heart has been mysteriously opened. Make your list and give thanks. Then sing to yourself those four lines of the carol, beginning, "How silently, how silently," and ending "the dear Christ enters in."

A heartfelt Christmas to all!

John

Exercise 3: Life Events

The above letter contains a list of life events, some recent and some decades ago. In this exercise I am to make my own list and reflect upon it.

1. I write down, in a few words each, the 4-6 most impacting events in my life over the *past year*.

2. I divide my life-line into four phases. On the chart below I list 10-15 of the most impacting events of *my life* and list them under the

proper phase. Under the last phase I list two of the events from question #1 (past year).

3. I list 2 books, 2 movies and 2 global facts that have impacted my life.

I put one of each on my chart in #2 in the approximate phase.

4. I look at my list and determine intuitively whether more of my events are joyful or painful. Which was the most joyful? Most painful?

5. I circle the key 3 events on my "big list." I write a sentence about the significance of each event:

   a.

   b.

   c.

6. I place a star by 3 events that most "opened my heart."

7. I double circle 1 or 2 events that turned my life around. From what to what?

8. Above the chart, I poetically name the four segments and an overall name for my life.

9. Which of the "big list" events was a *Christ event* for me? How would I talk about that in a few sentences?

10. What have I learned from this exercise about *my* life?

11. What have I learned about *life* from this exercise?

12. How does a *Christ event* work or what are its dynamics?

23. Review: Fifty Considerations for Your Credo

When asking the question Who was Jesus? we must expect different answers because only part of the response can come from history. The other part comes from the heart of the person answering the question. The query is both historical and personal, so the answers will be as well.

—Harvey Cox[1]

Exercise 4: Review

As I review in order to prepare to write my own Christ-image or christology, I begin by reading these fifty considerations, pulled together from the eleven theologians, plus Wilber and Berry. I pencil a "+" beside considerations that make sense to me, a "?" beside the ones that make little sense to me, and no mark beside the rest.

Chapter 4: Ogden

1. Christology deals with our relationship to God, not our faith in Jesus.
2. Jesus re-presents God's Word, which is built into existence.
3. Jesus shows us God's love, calls us to receive God's love, and sends us to love that which God loves.
4. Everyone experiences God's love explicitly through Jesus the Christ or implicitly through the way existence is created.

Chapter 5: Bultmann

5. *Demythologizing* (his interpretive method) allows for authentic encounter with the Word, neutralizing the confusion of unbelievable mythology.

6. That mysterious power that drives us this way and that is the God of grace and love.

7. The "Christ event"—the Word as the event of God—brings a present crisis of decision for or against faith in God.

8. Confession of sin and forgiveness are integrally bound up with receiving the Word—the Christ event is not complete without our *Yes* of faith.

9. The *Yes decision* out of the encounter of the "Christ event" is requisite for authentic life.

Chapter 6: Niebuhr

10. God brings our faith in little gods to a dead-end, where sometimes the miracle of faith happens and our faith is transformed into radical faith in the one God.

11. We join Jesus in his radical faith in God; God joins us in his radical faithfulness toward Jesus.

12. Denied, betrayed, abandoned, Jesus demonstrated radical faith in God, not knowing for certain that God was powerful and good.

13. Jesus demonstrates that radical faith is possible for every conscious person.

Chapter 7: Sobrino and Segundo

14. The faith of Jesus is the crux of discipleship, where we find out who God is, who Jesus is, and who we are; therefore, the *history of Jesus' faith* is more important than other facts of his life history.

15. The journey of discipleship is where faith happens—not in illumination, experience, or rational insight, in the first place.

16. "First born" is a key to christology, suggesting Jesus' relationship with the Father—as son—and his relationship with us—as brother.

17. *Hermeneutics* (the method for interpreting the source of our faith) is done in the context of the change in our individual/social

understanding of reality; or interpretation is grounded in our faith.

Chapter 8: Gogarten

18. Jesus lived and died to abolish the illusion or *lie* that this world will give us our heart's desire; Jesus said we are enslaved to the reign of the world.
19. Jesus' event of faithful obedience saves us: transforms our "responsibility to the world" to our "responsibility to God" alone; Jesus frees us from the doom of the world.
20. Jesus calls us to re-express his faith in God and showed what it looks like to take responsibility *for* the world: freeing those under the reign of the *lie* to live under God's reign.
21. Jesus occasions our crisis of faith: with him we can decide to be responsible *to* God and *for* those doomed to the world, or not.

Chapter 9: Perrin

22. Historical knowledge of Jesus is not faith-knowledge of Jesus.
23. Our encounter with Jesus as the Christ is the eschatological act of God, the encounter that brings our old world of sin to an end and gives us a new world of grace.
24. One's christology is a product of experience, reflection, and decision.
25. Jesus' resurrection is a present experience of God's vindication of Jesus' death and the promise of Jesus' risen presence with us.

Chapter 10: Kierkegaard

26. Christology has to do with our decision of faith more than it does with the history of Jesus and the doctrines of tradition.
27. Christianity is a mode of existence more than a teaching about God.
28. Faith is not believing there is a God, but is radically abandoning one's existence to God's will, as did Abraham and Jesus.
29. Christology is not knowing the truth but being the truth, being on the Way.
30. We become contemporaneous with Christ when our lives are transformed by the leap of faith toward God—like Jesus' leap.

Chapter 11: **Tillich**

31. We must *deliteralize* the myths of the tradition so as not to stumble over beliefs.
32. The gospel is "we are acceptable in spite of being unacceptable" in our state of separation from the Ground of Being, others, and self.
33. Grace strikes everyone, especially when they are separated ("while we were yet sinners") and brings us to reunion with the Ground of Being, others, and self—all this through the event of the New Being that happens in our existence.
34. Faith is accepting the fact that we are accepted, saying *Yes* to grace.

Chapter 13: **Mathews**

35. Jesus "collided with, encountered, invaded, broke into, and penetrated" established patterns of individual and social reality, bursting the illusions and false-Christs (*Everyman Christs*) of those he contacted, delivering them back to reality.
36. This bursting of illusions is the external happening of the Jesus-Christ-Event that brings a person or a social group to reality and internally forces a new decision about life—the decision for or against life *as it is constituted.*
37. The *no messiah* Messiah has come when one gives up illusions and faces reality, when one surrenders the search for some ultimate truth.
38. The cruciform principle of "to die is to live" points to two realities: an existential death to illusions and a missional death of expending oneself on behalf of. Both possiblities come as final truth in the encounter with the Jesus-Christ-Event.
39. To follow Jesus is not to imitate his words or reproduce his deeds, but is to *be* and *do* as a free person—walking on the waters of life in humility, gratitude, and compassion, confident that such walking is the meaning of life.

Chapters 17-19: **Cock**

40. The event of Jesus the Christ transparentizes life to its realities, bringing one to see that meaning is at the heart of life, always present.
41. Transrationality is experiencing and living in the reality of union

with the One, the Neighbor, and with the self, that comes in the transparent event of grace: broken life becomes transformed—glorious broken life.

42. The Other World becomes conscious to us in This World in extraordinarily ordinary ways and makes sacred our sense of mundane reality.

43. The transestablished one lives a profound, intentional, futuric, and universal style (that is triggered by the transparent event), catalyzing reconciliation where he or she goes.

44. *The way life is* transparently reconstitutes itself as good in one's consciousness through the Jesus the Christ event of grace.

Chapter 18: Wilber

45. Existentialism can be the doorway into the transrational (transpersonal) reality of life.

46. Spirit is always, already present, whether or not one recognizes *It*.

47. The Great Search is a dead-end, for Spirit is always, already present.

Chapter 19: Berry

48. The universe is the context for our life mission.

49. Universal rights transcend human rights.

50. The sacrificial mode of the universe calls for our interdependent sacrifice.

---

1. I check 15 of the 50 considerations that make the most sense to me.

2. I circle the numbers of 5 of the 15 considerations that make the most sense of all.

3. What do my 5 have in common? In a phrase, what is their theme?

4. I study the chart of the 11 theologians in Chapter 15, on pages 152 and 153.

5. On the two-page chart, I underline words and phrases that make sense to me.

6. From my underlining, I circle the 5 words/phrases that make the most sense. What is their theme in a phrase?

7. I circle the theologian's name whose christology makes the most sense.

8. I write a few sentences to begin to articulate my present Christ Image.

9. I re-read the following summary from Chapter 15 of their christologies taken together:

- All eleven are struggling to articulate christology in the post-Nicea and post–Chalcedon worldview of the authentic humanity of Jesus, who historically lived.
- Theirs are "christologies from below" which do not *assume* Jesus' divinity but indicate our relationship with the divine reality in life, through faith.
- All eleven are Christian existentialists, asking the question of human meaning to be found in our existence rather than beyond it, i.e., metaphysically or supernaturally.
- Jesus is not God for any of the eleven theologians.
- They base their christologies on the life-changing event initiated by Jesus—the event then and now.
- Most of them believe Jesus, as a human being, had faith in God, as we can.
- For them *sin* is not a moral category—first of all—but an existential one, i.e., *separation*.
- Christology has to do with *our* relationship with God, not Jesus' identity with God.
- Jesus as the Christ is a re-presentation and revelation of God's nearness, bringing God near enough to encounter us and demand our authentic response.
- For them Jesus occasions and catalyzes our decision for faith in God.

10. I compare the above summary sentences with my sentences in question 8. Where do I see gaps in my thinking or theirs? I add to and modify my sentences on the next page.

11. I look at the 11 theologians' chart again (pages 152-53). I fill in *my* Christ image categories (only a draft):

        a. Christology of _____
        b. Sin _____
        c. Jesus as the Christ _____
        d. Key to faith _____

12. I look back at my *Christ Image Evaluation* answers in Chapter 15, page 151. I go through my answers one by one. Would I change any of them now? Why or why not?

Where do I begin to see a new pattern in my thinking, a shift? From what to what?

What phrase would I use for *my Christ image* now as compared with then?

13. I do any needed revision of #11 above, a. through d. (I write to the left side of a. through d.)

14. What have I learned about *my* Christ image?

15. Which of the marks (next page) of *transestablished style* (from Chapter 18, pages 194-96) make most sense to me and my style out of my Christ image? I Check 5, then circle the 2 that I wish to internalize, symbolize, and embody.

Commandeered by the All
Radical self-understanding
Radical faith
Gives up certainty
Decisive in Spirit
Does the Free Deed
Turns matter into Spirit
Ready at a moment's notice
Reconciles the establishment and the dis-establishment
Directed at the underlying contradiction
Cruciformity
Sign of the Kingdom
Creates the New Decalogue

16. I intuitively write a draft (not the final) paragraph to articulate *my Christ image*.

CHAPTER 23 NOTE

[1]*Op. cit.* (Chapter 15).

24. Your Credo

This chapter is to help the reader come to an explicit credo, if she or he so chooses. The authenticity of the credo depends upon the reader. Through this method of composition and through this form, hopefully, the reader can articulate the deepest statement of faith yet. An expression of the center of one's commitment is the desired result of this exercise.

For the word "credo," I take the 11th century understanding: *that to which I am committed*; not the present-day understanding: a set of beliefs that I affirm intellectually. *Commitment* includes the intellect, which is only one part of a human being, but it also includes faith, heart, will, and embodiment. One's credo usually takes no form but is implicit. On the other hand, through creeds of the church or other covenant groups, through family and church training, Christians come to a more or less self-conscious credo.

The reader's credo follows—in response to all the 1) Christian writings, 2) Christian history, 3) conscious reflection, 4) church or covenant group experience, 5) personal experience, and 6) reflections from this book and its exercises.

Exercise 5: Credo

*To this point I have flipped through the book several different ways, reviewing my reflections on my notes, the imbalances triangle, the evaluation, the work of the 11 theologians, the 50 considerations, the marks of the transestablished one, my meditative council, my list of companions of Jesus, my life events, etc. This swirl has brought me to the moment of a final draft of **my credo**.*

1. I will review some of the creeds, scripture, rituals, and hymnody of the church. I do this as a final reflection on the Christian tradition

understanding. I will listen for the phrases and poetry that have meaning for me and will jot them down here.

2. I will consider the brainstorm of *justification* and *sanctification* below as a review of crucial elements of the consensus of the Christian tradition. Beside the items of the brainstorm I will decide if these need to be included in *my credo* by jotting notes that amplify their meaning for me.

   Justification Brainstorm
   > God
   > Existence
   > Sin
   > Grace
   > Cross
   > Resurrection
   > Jesus the Christ
   > Faith

   Sanctification Brainstorm
   > God
   > Jesus
   > Spirit
   > Vocation
   > Freedom
   > Discipleship
   > Covenant group
   > Church
   > Mission
   > Embodiment
   > Future

3. I will reflect upon my last draft in Exercise 4, Chapter 23.

4. I will write down the 4-6 pillars of my faith, i.e., *God loves unconditionally, no faith without embodiment,* etc. Intuitively I will write these down.

-
-
-
-
-
-

5. I review some of my four exercise reflections again, and then come back and modify my pillars above.
6. I sequence the pillar phrases.
7. I refine the pillar phrases above.
8. I brainstorm *content* for the pillar phrases (pillars on blank lines).

   a._____:

   b._____:

   c._____:

   d._____:

9. Using my pillars as the frame of *my credo,* I begin to weave the brainstormed phrases of each pillar into a pattern.
10. I then write (below) an *intro.*; each *pillar* in any mode of writing I choose: free verse, paragraph, creed; and *coda (or conclusion).*

   Intro.

   Pillars

Coda

11. The title for *my credo* is_____.
12. I polish *my credo*.
13. I will share *my credo* with whom?
14. I want to put *my credo* in what form and keep it in what place?

15. The _____pillar is the most important for me.
16. I need to really rework the _____pillar.
17. My response to my credo at this moment is

18. How have I grown in my faith during these exercises?

19. The phrase that best holds my Christ image now is

20. The biggest struggle of faith for me now is

21. I now make a few faith resolves:

22. Jesus is the Christ for me because . . . (I write a few phrases).

23. What I am most thankful for about my "Christ image re-creation" is . . . (I write a few phrases).

Section Six:

Edifying Discourses

25. DID WE OUTGROW JESUS?

[The Jesus hero] represents the way things are for all [humans]. He is the paragon. . . . He is a model of faith-filled living. [P]erhaps the 'exemplar' would be a more fitting term. . . . To follow in the steps of the representational Jesus is not to imitate his words or reproduce his deeds. It is to be and do as a free [human]. . . . It is to walk out across the uncertain, ambiguous, anxious deeps of my life in gratitude, humility and compassion, with the sure confidence that this very walking is the meaning of life. . . . The New Testament writers think of their Jesus hero as the pioneer who blazes the way; the elder brother who goes on before; the first fruit of a mighty harvest to be reaped. The followers then see themselves as the second wave of explorers, the younger brother [or sister], the latter harvest, yet as embodying the same life, traveling on the same way, participating in the same mission. As he lived his life as the meaning of his life, and announced the cosmic permission for all . . . thus to live, so the church understands that she can and must go and do likewise. As Luther said, the Christians are to be little Christs.

—J. W. Mathews, Chapter 12 of this book, pp. 121-22

There is a force in life that compels us to be fully human. It is not so much something within us that we are bent upon fulfilling as something that draws us forth, that calls us. Each of us has a *primal hero*, one who has lived our vision of what it means to be authentically human. That primal image may be a composite of many great persons, but the image of Jesus alone has informed a large part of humanity for the last two millennia. Therefore, many of us today are focused on Jesus, whether we admit it or not. Does this mean Jesus is the high-water-mark of humanness? For me, yes, he is the meaning of life.

As I reflect on Jesus in regard to the image of humanness needed for our time, I am appreciative of but not inspired by the sketchy facts of historical Jesus research. More, I am put off by those who believe literally that Jesus was *God's* only Son, divine upon arrival. This is a major reason Jesus is not taken seriously today—that is, as a divine, mythical creature, not like us in every way. Such a "divine" story of Jesus does not make sense to us who live in this post-modern age. What needs to be emphasized is Jesus' faith, his freedom, and his love.

Jesus' faith in *God* is where it all starts, remembering that his faith was called forth by the Spirit of *God*. Faith-filled living was the key for Jesus, and consequently the key for those who would follow him. In the midst of experiencing being driven this way and that by the power of *God* and being limited as we all are by doubts, loneliness, and death, Jesus lived the great *Yes* of faith. Though he was tested in every way, he did not lose faith in that One whom he obeyed and worshipped.

Out of Jesus' faith flowed his freedom to radically obey his Father. It was Jesus' free decision to go to Jerusalem. He did not have to go. It was Jesus' free decision to be crucified. Pilate would have let him off: "Don't you know I have the power of life or death over you?" Jesus replied, "No one takes my life from me. I decide for what cause I lay it down." And he cried in his human freedom from the cross, "If this cup will not pass, then into Thy hands I commend my spirit."

Out of Jesus' faith in *God* flowed his love for Neighbor. Through word and deed Jesus gave us ultimate images of who is our neighbor and how to love our neighbor, even as the father did in the parable of the Prodigal Son, even as the Good Samaritan did, even as Jesus did on the cross. No greater love. And not only does Jesus talk about the human neighbor of outcasts, women, untouchables, but also the non-human— thus Neighbor with a capital "N," all of *God's* Kingdom.

The address of Jesus is that we can become like him because he was like us in every way. Jesus' humanity saves us, as it were. A super-human Jesus takes away our faith, freedom, and love and makes us dependent on miracles and magic. If his experience of life was not like ours, identifying with him is out of the question—let us just wait to be saved. Many have narrowed the choice down to this: either concede Jesus was a human baby, or throw the divine baby out with the bathwater of supernaturalism.

What about Jesus' divinity? We are confused if we think his

divinity is a supernatural something. His Father commandeered him as that same *One* calls us today. The address upon us, therefore, is that Jesus chose to be the commandeered one with all the power of his 100 percent human being. He was *not* a deity masquerading as a human. He *was* human.

The scandal of the cross that encounters us is this: Jesus was absolutely human, else why all his sweating "blood" in Gethsemane? He agonized, like us, in deciding to go or not to go, to do or not to do his Father's will. The divinity of Jesus comes from his faith, freedom and love, even unto death. He could have done no more, for what he did was the utmost of what it means to be human: to lay down his life on behalf of, out of his understanding of his Father's will.

As it turned out, history conspired to sanctify his deed. His free deed of the cross became a "visible sign of an invisible grace," as Augustine wrote about the meaning of a sacrament. Jesus' followers understood his cross as a symbol of the grace of *God* erupting in history through his resurrected presence with them; yea, that *God* had raised him from the dead to be with his followers eternally and universally as a living presence. The power of *God* shown through in Jesus' willing one thing. Jesus became transparent to *God*. He made grace visible. The result for us? Through Jesus, *God* makes things new. He changes lives.

How do we know authentic life? Look at Gandhi, at Dietrich Bonhoeffer, at Joan of Arc, at Dag Hammarskjöld, at St. Francis, at the martyrs of the early church, e.g., Polycarp. Look at the *God*-awful power that is manifest when history judges that one gave his or her life to do the will of the *One* who calls and sends. History is changed.

St. Francis' image of what it means to be fully human—*giving is the divine action of us humans*—came from Jesus. That is what "he so loved the world" means, "that he gave" himself. When that giving is seen and experienced in its awesomeness, sometimes history perceives the grace of *God*, a sacrament, a sign of the invisible—and calls it divine. In that human perception divinity is born. But something is not divine for me just because somebody says so. It is not divine for me until I believe it and act out of it as very truth itself. Jesus is only divine for me in my decision of faith. He was not divine as a baby in a manger. An immaculately conceived baby makes no sense to us 21st century humans.

Some called Jesus' cross the deed of *God* and interpreted it through their experience as the meaning of their new life, as the symbol of resurrected power. No cross, no resurrection. To die is to live. No divinity without the faithful human deed. The divine conspiracy happened through a human's faithfulness. Maybe this brings us closer to the story about Jesus that we can operate out of and communicate honestly in this post-modern era.

Jesus was more than Crossan's dis-established sage. I do not even see Gandhi, Bonhoeffer, or St. Francis as dis-established, much less Jesus. Let's call them trans-established. They were out to reconcile the dis-establishment and the establishment, even if it took their lives. They did this out of the understanding of freely and lovingly doing the will of that *One* that called them and sent them—they all were guided by the Jesus story, even Gandhi, the Hindu.

They are all part of the sacrament of "reduplicating the deed," as H. Richard Niebuhr says. Reduplicating the deed is doubly radical: one is seen to have done a powerful deed, and then history says one's deed is transparent to godliness. When we see the *Jesus deed* going on in the lives of those who came before or after him, we have no problem understanding the meaning of faithfulness and holiness—sometimes we even say *divinely inspired*. Divinity for me is not a supernatural thing, it is a *faithful to* and an *on behalf of* thing.

If Jesus' deed is not reduplicable, it has nothing to do with us and should be dismissed out of hand as magic. The new human story of our time would rest on the foundation of the reduplicable deed of Jesus, without any divine strings hanging down from heaven. These others I have mentioned—Gandhi, *et al.*—had the vision of the resurrection of their people, on behalf of whom they lived and died. We can even say they also died for all.

Therefore, the *divinity of Jesus and his followers* is *the* indicative understanding of what it means to be fully human. If we can't say, "Go and do likewise," Jesus is not authentic for us. He is only a mythic figure. What we are talking about is the new human story that calls forth the mystery, depth, and greatness of creation and creaturehood. Jesus showed us that grace-filled living is at the heart of *the way life is*. He showed us that faith is possible, freedom is possible, that being a part of a loving-giving community is possible. He showed us that when these possibilities are embodied, divinity flares forth on Earth.

Some of us therefore call him the *Christ*, the transparent one, *the* sacrament of life. He made invisible grace visible through his faithfulness to the *One*, on behalf of the many. He is and always has been the *new human* when he is seen without the distraction of supernatural powers. Then he is given back the power to encounter the rest of us humans with his call to live the great double-commandment of life: faithfulness to the *One* on behalf of all.

Teilhard de Chardin has written, "The task before us now, if we would not perish, is to shake off our ancient prejudices [including our old myths] and to build the earth." We might add a strategem within the context of his words: "The task before us now, if we would not perish, is *to recreate a new human style and story that motivate humans to build the earth*." Jesus can be the source of that motivation for Christians and non-Christians. For me, the new story is transparent to the ongoing Jesus deed and the Christ event happening in our universal history.

What does all this say about christology? Joseph Mathew's phrase "Cosmic-Historical-Jesus-Christ-Man-Figure" sums up Jesus the Christ. The five sections of his *Christ of History* (Chapter 12 of this book) equal what he calls the "total historical complex":

1) THE EVERYMAN-CHRIST = historical illusion
2) THE JESUS OF NAZARETH = historical Jesus
3) THE JESUS-CHRIST-EVENT = historical event
4) THE CHRISTIAN STORY = historical story
5) THE ESCHATOLOGICAL HERO = historical hero

The big point here is that not only is Jesus historical, but the Christ is even *more* historical as far as we are concerned. As Kierkegaard said, we are "contemporaneous" with Christ. The Jesus-Christ-Event-Story-Hero is more real today than in the 1st century, as are false Christs or gods that call for our allegiance.

Mathews gives us these pillars of the new story that we can build on, coming at it from every existential angle—which means we have a story here with more than enough for authentic living if we respond to the event-Word in faith and become a follower, a "little Christ."

Again, Jesus is the Christ *only* for me, in one sense. He is not some cosmic Christ who engulfs us mystically. For him to be the Christ, I have to decide that in him and through him I see *the meaning of life*. At least then it might communicate to say, "I see *God* through Jesus." Not that Jesus is *God*, but without Jesus I do not have the most profoundly human understanding of the significance of life as given, lived out, and sustained by the grace of *God*. What is *godliness*? My best answer is Jesus, who personifies grace, faith, freedom, and love.

How do I enter the kingdom of *God*? In communion with Jesus. Through grace I become a "new being in Christ," as Saint Paul and Paul Tillich have said. I quite agree and would add what they also say, that we become new beings through the *Christ event* that occurs from everlasting to everlasting, to all people. This secular, contentless, universal, and transparent event is the starting point of the new human and the new human story, when it brings us to reduplicating the deed of Jesus, to embodying the faith of Jesus, to becoming little Christs.

The story of Jesus is not a fairy-tale. I think the deed of Jesus is the cornerstone of the new story of our time. The Jesus deed—when lived in his kind of faith, freedom, and love—is on behalf of all and comes from the inspiration of the invisible grace at the heart of the very good creation.

We may have outgrown the *mythological* story of Jesus, but we are just beginning to take the *true* story of Jesus seriously as post-moderners. He is not dead facts. He is not a supernatural myth. He *is* our primal hero. He relates us to *God*, calling us to be authentic sons and daughters. As little Christs in faith and deed we are fulfilled human beings.

We have not outgrown Jesus.

26. The Meaning of Existence

Ezekiel 16

The meaning of existence is faith in *God*. I will say this many times during this discourse: *the meaning of existence is faith in God.*

Meaning is a life of fulfillment as opposed to a life full of unhappiness. Is my life meaningful? Am I happy? These are most basic human questions. They get to the heart of quality of life.

Every person longs for meaningful existence. As we humans become conscious we start looking for gods who will give us meaning. We understand that meaning is a gift from a god. Therefore, we are god-worshippers by nature. If it's not *God* almighty, the maker of heaven and earth, then it's some "lesser god," with a little "g." We could list dozens of them. The most obvious ones are self; career; family; sex; wealth; status; country; ideology (such as democracy); civilization (such as our Western civilization); church (such as our denomination); truth; moral values; social values; and religion itself (including history, holy writ [the Bible], creeds, and sacraments). All these lesser gods demand our devotion and worship in exchange for the promise of meaning.

Each of us has gods by the dozens. Therefore, we are never without faith; we have faith in some god all the time. This is absolutely human. And our gods define who we are. If one worships her children, she is a *mother* first and foremost. If one worships wealth, he is a *rich man* first and foremost. If one worships self, he or she is *self-centered*— centered in one's god. So our problem is never the *lack* of faith, but the *object* of faith: In which god do we put our faith? Which god delivers the most meaning? Which god will deliver us from a meaning-less life?

How do we figure out which gods we worship? Here is an interesting little test: show me what you can't or won't give up, and I'll calls us to a mission in Indonesia, then our family is god. If we won't give up our investments for almighty *God's* holy cause, then our wealth is our god. If we won't give up our interpretation of the Bible even if it is dividing the church, then our interpretation is our god. If we won't give up our career if it interfers with our family and doing the will of almighty *God*, then our career is our god. You understand what I'm saying. Show me what you can't or won't give up and I'll show you your real god, the one you worship and are devoted to in your heart.

What do we know about these *lesser gods*? Each one is *selfish*, wanting absolute devotion from us. Each promotes itself by promising us fulfillment and meaning if we bow at its altar. The lesser gods also threaten us if we deviate in our devotion, giving us over to fear and guilt. For example, if my god is wealth, if I give it up I am told that I could starve or will not have enough money for catastrophic health costs or retirement.

Besides being selfish, each lesser god is *divisive*, separating us within ourselves as we try to worship many gods. If I am career oriented, and if I am a mother of two, and if I am a daughter of an invalid mother who is mostly home alone, and if I am trying to fund my future needs, and if I am single and dating a really lovable man—what is going on in my life? All these lesser gods are "drawing and quartering" me. Do you know where that phrase comes from? A person's feet and lower body were tied and secured to one horse; then the person's hands and upper body were tied and secured to another horse headed in another direction. When the horses were whipped to move out . . . . You get the picture. Our lesser gods are "drawing and quartering" us. Likewise, they are dividing us from others. If your god is democracy and mine is Nazism, then we are divided, even at war in Germany. Or if your god is Allah and mine is Jehovah, then we are divided, even at war in the Middle East. Or if your god is "white is supreme" and mine is "black is the most authentic," then we are racially divided in the USA.

Besides being selfish and divisive, each lesser god is *finite*, or passing away. Does one's family pass away (look at one of your family photos when you were a child—how many of your immediate family are left)? Does one's wealth pass away (ask anyone who's settled a family estate; does the deceased own anything)? Does one's career pass away (ask any retired person)? Does one's ideology pass away (ask the Russian communists)? Does one's church pass away (ask the mainline churches in Europe and Australia)? Does one's interpretation pass away (ask those who believe literally the Bible, that creation was about 6000 B.C., instead of the scientific consensus of 15 billion years since the Big Bang)? Do you and I pass away (I buried twenty-four persons in my first year as a pastor)? Yes! All lesser gods are doomed to pass away.

If the lesser gods are selfish, divisive, and finite, then we can add a summary attribute: the lesser gods are *false* gods. If this is the Age of Falsification (*Atlantic Monthly*, May 1998, 107), it all starts with false gods. What proof do we have? If our lives are meaningless and unhappy, then the false gods we are worshipping are failing us. Likewise, if our lives are meaningless and unhappy, then the false gods are not worthy of the faith we have in them. They are obviously not the real thing. None of them delivers ultimate meaning. None of them saves.

So you guessed it. Better, you knew it all the time: *the meaning of our existence is faith in* "God," with a big "G." Who is this *God*? Certainly not myself, my career, my family, my ideology, my country, my race, my church, and not my religion. But, yes, the *God* of Jesus, the *God* of Buddha, the *God* of Mohammed, the *God* of Abraham, Isaac and Jacob, the *God* of Chief Seattle, *et cetera*. This *God* is no religion's God, but G-O-D—let's use all caps and hyphens in between the letters to differentiate the one, true G-O-D—above all gods. Who? From everlasting to everlasting I AM. There is to be no other god before the one, true G-O-D. "Our hearts are unfulfilled until we find our fulfillment in Thee, O G-O-D," to paraphrase religious wisdom.

And how does our worship of and devotion to the one, true G-O-D come about? Usually, it's not a pretty sight. In fact, it's usually hell to pay. The one, true G-O-D lets us work it out the hard way. If our lesser gods are tearing us apart, then be sure that great G-O-D almighty allows that to happen, for our freedom is not to be violated. We can try to serve as many masters as we choose, but we really can't serve the one, true G-O-D and lesser gods at the same time. Listen to these words from the prophet Ezekiel to Jerusalem (16: 30-36; 41). You could call this passage "god hopping," but I will use hard Old Testament language and call it "whoring after false gods":

> This is what the Sovereign Lord is saying: 'You have done
> all this . . . [chasing after false gods] like a shameless prosti-
> tute. On every street you built places to worship idols and
> practice prostitution. You are like a woman who commits adul-
> tery with strangers instead of loving her husband. A prostitute
> is paid, but you gave presents to all your lovers [your lesser
> gods] and bribed them to come from everywhere to sleep with
> you. You are a special kind of prostitute. No one forced you to
> become one. You didn't get paid; you paid them. . . !
>
> Now then . . . , you whore! Hear what the Lord is saying. . . . 'You
> stripped off your clothes, and like a prostitute, you gave your-
> self to your . . . disgusting idols [false gods]. . . . 'I will make
> you stop being a prostitute.'

I told you this process is not pretty, the process of coming back to
our "husband" (reminds us of Hosea), back to the one, true G-O-D. We
have to whore around with other gods until we learn the hard way that
they do not satisfy, but lead us into a hell of meaninglessness and
unhappiness. To paraphrase Tolstoi in his *Confession*, "If we can no
longer have faith in the finite gods, then we will have faith in the Infinite
God, or else die." Too often we have to hit the wall—the dead-end of
our lesser gods—before we return to the one, true G-O-D. This is the
purpose of Jesus, to put *lordship* back in the hands of his Father rather
than in the hands of our lesser gods. And often when we experience the
saving Jesus Christ event in our lives, it feels just like hitting the wall,
bringing to a dead-end our lesser gods. In this process of life we are
finally brought to the crisis of decision for faith in G-O-D as our only
lord. And who planned life this way? Our one, true G-O-D. It looks
like we would have learned by now, participating in all this and watching
all the others hit the wall as well. But no. We are slow to stop prostituting
ourselves.

We go on in our "bad faith," whoring after lesser gods, until we
cry out with the Psalmist for the one, true G-O-D. And more often than
not, it is the cry of desperation, in a fox hole, so to speak, or even at the
moment of our death. "Who will deliver me?" "Woe is me!" "O God,
come to my assistance; O Lord make haste to help me." And sometimes

at those moments we get it right and make solemn promises and depth decisions to be the person/people of the one, true G-O-D. Is this bad? No, but it sure is a waste, dragging everyone and ourselves through the hell of it.

Why can't we just figure it out without all the carnage of wars, ethnic cleansings, racial lynchings, split families, and personal breakdowns? It seems so obvious. Against the one, true G-O-D there is no defense. This REALITY abides when all else passes away. We seem to know this at funerals, we seem to know that we are but grass that withers and blows away in the wind of this final REALITY. The lesser gods' seeming ENEMY, in Whom we live and move and have our being, has chosen us from the beginning and waits till we choose back. Almighty G-O-D wants us to choose, to decide for ourselves, who will be our god.

And will almighty G-O-D ever be defeated? Of course not. Will the one, true G-O-D deliver what is promised when the lesser gods do not? Absolutely. Will the one, true G-O-D ever let us down? Of course not. Can we trust almighty G-O-D? With our lives, Jesus says. Will G-O-D be there for us? All the way up to and through death, Jesus says. Will G-O-D take care of us? Jesus asks, does my Father care for the sparrows? Does the one, true G-O-D love us? Like none other, Jesus says. Is Jesus' Father our final hope? Absolutely! Is Jesus' Father worthy of our faith? Positively! Is faith in the one, true G-O-D the meaning of existence? Jesus answers

> I came to show and tell you the meaning of the way, the truth, and the life. That's why they call me the Christ. I proved that G-O-D can be trusted: I trusted G-O-D with my life; and I trusted G-O-D in the agony of my death, with absolutely no assurance of resurrection. I came to show you the meaning of faith, that you too might be reunited in faith with my Father. *Faith in G-O-D alone is the meaning of existence.* That's it. Stop your searching around. You want to be happy? Worship only my Father.

What are the consequences of this *faith only in the one, true*

G-O-D? Later on in Chapter 16 of Ezekiel we read, "Well, I restored Sodom and I can restore you. . . . The sovereign Lord says, 'I will treat you the way you deserve, because you ignored your promises and broke the covenant. But I will honor the covenant I made with you when you were young, and I will make a covenant with you that will last forever" (Ezekiel 16: 59-60). That's as good as it gets, folks: the sovereign G-O-D has promised to be our G-O-D forever. And *forever* is the biggest word.

This is "good faith," built on a reciprocal covenant. There is a big catch here in the way our sovereign G-O-D has created life to be: the only way we can serve almighty G-O-D and our lesser gods at the same time is to serve G-O-D alone—not G-O-D *and* mammon, but G-O-D *alone*. That's the way life is created: "We are torn apart by lesser gods until we find integrating wholeness in Thee, O *God*." G-O-D is the *integer* of our life. Most of our lesser gods are worthy of some allegiance, but only through integrating them under the banner of the one, true G-O-D will our relationship to the lesser gods work. "Our selves, our families, our communities, our state and nation, our hemisphere, our planet, our universe are forever divided until we find our unity in Thee, O *God*."

When I have faith in almighty G-O-D, all else is taken care of, even transformed. If my attachment is single-mindedly to the one, true G-O-D—and in that way I am authentically detached from all the lesser gods—then my relationship with them can be given back in a new way. My self, career, family, community, and values can be reverenced, become sacred in a new way, not for what they are in themselves, but for what they are as gifts from almighty G-O-D. Whatever is, now, has value for us in a new way. If we are reunited with G-O-D, then everything else in our lives is transformed. For example, our marriage is transformed from a lesser god to a gift from G-O-D if the two of us have faith in the one, true G-O-D.

But on the other hand, if we've got to have these lesser gods, and we treat them as our *true god*, we can't have them. This is at the heart of the meaning of infant Baptism, when we dedicate our child to the one, true G-O-D. If we really give the child up, like Abraham did Isaac, then we can have him back to raise. The child is no longer a god, but the gift of almighty G-O-D. This seems to be the strange economy of the one, true G-O-D. The Old Testament says it well, "Thou shalt have no other gods before Me."

What is the meaning of existence? Faith in G-O-D. Faith in G-O-D alone. Lesser gods promise meaning and happiness. Only the one, true G-O-D delivers it. So what is holding up the deal for meaning and happiness in our lives? Nothing except our decision to choose this day whom we will serve. The G-O-D of heaven and earth, or our false gods? Good faith or bad faith? Either way, the one, true G-O-D will not let us go.

In this context, there is only one prayer: "*O* **God***, bring me to faith in Thee, alone, so that I may know the meaning of existence. Through Jesus the Christ.* **Amen***.*

27. Waiting on the Messiah?

"Man by the Pool," *John* 5: 1-9

The bad news is that no more messiahs are coming. That is also the Good News, for *your* Messiah has already come. Joseph Mathews, in *The Christ of History*, put it this way:

> The need to 'make sense' out of our sufferings and actions is deeply human. Apparently humans every where and time have sensed themselves as pilgrims looking for a way to really live in this world. In the language of the poet, ALL quest after some light, way, truth, door. More or less awarely, they search for a bread or word of life. They dwell in hope that some tomorrow will bring a delivering power, an illuminating story, some saving event, a final blessedness. When that day comes, so they dream, then surely in some way the essence of life and the living of it will be different. All peoples have forged signs and symbols of this human characteristic. For the Hebrews of old, one such image was the coming 'anointed one,' the Messiah, translated into the Greek as the Christ [*edited for gender sensitivity*].

THE SITUATION: Human Longing

We are very human. That is our joy and our sorrow. To be human is to long for deliverance from our day-to-day situation, to want to escape from our life the way it is. To be human is to wish upon a star, to wait for our ship to come in, to yearn for a life without the limits we experience, such as dying. This is all very human.

We humans, male or female, young or old, rich or poor, are driven to live out of illusions instead of our real lives. We say to ourselves or to those we trust with our secrets that one day we will really start living . . . when we are older, have a job, a family of our own . . . when we get that raise . . . when the kids are gone . . . when we retire. "The grass is greener" is an illusion we all know firsthand. The big *lie* is another way to talk about it. We lie to ourselves. We make excuses for why we can't live our real life in our real situation with our real relationships.

If only I had my health, wealth, and a new mate. *Then....* The "if only's" and the "then's" are part of our human language. *If only* my mate enjoyed my hobby, *then* our relationship could be saved. *If only* he would stop being a couch potato, *then....* *If only* she would lose about fifteen pounds and start taking care of herself like she used to, *then....* *If only* we had the preacher we used to have, *then....* If only our situation were different, we would really be living our lives. I'm talking about us all. It's not bad to be this way, but it sure is human.

THE OFFENSE: Truth

Charlie Brown and Lucy are heroes of my generation because they are "us." Lucy has her psychiatric booth set up in her front yard and along comes Charlie. He tells her problem after problem: if only he had more friends, a better ball team, etc. She listens and offers the cure: "Charlie Brown, look out there in the blue. See any other worlds out there?" "I don't think so." "Is this the only world you see?" "Yes." "WELL, LIVE IN IT! . . . Five cents, please."

Is that good news or bad news? It's like standing at the bus station at the corner of Center and Jefferson waiting on the Trailways Bus for Roanoke, waiting and waiting. Someone finally comes along and asks us what we are doing. We tell them we're waiting on the bus. They say, "There ain't no bus to Roanoke anymore." Is that good news or bad news? Either way, it's the truth. We will have to make a new decision, to continue waiting or to look for other transportation.

That was similar to the way Jesus operated. Again Joseph Mathews wrote,

> Jesus collided with the lives of all he encountered. He invaded, broke into, penetrated their worlds, leaving them painfully unsettled. To the proud he seemed humble and they were threatened. If they hated life, he loved it. To those who hung desperately onto living, he appeared nonchalant about it all. If

they thought of life as detachment, he was utterly involved. If
their living was a bondage, he was too obviously free. . . . To
conservatives he was manifestly revolutionary; he impressed
the radicals as a reactionary. Obviously, the life of such a human
being would be in jeopardy. When persons' lives are audited
to the quick, either they must redo their lives, or destroy the
occasion of the audit. Jesus was executed.

We don't appreciate anybody's saying "that bus doesn't run
anymore." That comes to us as bad news. Likewise, we don't want
anyone to point out our little neuroses, much less examples of our glaring
self-centeredness.

A campus minister at a Texas university, a number of years
ago, tells a story about Sally that illustrates Jesus' type of therapy or
healing. She was very tall and did all she could to cover up that fact.
She walked humped over with her long hair falling straight down over
most of her face and neck. She wore no heels. She obviously thought
she had problems, and she came into his office frequently to share them.
She began to get to my friend. One day after she "dumped" on him
again, he lost control. He snapped, "Sally, do you know what your real
problem is? You've got a long neck and you refuse to accept that fact!"
As he said the word "fact," her long, raised arm came down with a
vengeance. She left fingernail marks down the left side of his face. As
he pulled out his handkerchief to see if she had brought blood, he saw
her run past his window, her coat flying.

He looked all over for her, asked everyone he knew that might
know where she was. Nobody knew. A couple of days went by. No
word. He feared the worst. Then, he caught sight of a tall woman
walking down the sidewalk. She was very attractive with low heels,
hair pulled back, head held erect, walking with a sense of pride. She
wasn't beautiful but was a captivating presence. Lo and behold, it was
Sally. He couldn't believe the transformation.

Had his careless remark been somehow responsible for this?
Yes, indeed. After her rage, her flight, her hiding out, feeling sorry for
herself, in despair over the situation, something clicked. She said it was
like a word got spoken, a word that communicated to her that she was a
tall, long-necked lady who could accept or refuse to accept that fact that

had become so fundamental to her life. And in the flash of a moment she was enabled to accept that fact. She became "Long-necked Sally" with passion. Reality broke into her life. "If this is who I really am," she said to herself, "I will be my tallness with grace." She was like a new person after that. He said she didn't come by his office anymore but spoke pleasantly with him when they met in passing.

The therapy of truth was Jesus' way. What came as bad news was often the good news of *the way life is*, the way our lives really are. Do you remember the story of the man by the pool? He had to be brought to Jesus on that rotten stretcher that he had lived on for over thirty years. It must have stunk! Jesus noticed him and opened the conversation. "What's your problem?" (Jesus wasn't much for small-talk.) The man said, "Oh, I've been sick for all these years, and nobody cares." What did Jesus say? "Bless your heart! Here, let me help you?" No. He said with authority, "Do you want to get well? Then pick up your bed and walk." And did the man do it? First, he rehearsed all his excuses, one more time, why he couldn't live his life as it was. When the angels stirred the pool, the first one in was healed. "I have tried hundreds of times but was never able to get into the pool first." Jesus just looked at him while the man rehearsed the reasons he couldn't get well. Jesus said again, "What are you waiting on? Pick up your bed and walk." "But . . . but." "Pick up all your excuses and walk. Stop blaming anyone for anything. Pick up your life—which is all you've got—and get on with it. You are going to die lying around being a victim. I can't believe you've been here thirty-eight years. Get up!" And what happened? The man picked up his bed and walked. He didn't even know what happened, or who it was that told him to pick up his life.

Do you suppose Jesus' healing command came as good news at first hearing? Jesus had that way about him that called people to live their real lives here and now. His command cut to the quick. He brought people in touch with the truth of their lives. He brings the truth and we have to say, *Yea* or *Nay*. Will we live out of the truth, or will we, like Sally, attack the one who brings the truth?

GOOD NEWS: Possibility and Hope

Whatever our situation is at any moment, our lives are livable.

We can live our lives as they are—as long as we are conscious. Our lives, just as they are, are our real lives. We can deny our lives the way they are, as bad, or we can accept them as they are, the good gift of *God*. "And God looked at all He had created and pronounced it good. Very Good." *God* does not look at you and say you could live your life if only something were added. That is not *God's* Word to you or me. *God* does not say, "If only you did not have that malignancy, you could live your life." *God* does not say, "If only you had not lost your job, you could live your life." *God* does not say, "If only your wife had not left you, you could live your life." *God* does not say, "If only you did not have a long neck, blotched complexion, a dull personality, or were not 80 years old, you could live your life."

Consider our dear friend Margaret, who died so young of cancer. She was the mother of three children, a great wife and family member. She loved her church and community. After learning of her fate, she started a Day Camp for preschool children and took on the task of leading the recreation program at the Vacation Bible School immediately after her first treatment series. She rescheduled her last treatment till after Christmas to make sure her children had that last great family memory with her. She was an inspiration to the entire community and that's why her memoiral service was packed—she exemplified faith in *God*. Her doctor spoke at the service of the deep impact of her faith on him and others. The service was a triumphant celebration of life and death (that she helped write as she was most consciously living and dying). Did she see life as bad? Did she stop "living" because she could no longer do the things she used to do? Did she lose faith in *God* for allowing this to happen? *Through her faith she was enabled to live the life she had as the good life she had left.* And isn't that the way it always is, for all of us: the good life that we have left? My life is just the way it is, and by *God*, it's good! It's always the good gift of *God*.

You see, *God* didn't goof, or mess up on creation. What is, *is*, and is possible. We may have rotted over the years like the man by the pool, or the rot may have just set in. We may have lain around in our stinking excuses for years, pointing the finger at someone for doing or not doing something to or for us. And quite often we blame *God*. And then along comes the Truth, along comes Possibility and says, "Pick up your bed and walk!"

Or he might say it another way, "No situation is hopeless. The truth is, nobody is going to come along and help you escape your real life situation. That's good news. Waiting on the Messiah? No messiah is coming and I'm it [paraphrase of J. Mathews, Chapter 12]. What you see is what you get. Just as it is, this is your life to live or to rot in."

Every situation is full of hope, even though it seems hopeless. Consider the concentration camps of Nazi Germany. There was hope even there. Not the hope to escape the seemingly *God*-forsaken camp and its certain death. I am reminded of Victor Frankl who wrote of those whose spirits would not die in that hell. He came out alive, and having experienced the possibility for life in that humanly impossible situation, he began his school of *logotherapy*, which loosely means the dark cannot swallow up meaning.

And I am reminded of Etty Hillesum, a young Jewish woman who became a saint on her way to the gas chamber, feeling her vocation was to give love and meaning to those suffering the most evil of deaths. In her diary she wrote,

> They are out to destroy us completely . . . we must accept that and go on from there. . . . God take me by Your hand, I shall follow You faithfully, and not resist too much, I shall evade none of the tempests life has in store for me, I shall try to face it all as best I can. . . . I shall try to spread some of my warmth, of my genuine love for others. . . . I vow to live my life out there to the full. [*An Interrupted Life: The Diaries of Etty Hillesum*, 1941-1943 (New York: Pantheon, 1983).]

Her time came, also, but what a witness to the power of the presence of *God* in that seemingly *God*-forsaken situation. There is no human situation that is hopeless. It is possible to live our lives to the full in any situation.

Ask those couples who saw no hope in their marriages, but like Abraham, hoped against hope, and discovered marriages full of hope. We do go blind at times and do not see the possibility that is really there. Ask those parents who are told their child will soon die of leukemia and discover months full of joy and wonder as they really live those last days with their child. Every situation is full of possibility for those who have been given the eyes to see, the faith to dare to hope—not false hopes—but to hope for fulfillment of real life in the *God*-given situation of the moment. Every situation is a *God*-given situation. Every situation is a gift of *God* with life in it, to be picked up and lived. That's the way *God* made it, mysterious as it is. All creation is "very good," remember. It may sound cruel to say this or that situation is very good, i.e., concentration camps, dying of incurable disease, broken family. What we are saying is that *God* has created every situation full of hope and possibility—to be lived fully, as worth living.

Don't you see? Jesus brought Good News, especially when he was hanging on the cross. He lived his cruel dying as a gift from *God*. Did it redeem anyone? Yes, those on the crosses on either side, the Roman soldiers nearby, and most of his disciples, even those who ran at first. That was the beginning of the Gospel that was shed abroad, that any situation, even death, could be lived triumphantly. Jesus did not finally give up, even when most others would have. He continued to believe in the faithfulness of *God* even when it looked like *God* had forsaken him. *And* God *was faithful.* This is the Good News: *God* can raise us from the death of our hopelessness; *God* can raise us from our giving up on the situation we're in; *God* can raise us from death to life—right here, right now, in our seemingly *God*-forsaken situation.

This is what it means when we say our Messiah has already come. The waiting is over. Right here in the middle of our lives, in the middle of whatever situation we find ourselves, truth, hope, and possibility are present whether we can see or not. We have all that we need to really live our lives as they are given, right now. Good News says to us,

> Stop waiting on another messiah. Stop waiting for a miracle. Stop waiting for anything. The Messiah has already come. This is God's mysterious yet gracious trick: if you're waiting on something to happen or someone to come and save you before you start really living, then guess what. *There isn't any messiah coming to save you, and that fact is the Messiah.* He has already come. He is here. Lest you die waiting, pick up your life and walk. Now.

DECISION: Yes or No

We are left with a big decision: to live our given situation to the hilt or to go on waiting, which is blasphemy. Blasphemy is waiting on some other god to save us and not believing that our one, true *God* already has. Blasphemy is saying *No* to our life as it is, saying *No* to our situation as impossible, hopeless. It's saying *God* is not present here, or *God* doesn't have the power. It's saying Jesus may have redeemed the Earth, but he sure missed me and my situation. Blasphemy is saying *No* to *God* the creator. It's saying, "He created my life and afterwards said 'It is very bad.'"

But we can say *Yes*. "Oh Lord, come to my assistance, make haste to help me." Is that a plea of unfaith or faith? Of faith. It's the stance "We can live this situation together, Lord." It's Etty's prayer, "God, take me by Your hand; I shall follow You faithfully and not resist too much." That's what Jesus meant when he said, "Into thy hands I commend my spirit. You and I, Father. We're in this together."

We have the advantage over Jesus in our dying. How so? He has shown us the way of faith up to and even in death. That is advantage number one. Advantage number two: we are sure *God* will be faithful to us and present with us, even as he was with Jesus. That is the promise.

Therefore, there is possibility and hope in any situation, bar none. Why? Because the Messiah has come. Christ is born in our lives.

Life is possible. As the saying goes, "It's easier to love what you have than what you ain't got and wished you had."

I can say *Yes* to my life as it is, for *God* is with me. The Messiah has come. Is here. I will wait for no other.

*Let each of us call to mind one situation that Jesus is telling us to pick up and live, knowing we can say **Yes** to that situation; for* God *through Jesus the Christ will empower us to live that situation fully and triumphantly.* **Amen**.

28. My Christ Image

It Happens

Ever since "God" formed
"the way life is,"
the transforming "Jesus Christ event"
has been happening—
once and for all and ever again.

When it happens to me,
I experience
reunion
with "God"
and Neighbor
and self.

When it happens to me,
my corrupted faith
is transformed into
radical faith:
faithful only
to the one, true "God"
for the very good creation.

All this is
the quintessence
of gracious existence.
                    —j.p.c.

Why did Jesus come? St. John answers, to reveal to us the way, the truth, and the life. Were the way, truth, and life not known before his coming? Are they not known today? Did *the way life is* change when he came? Was *God* unable to communicate completely the way, truth, and life before Jesus came? Is *God* unable to communicate the way, truth, and life outside the Jesus tradition? Does *God* only communicate his ultimacies through one religion? Do we know more about *the way life is* today than they did 2000 years ago? These are the types of questions 21st century folks will be asking.

The way life is began with *God* and is therefore from everlasting to everlasting. To say that Jesus the Christ was pre-existent with the Father is a classical tenet of christology that holds that "He was in the beginning with God; all things were made through him (Jesus the Christ), and without him was not anything made that was made" (Jn. 1:2-3 NSV). This is the theological assumption of both John and Paul.[1] Bultmann says in his commentary, *The Gospel of John*, "In reality Paul and John, independently, . . . give clear expression to the early Christian understanding of time and existence that in its essentials was already in existence before both."[2] If one does not assume this—and of course Christ's pre-existence is not a historical fact—then he or she would simply say that *the way life is* began with *God*, another non-historical fact.

Yet, my confession is historical. It starts here: first, to say *God* created *the way life is*, second, to say that creation is grace-filled, and third, to say that life is gracious existence—and in particular my life (my very name, "John," means "God is gracious"). Juan Luis Segundo writes that "this existence is a gift, a grace."[3] This makes sense to me out of the truth of my life and the truth of those whose lives and reflections are credible to me.

Of course, I speak about levels of truth, historical and existential. For example, I do not believe that Jesus was born of a virgin. But his birth is most significant to me existentially, interpreted that we too can be "virgin-born," as the Gospel of John (1:12-13) says: "But to all who did accept him . . . he gave the right to become children of God, born not of human stock, . . . but of God"—so we too come straight from the source of life itself. Therefore, the virgin birth is absolutely true and absolutely not true, depending on which level of truth we are talking about.

Something is true to me, factually or symbolically, if it has meaning for my life. I do not need to go into what Bultmann means by *demythologize*. (St. John and I just demythologized the virgin birth.) In case we tend to be lazy or dishonest in our thinking about the levels of truth, we need to memorize Tillich's admonition: "Faith, if it takes its symbols literally, becomes idolatrous!"[4] In this regard there are millions of idolatrous Christians who are seeing the symbols (i.e., virgin birth) as objects of faith rather than looking through the symbols to grasp final reality.

No wonder traditional and fundamentalist Christians began to howl when Bultmann and his kind wrote that the following are primitive, mythological images and therefore not historical: pre-existence of Christ, virgin birth, incarnation, sinlessness of Jesus, miracles, blood atonement, bearing our sin, bodily resurrection, second coming, heaven, hell, angels, satan, etc. Even before I began to doubt historical "facts" in the New Testament, Bultmann said bluntly it is "no longer possible for anyone seriously to hold the New Testament view of the world—in fact, there is no one who does."[5]

We have to get into our own worldview and speak out of our own idiom. As a thinking 21st century person, is Jesus as the Christ the secret to my life? This is the question. I cannot enter the christological dialogue without saying why Jesus is or is not the Christ for me.

What is the meaning of Jesus the Christ for the next generation— that of my sons and my grandchildren—many of whom vaguely believe in *God* as a force that impinges on their lives, but with whom they have no conscious, intentional relationship? Jesus the Christ makes little sense to them, especially if they have to try to hack their way through all the New Testament mythology. They ask Why bother? What is the meaning of Jesus the Christ for those in the historical Christian church and those outside it, the Buddhists, agnostics (also in the church), atheists, and everyone who is searching for meaning?

What is the truth of *Jesus the Christ*? Have we outgrown that question? What is our ultimate statement of faith, our ultimate human confession? If Jesus is the Christ for us, the ultimate possibility of life for us has come—for me, the next generation, and everyone who has ever lived. And if it is so and makes our lives full, we have to share this ultimate truth or wither away.

In the New Testament there is not one christology but many—

christologies, plural. In addition to the christologies of John and Paul, there are also the christologies of Mark, Matthew, and Luke. All are different. The christologies of Paul and Mark are not as embroidered, and probably were earlier than the other three Gospels in composition. Most scholars now agree that Paul wrote first, then Mark, then Matthew and Luke, and then John.

First century christologies are of a supernatural nature: a redeemer is sent from heaven to live with mankind on earth; while here he atones for our sins; he is raised from the dead; he ascends back into heaven; and he is to come again to finish his redeeming work. Early on in the tradition the historical Jesus is framed by this supernatural understanding of Christ. D. F. Strauss—a hundred years before Bultmann—argued that many events and sayings in the New Testament do not represent fact but were added to show that Jesus was the Messiah, to fulfill the messianic predictions of the Old Testament[6] and therefore to legitimize the new church.

For centuries the Jews had been waiting for the messiah to appear, hoping each boy baby was the one. The surrounding cultures of that time were also of a similar anticipation, for there were other messianic proclamations. It is understandable, then, for the New Testament to put so much emphasis on the messiah's birth and to cast his words and deeds in traditional messianic utterances, e.g., the Old Testament book of Isaiah.

Add natural human expectation. There is that expectant longing in human beings of all ages for one to come and solve the human predicament, or better, to transform our human struggles.

Mixing this human longing with a traditional religious and cultural expectation, the context for Jesus the Christ was set. The long-expected Messiah, the *Christ*, happened through a human being from Nazareth so powerfully that a movement, church, and tradition emerged that came to be called *Christ*-ian: followers of the Messiah named Jesus.

Is it any wonder that the New Testament was written on the foundation of the confession "Jesus is the Christ," meaning Jesus is the all-determining fact of history? All other parts of the story of Jesus—his birth, his baptism, his ministry, his words and deeds, the cross and resurrection, and his coming again—are to drive home the message that this common-born human, Jesus, was chosen by *God* to be the Christ for all creation and in all times, truly the Lord of the world and our personal savior. This said—even without most of the mythological statements—theological abstraction and churchy talk remain.

In the midst of this, the big existential question is always How does one relate to that mysterious power who brings us into life, drives us this way and that, and eventually takes us out? This human question is far bigger than Where will we spend eternity? How we relate to that power and therefore what we call it is at the very heart of what it means to be human. Is it any wonder that relating to that awesome power that brings us into life without our permission and then limits us in every human way—even unto death—is the primary cause of our despair and joy?

Jesus showed us how to relate to that power most humanly. Possibly, we can relate to Jesus as he related to that mysterious power, for his life and message were an absolute *Yes* to that power, even calling it "abba"—a very endearing name for one's father, the kind of father who loves his child and will absolutely do it no harm. Said positively, will absolutely do it good. "Abba" illuminates Jesus' faith in *God*.

What difference does Jesus make in *my* relationship with that mysterious power he called "Father"? First, Jesus demonstrated the authentic human style out of his understanding of the goodness of life from his Father. Second, Jesus presents to me this same possible relationship to *the way life is*, so that I too can see through to its source and say a radical *Yes* to life as he did. (This is not an exemplarist christology but a transparent christology.)

What does this add up to? The event which occasions this transformation is presented through Jesus of history. It was presented to those who followed him, who came to understand in the midst of their most devastating despair that life conquers death and is to be lived in grateful surrender to *the way life is*, knowing it to be the gracious Kingdom of the Father, into whose hands they too could commend their existence. That event which changed their lives came to them through Jesus. They therefore called him the *Christ*.

Afterwards they told the *Jesus-is-the-Christ story* so many times and with such conviction that a larger following grew and became the movement. They confessed who Jesus was for them orally and then wrote it down many different ways.

And I who also heard their *story* and became a part of their tradition am called to witness to who Jesus is for me.

In my real existence, when I see the way my life is and want to scream out of my despair at how bad life is, sometimes a voice comes saying, "You are my son in whom I am well pleased, just the way you are. I receive you back home again with all the rights, privileges, and responsibilities of sonship." And if I take that voice at its word and become the son again—with open eyes and joyous heart, just as I am—I also understand the event of a lifetime and call it the *Christ*, as did Jesus' first followers. Out of this tradition, the *Word*, no matter how it comes—through the red-lettered words of Jesus in the King James Version or through the hateful words of a worst enemy [e.g., Ma Greeny in *Requiem for a Heavyweight*]—if I decide to let it transform my life, it is the *Christ Word*, a divine word for me.

This is a very human event, meaning it happens to all human beings whether they understand it or accept its blessing. I confess it to be the *Christ event*, some call it the *God event*, and others call it *the transforming event* in existence. Whatever we call it, it keeps on happening. Because of it we can relate reverently to that mysterious power that brings us into life, drives us this way and that, and then takes us out of this form of life. Because of the *Christ event* I have the possibility of saying *Yes* to my life journey, to live it as a blessing. Through the *Christ event* I can relate to that mysterious power as *Thou* from whom all blessings flow. I am afraid this generation is relating to the mysterious power as *it* and living in grimness rather than in the blessing of *Thou*.

Although grace did not begin with Jesus, through this understanding of the *Christ event* I can say that the *grace happening* that gave me new life came through *Jesus the Christ*. That transforming event in my existence—that gives me the new possibility to embrace my life as it is and to say *Yes* to life as "very good"—convinces me that *the way life is* is calculated to transform my life through such an *event, impact, occurrence, happening, encounter, confrontation, address*—whichever word makes the most sense.

Such an *event* is a secular, non-religious encounter that happens to anybody, at any time, throughout history—even eons before and after Jesus. Upon reflection, a person can most certainly relate to the transforming *event* through the hologram of a so-called religious experience and say it was the *Jesus Christ event*. Nevertheless, it is still an absolutely secular event. It is part of *the way life is*, which is absolutely secular, even though I interpret it as holy. The *Jesus Christ event* is built into the very dynamics of life from the beginning. (Only in this sense does the pre-existence of the Christ make sense to me.)

We must look at the *dynamics* of this *all-determining event* in order to get hold of its meaning for every person in every time. This is our interest, not a static, ontological second person of the trinity. Ontological debates are boring, seldom life-giving.

It is enough to say that the biggest question of my life is How do I say *Yes* to my life—the way it is—not cynically or stoically, but gratefully, and live it with great passion and compassion? I confess that the answer to that question is through the *Jesus Christ event*, which has transformed my life many a time, and promises to again and again.

CHAPTER 28 NOTES

[1] Rudolf Bultmann, *Theology of the New Testament* (New York: Scribner's, 1951), p.131.
[2] Rudolf Bultmann, *The Gospel of John: A Commentary* (Philadelphia: Westminster, 1971), p.10.
[3] Juan Luis Segundo, *Grace and the Human Condition* (Maryknoll, NY: Orbis Books, 1973), p. 12.
[4] Paul Tillich, *Dynamics of Faith* (New York: Harper & Row, 1957), p.52.
[5] Rudolf Bultmann, *Kerygma and Myth* (New York: Harper & Row, 1961), p. 4.
[6] John Macquarrie, *The Principles of Christian Theology* (New York: Charles Scribner's, 1966), p. 253.

29. Vocational Odyssey

I am I, Don Quixote,
The Lord of La Mancha,
My destiny calls and I go;
And the wild winds of fortune
Will carry me onward,
To whithersoever they blow . . .
Onward to glory I go!
        —Man of La Mancha[1]

We begin our vocational odysseys in strange ways. A rifle bullet in a President's head in 1963 re-occasioned mine. Deep dialogue goes on at such times. For weeks I tried to shut it off. I could not. I got orders to leave my three-year, plush Ph.D. scholarship program at the unversity. I did, against the wishes of my wife, my family, the university, and my country—the one footing the bill. I went to seminary to prepare to change the world. After three years there, I spent three more years pastoring two churches. I rehearsed my vocation: renewing the church to change society. I intended to change those people that they might change their communities, but I did not know how. So I started looking for more training to do my vocation. My wife and I attended a seminar that was immensely helpful. We took the seminar leaders home for dinner and told them about our struggles to renew the church for mission in the community. One of them asked us how many communities there were in the world. We didn't have a clue. He clearly was raising the question of our seriousness to change the world.

Somehow that question was a springboard for our "destinal leap." Soon after that we joined their group in the big city where they were living in the ghetto, researching and building models for churches to care for and change their communities. After we got there in 1969, I watched TV with the nation that summer, and lo and behold, we were looking at the Earth from the Moon. Transparency happened and something said to me, "That's your vocation." I fell into a profound state of universal gratitute as the Earth claimed my life. The dialogue in my being said to me, "All the money your country spent on getting that man on the Moon was spent for you." I had my symbol and I've been carrying that symbol of the Earthrise with me ever since.

That most significant piece of my vocational journey took about seven years to happen. I contend that every person is called to such a journey. About eight years later, I was living and working with the leaders of tens of villages in India. One night a young leader, Udesh, and I talked the night away. He was one of the lucky ones, with two years of college education.

As we sat on the ground outside his very humble dwelling—if we had gone inside we would have still sat on the ground—he told me about his studying mechanical engineering and going to Bombay to get a job. He began to make money and was taking on the middle-class urban life-style. One day a beggar came up to him—a man from a village like his—with his hand out. That was *the event* in Udesh's life. As we talked about our struggles to make our vocational decisions, we shook our heads knowingly. By that time he had become a leader in his village. He told me his vocation was living on behalf of the 500,000 villages of India. A few days later, in a speech to villagers and government officers from that area, who had come to visit his demonstration village, he said, "I am developing my village on behalf of the 2,000,000 villages of the Earth." I knew his symbol had taken a leap, from 500,000 to 2,000,000.

This song, written by colleagues about 1970, held the story of our two journeys, especially the refrain:

Local People Rise Again

Tune: *Country Roads*

Born in plenty, raised up blind,
All turned hollow, something there was wrong.
Human suffering over all the world—
Five billion people die and never live.

Refrain:
All the earth belongs to all:
That's the vision and the call.
Local people rise again
To build the earth, the common earth. . . .

At the center, aweful calm;
Born of spirit, then my life was gone.
Human suffering over all the world—
Five billion people die and never live.

From the center we shall stand,
In every nation, throughout every land;
Building patterns to release the new—
Dying daily that the new may live.[2]

He was a Hindu and I was a Christian; he was a brown man and I was a white man; he was about thirty and I was forty-two—each deeply understanding the other as we talked about the vocational odyssey of our lives. We talked about the occasion of our calling as an address that led to despairing wrestling with our decisions, and the symbols that declared what we were living on behalf of. We talked of how so many people never seem to get past the event that raises consciousness and deep wrestling. It's as if they get blocked for whatever good or bad reasons and slide back into the shallows of life—and try to forget their calling.

Or we both knew what Dag Hammarskjöld was talking about when he wrote,

> *I don't know Who—or what—put the question. . . . But at some moment I did answer Yes to Someone—or Something—and from that hour I was certain that existence is meaningful and that, therefore, my life, in self-surrender, had a goal.*[3]

After saying *Yes*, Udesh and I often stalled on a seductive plateau. Believing our vocation was one community, for example, something happened again from outside which occasioned a new leap. Later we were enabled to name and symbolize our vocations: we declared to each other that we were sent to care for all.

Hammarskjöld was a vocated man. Just re-read his autobiographical *Markings* to get the sense of one who made a covenant with "Someone."

> *We are not permitted to choose the frame of our destiny. But what we put into it is ours. (55)*

> *You told yourself you would accept the decision of fate. But you lost your nerve when you discovered what this would require of you: then you realized how attached you still were to the world which has made you what you were, but which you would now have to leave behind. It felt like an amputation, a 'little death.' . . . You will have to give up everything. Why, then, weep at this little death? Take it to you—quickly—with a smile die this death, and become free to go further—one with your task, whole in your duty of the moment. (158)*

> *What next? Why ask? Next will come a demand about which you already know all you need to know: that its sole measure is your own strength. (129)*

> *Life only demands from you the strength you possess. Only one feat is possible—not to have run away. (8)*

> *Do not seek death. Death will find you. But seek the road which makes death a fulfillment. (159)*

You say to yourself, as you read these lines and hear Udesh's and my stories, "Those guys are the exception." You say, "I've got a job. I've got two kids in school depending on my job. I've got a thirty-year mortgage on my house, I've got an aging mother, and I can't leave my golfing buddies, etc., etc., etc. Anyway, I'm not leaving. I am not going anywhere."

So be it. Stay where you are. You can be *the chosen* from anywhere, else vocation is not a quality of universal humanness. Imagine six billion people going somewhere else to do their vocation. "When the imitation of Christ does not mean to live a life like Christ, but to live your life as authentically as Christ lived his, then there are many ways and forms in which a man can be a Christian."[4]

We have two vocations, if you will: our real vocation and our assigned vocation. *Those Who Care* is our primary vocation, but we have been assigned to a secondary vocation, some particular division— lawyering, plumbing, priesting, teaching, stay-at-home momming, etc.— but none of these is our primary vocation, which is to be *Those Who Care*. A strange thing often happens out of this understanding of primary and secondary vocation: one pours more passion into the assigned career, sensing it to be what it was created to be, a vocation, a human form of caring.

Everyone is born to care. And if so, then we must be awakened to that fact—that is always there—before we can make a vocational decision. The Order: Ecumenical, that group in the ghetto we joined, understood its primary vocation to awaken as many as possible to choose vocations, and to indicate forms of engagement and sustenance for the vocated—this is a chief responsibility of religious institutions that seems to be overlooked these days as they fight over such issues as homosexuality and female ministers.

The bottom-line is We don't have to go anywhere. And yet . . . if we hear the call to move out and decide not to, we know what happens. We stop the journey. Vocation is an intentional decision in response to a call from beyond ourselves. And sometimes we decide to say *No* to the journey, but always have the possiblity to re-decide to be on the journey of *Those Who Care*. None of us wants to just have a job. All of us yearn to give ourselves on behalf of something that is worth our lives. Vocation is an awesome thing, an every-person journey into the deeps of care. If we allow ourselves to go on the journey and don't short circuit it or stop it, it will fulfill us as promised.

We can take our *Those Who Care* image and turn the dial one more notch and stand in awe of the varied band of *Those Who Care* . . . *For All*. How can a villager care for all? How can a ghetto dweller care for all? How can a church member care for all? How can a lawyer care for all? How can a mom care for all? Is it possible? Of course. I have been part of a group that worked with villagers around the world that were tangibly linked together through a movement of village development;

they knew they were doing their village demonstration in concert and on behalf of all the other 2,000,000 villages. I have been part of a group that worked with rural and urban communities that were down and out; they too were linked self-consciously to care for all. I was a part of a group that worked with congregations in an experiment on behalf of all congregations; that network of care vocated all participating members in a common destiny. I was part of a group that linked professionals—whether lawyers or carpenters—in guild-type associations that shared their expertise to those in need around the world; they sensed themselves as vocated people caring for all.

Through such networks of care the major contradiction of our time is being dealt with, the great gap between the 85 percent who don't have the resources and the 15 percent who do. As Teilhard de Chardin says, we are human when we know ourselves to be engaged in building the earth. Anyone can swim in the deep waters of vocational caring for all. The kingdom can come on earth in large and small ways, but not through us unless we sense ourselves as faithful to our calling. As the hymn says, "I hear the cry of brothers doomed to die/ And that's the cause of my return."[5]

What does this have to do with Jesus as the Christ? Listen to Paul van Buren: We sense the *Presence of God* when we are encountered by Jesus (p. 131). The call of Jesus to discipleship is heard as the call of God (p. 2). "Christology, as an understanding of Jesus that is nothing less than an understanding of oneself before God, gives the Church and every believer their identity."[6] When we bump into Jesus, the one of radical faith in *God*, and the one who lived his life on behalf of Jew and Gentile alike, we understand the meaning of human existence, to be vocated to *God* and *God's* creation. From Jesus as the Christ I know where the image *Those Who Care For All* comes from. A Buddhist knows the same. And one who professes no faith knows that the understanding of *Those Who Care For All* is in the genes of humanness, epitomized in the likes of Gandhi, Hammarskjöld, Martin Luther King, Jr., and Mother Teresa. Vocation is the tap root of what it means to be human.

To try to save part of an old hymn, *Once to Every Man and Nation*, that was omitted from the last United Methodist hymnal because of its bad theology, let me amend it according to our discourse:

Come to Every Soul and Nation

> Tune: *Ton-Y-Botel*

> Come to every soul and nation
> Those great moments to decide,
> For the care of God's creation
> And our lesser gods deny;
> Some event, God's true Messiah,
> Calling each to *Yea* or *Nay*,
> And the choice becomes our future,
> Our vocation grasped in faith.

> Though the cause of evil prosper,
> Yet God's Word alone is strong;
> Though his portion be the scaffold,
> And upon the throne be wrong;
> Yet that scaffold sways the future,
> And, behind the dim unknown,
> Standeth God within the shadow
> Keeping watch above God's own.

Following is one of many songs members of the Order: Ecumenical were writing and singing to known tunes back in that Chicago ghetto around 1970. I include it here because it is a song about our *birthright*: being called to care for all.

The Sign

> Tune: "The Triumphal Entry March" from *Aida*

> Born to forge, out of the darkest night, the sign
>   of abundant life
> In the midst of strife, struggling, suffering, consuming awe.
> Born to join in the long march with those who love
>   the shattered earth,
> Calling forth new birth, loving all, serving all, unto death.

Refrain:
The silence has deafened them, the stillness enlivened them.
The future has chosen them to give their lives. . . .
Go forth in love for the mystery, beloved of history,
Blessed in the call, sign of faith, sign of hope, signal of love.

The cry to build the vision of common earth resounds in
the hearts of all
Across the sweep of time, echoing, echoing human need.
And hist'ry's saints with ageless voices claim the promise
of myst'ry's love;
Laying down their lives, following, following, giving all.[7]

One of history's saints is Gandhi. I saw the *Gandhi* movie about ten times within a couple of years as I led college students to discuss his significance for their vocations. Where did Gandhi's power come from? Is his power available to us? Where does the vocated one need to show up today, in what situations, and even in what geography? Those were the kinds of questions we asked them after the three hours of transparent vocation on the screen.

Gandhi's power came from his decision unto death. Another way he said that is, "Over my dead body will this cultural and religious violence continue!" That was the message of his avowed 40-day fast in Calcutta that almost took his life, on behalf of all of India and Pakistan. We might say he was a dead man already, having decided what he would live and die for—his power came from the depths of his consecrated decision. He was using his awesome power to defy the masses in their mayhem. He made that world stand still, literally.

Awe here is when life jumps up and grabs us or shocks us. Our attention is rapt. Life stops us in our tracks. When Gandhi told the repentant Hindu man there was a way out of "Hell" for him—to take a small Moslem boy and raise him a Moslem—that man was awe-struck. We could see it in his eyes and in his body language. He had bumped into the consecrated style. It transformed his life, almost instantaneously.

When we are enabled to see through a situation to the deeps of life, life goes transparent for us. At such times life is awe-inspiring. Profound insight sometimes rushes into our consciousness. That fifteen-minute movie clip of Gandhi's fast is an example. Watching it, we experience the power of the human spirit. We are afforded a peek at depth humanness. We are in touch with human fulfillment. We are ennobled just being a part of the same race as such a person, swelling a little with pride, knowing that all humans—including us—have a capacity for compassion and courage and sacrificial service. We experience fascination and, yes, fear.

At such times the vocated ones become heroes or saints for us: as ordinary persons they become transparent to the holiness in life. They become instruments of peace, as St. Francis says—as Gandhi did in this instance—or instruments of the call. They show us what it means to follow life's bliss.

How do we recover the profound journey of vocation, that has to do with destiny, with consecration, with turning sometimes violent matter into spirit? Not finally through enlightenment means such as education, but through the transparency of vocated lives.

Nelson Mandela said in a speech in 1994,

You are a child of God.
Your playing small doesn't serve the world. . . .
We were born to manifest the glory of God that is within us.
It is not just in some of us; it's in everyone.

Another writes,

Saying yes to the calls tends to place you on a path that half of yourself thinks doesn't make a bit of sense, but the other half knows your life won't make sense without.[8]

I send us out with Hammarskjöld to say *Yes* to the call, to find the certainty that existence is meaningful and that, therefore, our lives, in self-surrender, have a goal.

Repeat after me: *These are the Times.*
                        We are the People.
                        So be it.
                        Be it so.

CHAPTER 29 NOTES

[1] Lyrics, Joe Darion; music, Mitch Leigh.
[2] The Order: Ecumenical. At the time it was written, about 1970, the number was "three billion," or the greater part of nearly four billion persons on earth.
[3] Dag Hammarskjöld, *Markings* (New York: Alfred A. Knopf, 1964), p. 205.
[4] Henri J. M. Nouwen, *The Wounded Healer: Ministry in Contemporary Society* (1972; New York: Doubleday, 1979), p. 99.
[5] "The King's Business," stanza five, lines three and four.
[6] Paul M. van Buren, *A Theology of the Jewish-Christian Reality—Part Three: Christ in Context* (San Francisco: Harper & Row, 1988), p. 24.
[7] The Order: Ecumenical.
[8] Gregg Levoy, *Callings: Finding and Following an Authentic Life* (New York: Crown, 1997).

30. Good Evangelists

John 20-21

When I was a young man I decided that my secret name would be *John the Evangelist*, and that my secret animal of power would be the eagle, like St. John the Evangelist of the New Testament. Each Christian has been commissioned to be an evangelist, to share the *good news*; therefore, I keep asking What is a *good* evangelist?

Knowing

Instead of "You are bad and sinful," good evangelism assumes everyone is loved by *God* and is of the good creation. It assumes that life is sacred, that all time, space, and relationships are good, because the good is everywhere, and all is planted in it. Everybody and everything is a secondary symbol, pointing to and representing the primary goodness of life. All is essentially good, whole, and at one with the Good.

The evangelism I'm talking about is more than meets the eye. For example, many say that life appears tragic. Apparently earthquakes and hurricanes are tragic. Apparently death is tragic. But to good evangelism, what is apparently tragic is really good. It is like Dali's crucifixion (*Christ of St. John of the Cross*), the one above my desk. The Eschatological Hero is there in the dark, enlightening and hovering over creation. Maybe he's stuck in the Other World in the midst of This World, which is where the Other World has been since the Incarnation, since the beginning. Beneath him are fishermen at their boats, preparing their nets. All looks normal except for the dominating presence of Jesus on the exalted cross, but we know that reality is always more than what we ordinarily perceive.

Dali spent much of his ministry as an artist revealing the mystery in the mundane, allowing things like watches curled over boxes to illuminate the significance of the mundane. What seems mundane is really meaningful, more than it would at first appear. We see through the tragic when we are given the eyes to see, for life lived out of the understanding of goodness is never really tragic or meaningless. The movie *Life Is Beautiful* witnesses to this truth.

To put it another way, every created thing is a *portent*, or an indication of something important. What is the portent of a burning candle standing on the table? Someone might say, "It is expending its life," or another might say, "The dark can never put it out, at least in my imagination." Just mundane stuff of life showing significance. Everything and everybody is "im-portent." Every person is full of goodness, therefore, depth and greatness, uniqueness and wonder.

Remember all of that old brainwashing that the church is good and the world is bad, and the holiness of the church has to go out there and be with the unholy to bring it back to holiness. This mythology is still prevalent. But the truth is, the church is not good except as it is in the world, for the world is good. The church is good because it's a part of the world. Everything is finally the good creation, the good earth, and the church happens to be stuck in the good like everything else is. If it's created, it's good. Good evangelism is simple to understand ontologically, hard to understand morally.

Where does this understanding come from historically? At least from the scriptures. Remember Peter's vision? An unholy man, a fellow of the wrong religion, came to Peter. Peter had a vision which told him to eat all the meat. Peter said, "No, it is unclean." And then a big sheet came out of heaven and dropped down its four corners and enveloped all. Peter got the message: all is clean. All are clean.

"And *God* looked at all He had created and said, 'It is Good!'" Who would argue?

Doing

The people who are the church have a special *function*, built upon this understanding of good evangelism: to go round and say, "Lo, here; lo, there," and to point to the importance and the significance of all creation. The church has the supreme task of re-introducing the world to its essential goodness and glory. The church allows the world to see through to what is beneath what appears to be. The church objectifies the depth reality of creation—pure, good creation, by *God*.

Good evangelism is a new type of transforming or trans-
substantiating, out of the understanding that there is no such thing as the
wrong time, the wrong place, or wrong relationships. This is as good as
it gets, whatever *this* is at the moment. The people of good evangelism
in history are those who gave civilization the authentic image that all is
good. That is what happened in the Middle Ages. The church at first
was authentically pointing to the reality of the Other World in the midst
of This World. Later on they got fouled up, but not at first. That was a
glorious time in the western world because the church sort of baptized
all the structures of society and sacralized them, pointing to their greatness
in the eyes of *God*.

This understanding of the good creation is the foundation out of
which we begin to talk today about social revolution as transformation:
the old social vehicle is good, essentially, and is to be honored and built
upon—again, transformed, not destroyed. Transformation is a deep
resurgence of spirit within the people; violent insurgence loses sight of
the people's goodness. We are in the middle of such resurgence of the
spirit and social transformation today, in Eastern Europe, for example.
It was awesome after the collapse of the Soviet Union to watch 250,000
Lithuanians stand in silence for fifteen minutes, then begin singing hymns
in chorus as the church bells rang across their country. Their past,
present, and future filled the moment: "these are the times, we are the
people," they must have known in the depths of their souls. That moment
was good and glorious, though filled with incredible crisis. They
witnessed that "this mundane moment is extraordinary." As they sang,
they understood the goodness of creation, whatever happens, and stood
there evangelizing us who watched on TV.

What does transformational (good) evangelism look like in the
realm of our mundane encounters? I know an Irish priest in New Jersey
who understands good evangelism radically. He told a motorcycle gang
with their gals, about a hundred of them, to circle up in the church
parking lot, which they did. He brought out a big tub of water and with
a kitchen ladle hurled water all over them and blessed them, no questions
asked. And you know what? The gang, in their black leather jackets,
tattoos, long hair and sunglasses, walked down the aisle in the middle of
the Mass a few weeks later. That is real evangelism, no questions asked,

just planting the flag of the Kingdom of *God* anywhere and pronouncing everyone washed clean . . . good . . . and holy.

Another good evangelist is Don Quixote. He walks up to Aldonsa and says, "My Lady!" And she says, in so many words, "Shut up! I'm nothing but a whore. Everybody knows that." Remember how offended she gets? The Word is offensive. To go up to someone and say, "My Lady, you are good just as you are, whole and perfect; you are the salt of the earth, the light of the world, a royal priestess"—that would offend most anybody. The response more often than not is, "No, I'm nothing, I'm nobody." And Don Quixote and Sancho descend into the hell of that dank prison with their theatrical trunks on their backs. They open them, do a play, a dance, a miracle. All who watch are transformed in their images of possibility and worth. They understand again that they are good.

Then, of course, one man can do such an act and transform the lives of those condemned to die. Jesus is the Good Evangelist.

Being

The accounts of Jesus' resurrection appearances in the Gospel of John are stories of *awe*, which is the *presence* of the goodness of which we speak. The *style* of Jesus is transparent to the goodness of *God*. Consider this paraphrase of the events of the story.

> (John 21) Mary Magdala arrives at the tomb in a stupor and ends up reeling. The stone has been rolled away. Everybody starts running around looking for Jesus. Simon Peter notices the strange and awful scene inside the tomb: near the linen cloths is the handkerchief which had been round Jesus' head; and guess what: it is rolled up neatly; Mary is crying, desperately wanting to know who has taken him away, when the angels ask her why she is crying, as does Jesus standing there, whom she first thinks is the gardener; he calls her name and she jumps and throws herself at him, but he says, "Do not hold me now for I have not yet gone to my Father."
>
> Mary runs off shouting; the disciples come together in a locked room, yet Jesus comes right through the wall and says, "Peace

be with you!" as he shows them his hands and side; then he
breathes on them and tells them they can forgive anybody they
decide to forgive; Thomas wants to touch the nail holes and
put his hand in Jesus' side; a week later they are locked up
again, and Jesus comes right through the wall and says, "Peace
be with you!" and "Put your hands here, Thomas."

(John 22) Later, the disciples are out in the boat fishing, and
Jesus hollers for them to put their net on the other side, which
they do and can hardly pull all the fish in; Simon Peter immediately jumps into the water, making for Jesus; they all come
ashore to be fed bread and fish by Jesus, of whom none is bold
enough to ask again, "Who are you?" for each knows quite
well it is the Lord; then Jesus asks Simon Peter if he loves
Him, three times, and hears three "yes's" and tells him three
times to feed his sheep.

What a strange story. Here is Jesus with nail holes in his hands
and feet, a slit in his side, broken legs—some accounts say—a crown of
thorns pushed down tight on his forehead, whelps all over his back. In
this condition he walks around for forty days. Do you get the picture?
In this story only the one who is crucified is resurrected. And what a
strange dance he is doing. Is his presence not spellbinding? Do you
think anyone is awed? He is uttering strange sayings, doing strange
deeds, making preposterous claims, and getting the disciples clear on
their mission after he leaves them. It's as if Jesus has almost been with
the Father, but says, "No, not yet, please. I have to return to help take
care of all those doomed to die." A story of sheer, sacrificial service.
His only wish is to release the creativity of every being. The
transestablished style of the resurrected is what Jesus is showing the
disciples. He beckons them to follow, to be sacrificial servants. What
does the Gospel seem to be saying? That the resurrected style transforms
history by awakening, calling, and sending.

Now we are back to square one of good evangelism. The deepest
compassion comes when we realize that the "last fat lady," whoever that
is for us, has missed the experience of wonder, freedom, service, and
peace. We end up driven to responsibility for the world, which is
responsibility for those missing out on living gloriously. When we see

someone really taking responsibility for the world, really vocated, we see "miracles" being done. That someone seems to be taking every situation and releasing wonder. Such a person has authentic charisma, for the life given on behalf of others does turn matter into spirit.

Just think about following Mother Teresa around for forty days. She is one who prayed, "Not yet, please. Let me be about serving the dying a while longer until my Sisters are clear on their mission after I am gone." So she continued with her pacemaker, walking through walls into the offices of world leaders, demanding their support and concern for the poor and dying of their land. Her evangelism was undisputed, for the evangelist stood there as the symbol of those she served; she lived with her dying brothers and sisters; she made servants of the rich and powerful as they responded to her on behalf of the need of those doomed to die.

The *life-style* of the sacrificial servant is captivating. I read about Gandhi, and as a pilgrim I bowed at his monuments and ashrams across India. He was just a little Hindu who got commandeered by the Lord of history while he was becoming a successful lawyer in South Africa. He prayed, "Not yet, please, for I have unfinished business back home, brothers and sisters dying before they live fully." He spent many decades being the miracle worker of India, leading them to independence from the British Empire, demonstrating a simple but full way of life; walking into the middle of the most dehumanizing situations and saying something like "Peace be with you!" as he would sit down, wrap himself in cotton, put on his spectacles, and either start spinning thread, writing letters, or talking sensitively with some crushed human who came to touch the hem of his garment. They could not defeat him, so they shot him, which is too often the reward of the sacrificial servant; and just as often he or she becomes the martyr whose spirit is all the more powerful. This is evangelism that is irrefutable, for the life and death of the sacrificial servant is the ultimate human power. The presence of the word and deed in flesh is awesome. New life erupts as this resurrected style happens in history.

What is the way of good evangelism: 1) to *know* that life, as it is, is good; 2) to *do* good evangelism through word, sacrament, and deed; and 3) to *be* the resurrectional style, the sacrificial presence that transforms every situation it passes through and every life it touches.

Those who follow this Way are transparent to Jesus, who is transparent to *God*. They are the *Good Evangelists*, those who declare the good news with their lives. With this understanding, the word *evangelist* is given back to us anew.

Epilogue

*God is not an object. We blaspheme when we address that mysterious power as he, she, or it. **Anthropomorphism** is making **God** in our own image.*

*The **great Christian heresy** is making Jesus **God**. Jesus represents **God**, but is not **God**. To believe he is, is to try to get off the hook of discipleship, swapping faith for magic.*

*The **freedom of Jesus**, the **faith of Jesus**, and the **passion of Jesus** are our possibility as followers of the 100 percent human Jesus.*

*But **Jesus the Man** is not nearly so historical as **Christ the Event**, the transforming event of every person's existence.*

We have considered Jesus as the Christ from the perspective of theologians who have dominated the last half of the 20th century. (I could have added others. I considered three seriously: Paul van Buren,[1] Hans Küng,[2] and Marcus Borg.[3]) And we have re-created our own Christ images. What difference does it make if my Christ image is really mine? To me, all the difference relative to meaningful existence.

As human beings we have a general pre-understanding: the interrelationship of our cultural-mythological perceptions and our historical-real perceptions. How do we take the *mythological* and *real* seriously as we exist in faith, realizing that our sense of meaning is created in our lifetime, more or less self-consciously? Said another way, we inherit a story about the meaning of life and an "objective" picture of mundane existence, but these will not finally sustain us; we must figure out the meaning of life for ourselves, where we stand. This is the context for the journey of faith. How we interpret our human journey has everything to do with meaningful living.

The spirit malaise of our time is *the* contradiction of our planetary society. A fourth to a third of the world's population, more or less, emphasizes this cure: faith in *God* through the *Spirit event* of *Jesus* the *Christ* (or through the religion that worships *God* in Christ's name).

This seems so very complex, this trinitarian truth handed down by the Christian tradition. But in essence, what we have been trying to understand throughout this book is that Jesus was related to *God,* and through the power of his Spirit, so are we related to that power.

I am reminded of a story. A woman saw a boy barefoot in the cold of winter, took him into a shoe store and bought him shoes and sox. He asked, "Are you God?" She said, "No, but I am a child of God." He said, "I knew you had to be related." Herein lies the seed of christology and the journey of Christian faith. Through his deeds the early followers asked Jesus, "Are you God." He said, "No, but I am his son." They said, "We knew you had to be related." And he said, "And so are you his sons and daughters. That's who we all are."

We are the family of ultimate reality through the transparent event. The truth of the Christ image is that life is graciously good—as given—and is to be lived in humble and compassionate gratitude. Joseph Mathews said it well in the beginning poetry of this book: Jesus "opened the future, made new the past, and filled the present full of meaning." This is the fruit of faith in *God.* What it means for all of us to live in reality is to be able to see life, as it is, as a blessed gift. All else is a distortion of reality, an illusion. This *God*-through-Jesus-the-Christ-Spirit-poetry points to that which is worthy of our faith, worship, and vocation. We experience homecoming as we relate to this ultimate reality of life.

When we begin to genuinely give thanks for what *is* and who *is,* we are finally *home. Being at home*—not *going home* sometime, some place up there—is essential to the transformation of our planetary spirit malaise.

As D. H. Lawrence suggests, let us be *at home, at one,* and *at peace* in *this life,* which happens—this book maintains—through the transparent Christ event.

> *All that matters is to be at one with the living God*
> *to be a creature in the house of the God of Life.*

Like a cat asleep on a chair
at peace, in peace
and at one with the master of the house, with the mistress,
at home, at home in the house of the living,
sleeping on the hearth, and yawning before the fire.

Sleeping on the hearth of the living world
yawning at home before the fire of life
feeling the presence of the living God
like a great reassurance
a deep calm in the heart
a presence
as of the master sitting at the board
in his own and greater being,
in the house of life.

The name of the poem is *Pax*[4]—Peace. "Grace and peace" are ours, as Paul says, "from God our Father and the Lord Jesus Christ." That old poetry is the stuff of our real lives.

EPILOGUE NOTES

[1] Paul van Buren's *The Secular Meaning of the Gospel* (New York: Macmillan, 1963) was not taken seriously after publication, partly because of its unfortunate affiliation with the "death of God" movement of the time. His later works are worth reading as well, especially *A Theology of the Jewish-Christian Reality, Part III: Christ in Context* (San Francisco: Harper & Row, 1988). In both books van Buren considers christology from the Jewish covenantal understanding.
[2] Hans Küng's *On Being a Christian* (New York: Doubleday, 1976) is one of the most helpful Roman Catholic christologies.
[3] Marcus Borg's *Meeting Jesus Again for the First Time: The Historical Jesus and the Heart of Contemporary Faith* (San Francisco: Harper, 1994) is a helpful book for seekers. Key to Borg's christology in this book is the journey of discipleship in the context of the big themes of the Bible: exodus, exile, and the priestly tradition.
[4] *The Complete Poems of D. H. Lawrence* (1964; New York: Penguin, 1971), p. 700.

INDEX

*Selected Names
and Subjects*

Uses of the Study Guide

This Study Guide was written for a group of twelve South Carolina ministers meeting for their annual continuing education units. They met three hours once a month over nine months during 2000-2001.

A group can use the format as is or can use sub-divided time sections, picking and choosing which to study.

If a group were only to study six to nine sub-sections of the Study Guide, these are recommended ("heavier" sub-sections have been left out):

1.   Session 1: A. Introduction
2.   Session 1: B. Christ Image Evaluation
3.   Session 2: A. Journey (use assignment from end of Session 1)
4.   Session 2: B. Exercise: What Do We Believe about Jesus?
5.   Session 6: A. Meditative Council (after assignment, end of 5)
6.   Session 6: C. Companions of Jesus Reflection (after all done B.)
7.   Session 7: A. Life Events Reflections (after assignment, end of 6)
8.   Session 7: B. Big Group Reflection (on Life Events)
9.   Session 9: C. Review

STUDY GUIDE

Session 1 (90 Minutes)

A. 30 Minutes: Introducing the book

1. Pass out books. Print names on edges or somewhere prominent.
2. Turn to Table of Contents and read through sections and chapters.
3. Each group member flip through book and find a quote to read to group; mention page number and go around reading short quotes.
4. What section looks the most interesting?
5. Reflect as group on what you think the book is about.
6. How will the book challenge us?

B. 30 Minutes: Christ Image Evaluation

1. Each member take the *Christ Image Evaluation* on page 151. Date it. Feel free to write in books.
2. Which question (1-22) stood out, for whatever reason? Go around quickly, getting out the one question number per member.
3. Members share answers as will to (23) *a false Christ?*
4. Members share answers as will to (24) *Jesus is the Christ for me because. . . .*
5. Members share answers as will to (25) *phrase for my christology?*
6. Did I pass? Each member answers.

C. 25 Minutes: Presuppostions

1. Read the author's eight *presuppositions*, next to last paragraph, page 3.
2. Which one makes the most sense to each member? Each one pick one of the eight.

3. Members share reason why s/he chose that pressuposition. What makes sense?
4. What have we said christology is all about this session?
5. Why is christology the heart of Christian theology?
6. What is one thing members want to take with them from this session?
7. How will this study together make a difference to us?

D. 5 Minutes: Session 2 Assignment (read as a group)

1. Read from beginning through Section One, to page 29.
2. Think about *your* journey with Jesus Christ; write it out, if you wish, in notebook.*
3. Answer 1-25 (pages 16-17) statements/questions, including 100 word paragraph on *What I Believe About Jesus of Nazareth*. Bring with you to Session 2.
4. Really digest Chapter 3, thinking of examples for each of the 9 triangles, page 18.
5. Bring a special *Study notebook to write in for Sessions 2 through 9.

Session 2 (150 Minutes)

A. 30 Minutes—Conversation: Our Journey with Jesus the Christ

1. In a few words, each tells a memory about Jesus from her/his early experience.
2. In a few words, each tells about an early image of Jesus—what he looked like.
3. Take a minute for each to fill in the blanks about a shift in her/his perception of Jesus, from _____ to _____ (e.g., from nice to demanding).
4. Each reads his "from_____ and to _____ ."
5. What has occasioned the biggest shift in your christology (your understanding of the meaning of Jesus the Christ)?
6. Any who will, please share a life-changing experience associated with Jesus Christ.

7. Someone read the "Special 'Jesus the Christ' Note" on page 11.

B. 30 Minutes—Exercise: What Do We Believe About Jesus?

1. Each person has answered *Yes* or *No* to the first twenty-four assigned statements/questions, pages 16-17. Please share your answers by going *quickly* through 1-24, one number at a time, listening to each person say *Yes* or *No*—or *Pass*, if really in a quandary—then the next number.
2. Intuitively, what is our consensus about Jesus, in a sentence? Several please answer.
3. Several please read your assigned 100-word-belief about Jesus the man.
4. Now, what would you say is this group's consensus about Jesus of Nazareth?

C. 15 Minutes—Sub-Groups: Jesus, Christ, and Lord Imbalances

1. Divide into three sub-groups and move to corners of the room: Group 1 takes the "Humanism Triangle." Group 2 takes the "Christism Triangle." Group 3 takes the "Fundamentalism Triangle."
2. Sub-group goes through its three smaller triangles and gives an example of each, as assigned (e.g., 1. Historicalism: Jesus Seminar). Scan the paragraphs if stumped.
3. Talk about how each is an example of your bigger triangle: Group 1, Humanism; Group 2, Christism; Group 3, Fundamentalism.
4. Sub-group decides the imbalance of its larger triangle (Humanism, Christism, or Fundamentalism)—in one phrase—in regard to "Jesus Christ is Lord"?

D. 30 Minutes—Plenary: Jesus the Christ is Lord Imbalances

1. Each of three sub-groups gives examples of each of its three smaller triangles (1-3; 4-6; 7-9) and reads its bigger triangle imbalance phrase.
2. Reflecting on what you have been hearing, each person writes down, in a phrase, what is the key imbalance today in the "Jesus the Christ

is Lord imbalance" (e.g., worshipping Jesus) within Christianity locally and globally.

3. Each person reads her/his imbalance phrase.
4. Intuitively—from what you have studied in your assignment, heard here today, and feel deeply—what is the major imbalance (in a phrase) in our christology: our thinking about Jesus the Christ as Lord?
5. What difference does it make to let this imbalance continue?

E. 15 Minutes: Reflection on the Total Session

1. From all we've done in the *process* of this session, what was the one thing that stands out for you? Get short answer from each person.
2. What is the one *question* that you will continue to mull over after this session? Again, each person answers in a few words.
3. What is the *key insight* that has come to you in this session?
4. What is your *state of being* after this session?

F. 30 Minutes: Session 3 Assignment (read as a group)

1. Right now, look at Table of Contents, Section Two: Comparative Christologies.
2. Each one choose one of the nine theologians (treat Sobrino and Segundo as two) to read and report on next session. This makes 9. If there are not enough theologians, persons can double up, starting with Bultmann, Niebuhr, and Gogarten—double-ups do not split a chapter, please.
3. Prepare to make no more than a five-minute presentation on your theologian's chapter. Try to make it exciting.
4. *Guidelines* for your presentation: 1) use and refer to the book as your primary source; 2) present images more than concepts—use examples and illustrations, even graphics; 3) tell us what you like about your theologian more than what you don't like; 4) drive home the one thing about his (sorry no females, thought about adding Rosemary Ruether or Paula Fredrikson) christology that is all important—to you; 5) no comments about how hard it was/is to

figure out his christology—true of all of them. The author says these theologians offer the christologies of the 20th century (Kierkegaard considered ahead of his time) that have influenced his christology most.

5. Think about another 20th century theologian you wish the author had included in his book.

6. Please read the whole of Section Two. It is less than 100 pages. Session 2 (today) and Session 3 will be the most difficult, rationally, but maybe not spiritually.

Session 3 (150 Minutes)

A. 60 Minutes: Presentations on Theologians' Christologies

1. Each person, seated or standing, gives his/her five-minutes, or less, presentation, using the guidelines in the assignments on page 288. Each listener takes notes in notebook. (Before the presentations, as a group, read the **B.** procedures to know how to take notes.)

B. 75 Minutes: Reflection on Presentations

1. Each person lists in notebook one key phrase about each christology as presented.

2. Each person then reads list silently and comes up with three phrases that are key to him/her.

3. Each person reads his/her three key phrases to group. Group takes notes of insights.

4. In three sub-groups, decide the five key insights for the group.

5. Each sub-group reads five key insights to whole group.

6. Of the fifteen sub-group insights, the total group picks five key insights.

7. Group discusses new christological insights of the total session. Which of these insights is traditional or radical?

8. Which insight of Session 3 has been the most enlivening for you? Say a few words to explain.

C. **15 Minutes**: Session 4 Assignment

1. Read Section Three, "Dynamics of the Christ Event," pages 108-146.
2. In Chapter 12, "The Christ of History," by Joseph Mathews, which part is the most important to you? Why? Bring back one quote.
3. In Chapter 14, "The Christ Event in Life and Art," which presented art form in the chapter is the most powerful for you? Why?

Session 4 (150 Minutes)

A. **30 Minutes**: Chapter 12, *The Christ of History*

1. Each read short quote from Chapter 12. Group repeat the quote.
2. Each person tell which sub-section of Chapter 12 was the most important for her/him.
In the Five Sub-Sections of Chapter 12:
3. What is the EVERYMAN CHRIST? Give examples.
4. What struck you in the THE JESUS OF NAZARETH section?
5. What are other names for the JESUS-CHRIST-EVENT?
6. What is the cruciality of the CHRISTIAN STORY?
7. What is the significance of the "amalgamation" (bottom, p. 119) in THE ESCHATALOGICAL HERO section?

8. Someone read the last paragraph to the group.

B. **60 Minutes**: Chp. 13, Reflection upon Joseph Mathews' Christology

1. *Why* is the EVERYMAN CHRIST an illusion, page 126?
2. How does JESUS OF NAZARETH burst the illusion, page 126?
3. What are the dynamics of the CHRIST EVENT, page 127?
4. **20 min.**: P. 128, read, starting "Why did they call him the Christ?" to end paragraph. Discuss which answer speaks to you (each person).
5. Explain the process of the event, the story, and the church, page 131.
6. Who is the Christian HERO, page 131-32?
7. Why did Mathews name it *The Christ of History*, page 132?
8. *Jesus the man* or *Christ the event* is more historical? Explain.

C. 50 Minutes: Chapter 14, "The Christ Event in Life and Art"

1. Someone please read the Perrin quote at beginning, p. 134.
2. Of the art forms presented in the chapter (Marshall's quote, pp. 134-35; author's JFK example, pp. 136-39; *Requiem for a Heavyweight*, pp.139-41; Christmas greeting, pp. 142-43; *As Good as It Gets*, pp.143-46), each person say which one is the most powerful. Say why in a very few words.
3. In each art form, point out the *Christ event(s)*.
4. Describe what a *Christ event* is from these examples.
5. **25 Minutes**: When has a *Christ event* happened in your life? Each person give an example.
6. What are the life dynamics of a *Christ event*?
7. Would Mathews agree with you? Why or why not?

D. 10 Minutes: Session 5 Assignment

1. Read "Section Four: Rethinking My Christology," pp. 148-198.
2. Answer again the "Evaluation" on p. 151. Share in Session 5.
3. Write your own "Evolution of Christology" using the chart on p. 162. Share in Session 5.
4. Write a brief definition of how "transparent," "transrational," and "transestablisment" are used in the author's christology, pp. 160-98.

Session 5 (150 Minutes)

A. 45 Minutes: Christology Evaluation and Evolution

1. In the "Evaluation" on p. 151, how have you changed since you took the "Evaluation" in Session 1. Each shares a reflection.
2. Each share her/his chart on "The Evolution of My Christology" on p. 162.
3. Share reflections on the group's "Evolution of Christology." Listen for key turning points in each person's evolution.
4. Ask questions about the "Current Edge" of the evolution sharings.

B. 30 Minutes: The Transparent Event

1. Discuss the definition and examples of "transparent" on pp. 163-64.
2. What are group's examples of "transparent" re: to the author's definition?
3. Discuss the "dynamics of the profound, transparent event" listed at the bottom of p. 166. How would you restate the third and fourth statements of that list?
4. What is the "reason for taking Jesus to Muslims, Buddhists, Hindu, etc." (p. 168)?
5. Explain "Every person has a 'chirstology' in the sense I am talking about, Christian or not" (p. 169).

C. 40 Minutes: Transrational Spirituality

1. Read the quote by Ken Wilber (p. 171) and comment on the presence of Spirit.
2. When is the Spirit not present?
3. **15 Minutes**: If the Spirit is "always already present" (bottom half p. 181), what is indicated for us:
   a. How does this square with our understanding of creation?
   b. How does this square with our understanding of sin?
   c. How does this square with our understanding of salvation?
   d. Believing this, how might we act differently?
   e. Believing this, how might this understanding alter our spiritual practices?
4. **15 Minutes**: Scan pp. 179-82. Discuss how these paragraphs on "transrational grace" alter or confirm our understanding of Jesus as the Christ?

D. 30 Minutes: Transestablished Style

1. What strikes you about "The Big Context," pp. 188-90?
2. What does "Neighbor," with a big "N," mean?
3. What is the definition of "trans-establishment" (p. 190)?
3. Who are "Exemplars of the Transestablished Style" (pp. 191-93)?

5. Each person quickly say which of the thirteen "marks of the transestablished style" most strikes her/him.
6. Discuss why.

E. 5 Minutes: Session Six Assignment

1. Each person read Chapters 19 and 20, doing Exercise 1: "My Meditative Council."

Session Six (150 Minutes)

A. 45 Minutes—Sub-groups of 3 to 5: Meditative Council Reflection

1. Each share how many on your council are "consecrated religious."
2. Each share who are the 3 that you listen to most.
3. Each share why his/her number 1 is number 1.
4. Share what your meditative council has said in the past that has guided you in a crucial decision.
5. Share what your meditative council is saying relative to your mission.
6. What difference does one's meditative council have on one's life?
7. Do you feel you need to make changes on your council? If so, how would you do that?

B. 30 Minutes: Companions of Jesus Exercise (Individual)

1. As individuals, scan pp. 208-12. Then do Exercise 2 on pp. 212-13.

C. 45 Minutes—Sub-groups: Companions of Jesus Reflection

1. What is a "companion of Jesus"?
2. Each share a writer, a book, or a fictional character in question #2.
3. Each read list of 3 to 4 primary companions of Jesus, #3.
4. In #6, share how primary companions influenced your faith journey?
5. Each share how s/he has come to faith in *God*?
6. What have we learned about the journey of faith as we have listened?

D. **25 Minutes**—Big Group: Reflection

1. Share what you have learned about meditative councils.
2. What are our three key insights as the big group.
3. Share what you have learned about companions of Jesus?
4. What are our three key insights as the big group.
5. What have these two exercises brought home to us?

E. **5 Minutes**: Session Seven Assignment

1. Read Chapter 22 and do Exercise 3: Life Events.

Session Seven (150 Minutes)

A. **60 Minutes**—Sub-groups of 3 to 5: Life Events Reflection

1. Each read #6, "the three key events," to each other.
2. #7, share an event that turned your life around. From what to what?
3. #9, share an event that is a Christ event.
4. #10, how does a Christ event work or what are its dynamics?
5. Write out the dynamics of a Christ event to read to the big group.

B. **30 Minutes**—Big Group: Reflection

1. What was going on in each sub-group?
2. Each sub-group read its dynamics of a Christ event.
3. Discuss and come up with a big group consensus on the dynamics of a Christ event (read the 4 bullets at the bottom of p. 166 as an example).
4. Discuss what is your part in these Christ event dynamics.

C. **40 Minutes**: 50 Considerations for Your Credo (Group Review)

1. In preparation for Session Eight, review together pp. 218-22. Do this individually, using the "+" and "?" directions for Exercise 4: Review, p. 218. Sit in pairs in the big group to help each other.

2. Read the 50 Considerations again doing question 1, bottom p. 222.

D. 10 Minutes: Session Eight Assignment

1. Finish Exercise 4, pp. 222-25.
2. Do Exercise 5, pp. 226-29.

Session Eight (150 Minutes)

A. 60 Minutes: Considerations for Credo Reflection

1. Each read the five circled statements that make most sense to you.
2. Which considerations were the most mentioned?
3. Each share your theme phrase, #3.
4. Each person read the theme phrase, #6.
5. Each person share the theologian whose christology makes the most sense, #7.
6. Each read the bullet statement, #9, that is most important to you.
7. What new insights about christology have occurred in group sharing?

B. 45 Minutes: Credo Reflection

1. Each read your revised Christ image categories, #11, p. 224 (Ex. 4). Ask questions or make comments after each person's reading.
2. Each read your pillar phrases, # 8, p. 228 (Ex. 5). Ask questions or make comments after each person's reading.
3. Each read your Credo. Make comments after each person's reading.
4. What new insights about christology have occurred in group sharing?

C. 30 Minutes: Group Reflection on Christology

1. Each share the phrase that best holds your Christ image now, #19.
2. Share your biggest struggle with faith in this exercise, #20.
3. Each share why Jesus is the Christ, # 22. Comment on each.
4. What has been the gift of Session Eight for us?

D. 15 Minutes: Session Nine Assignment (read as group)

1. Each person read Chapters 25-30, pp. 232-79, including Epilogue.
2. Each person choose a chapter or Epilogue to report on, covering all seven chapters. Decide this in the group.
3. Prepare to make no more than a five-minute presentation on your chapter. Try to make it exciting.
4. *Guidelines* for your presentation: 1) use and refer to the chapter as your primary source; 2) present images more than concepts—use examples and illustrations; 3) tell us what you found helpful about the chapter more than what you don't like; 4) emphasize the one thing about chapter that is important—to you.

Session Nine (150 Minutes)

A. 60 Minutes: Presentations from Edifying Discourses and Epilogue

1. Each person, seated or standing, gives her/his five-minutes, or less, presentation, using the guidelines in the assignments on page 306. Each listener takes notes in notebook. (Before the presentations, as a group read the **B.** procedures to know how to take notes.)

B. 60 Minutes: Reflection on Presentations

1. Each person lists in notebook one key phrase about each chapter as presented.
2. Each person then reads list (#1) silently and comes up with three phrases that are key to him/her.
3. Each person reads his/her three key phrases to the big group. All take notes of insights.
4. In three huddles (chairs pulled together) decide the five key insights.
5. Each huddle read five key insights to the big group.
6. Of the fifteen huddle insights, the big group picks five key insights.
7. Group discusses new christological insights of the total session. Which of these insights is traditional or radical?
8. Which insight of this session has been the most enlivening for you?

Say a few words to explain.

C. 30 Minutes: Review of Book and all Sessions

1. Each tell which Chapter of the book was the most helpful for you and why.
2. Each tell which Session was the most meaningful for you and why.
3. **10 Minutes**: How has your understanding of Jesus the Christ changed and how might you change as a result?
4. What would be your title for this book now?
5. What would you say to recommend this book for someone to read or study?
6. What would you like to say to the author?

About the Author

John Cock wrote his memoir, *Called To Be: A Spirit Odyssey*, upon the completion of three careers: one in teaching, one in the service of the church as a minister and, along with his wife and two sons, as a member of the family Order: Ecumenical—living in inner-cities of the U.S. and in villages of India and Indonesia—and the third one back in his hometown in the Blue Ridge Mountains of Virginia as a shop owner and downtown revitalizer. In his fourth career he is a writer, having published his memoir, this his second book, and his third book, *Motivation for the Great Work: Forty Meaty Meditations for the Secular-Religious*. He is also a retreat guide and grandfather, who loves to pull Kaitlyn and Nolan in the *Radio Flyer* wagon.

www.ingramcontent.com/pod-product-compliance
Lightning Source LLC
Chambersburg PA
CBHW031826090426
42741CB00005B/149